AF840719

# THE LAW OF CONSULAR RELATIONS
## An Overview

# THE LAW OF CONSULAR RELATIONS
## An Overview

*Mark A. Sammut*
*LL.D., M.Jur. (summa cum laude), M.A., PGCert(Laws)(London)(Distinction), Cert. Diplomatic Studies*

*With a Foreword by*
*H.E. Professor Guido de Marco*
*President of the 45th UN General Assembly*
*President Emeritus of the Republic of Malta*

xpl

*To my parents*

© Mark A. Sammut 2010

*Produced*

xpl publishing
Suite 74, 17 Holywell Hill
St Albans AL1 1DT
UK

www.xplpublishing.com

ISBN 978 1 85811 375 3

All rights reserved. No part of this publication may be reproduced, stored in a retrieval system, or transmitted, in any form or by any means, electronic, mechanical, photocopying, recording or otherwise, without the prior permission of the publisher.

Printed and typeset in the UK

"Consuls are the Cinderellas of the diplomatic service."

– A Consul, quoted by Eric Clark.

*"The lawyer, like the diplomat,*
*deals in debate and compromise.*
*A knowledge of law is essential to the diplomat,*
*an ability to negotiate is essential to the lawyer,*
*and a knowledge of human nature is essential to both.*
*But when the lawyer turns to international problems*
*these similarities lead him to the false conclusion*
*that diplomacy is a form of law. His whole training*
*has accustomed him to presuppose legal from illegal,*
*and where there are police and jails to enforce decisions.*
*Moral as well as legal concepts govern his thinking...*
*He seeks to regulate affairs by hard and fast formulas*
*within a completely ordered system. None of these concepts*
*applies to international affairs. Even international law, which covers*
*only a tiny part of the field of diplomacy, has few sanctions."*

– Charles W. Thayer, 1959.

All quotations culled and/or adapted from
Chas. W. Freeman, Jr. (1997):
*The Diplomat's Handbook,*
United States Institute of Peace Press,
Washington D.C., United States of America

# CONTENTS

# Note on the Author

Mark A. Sammut (Malta, 1973) has been conferred the Certificate in Diplomatic Studies by the Mediterranean Academy of Diplomatic Studies, the degrees of Doctor of Laws, Magister Juris (*summa cum laude*) in International Law, and M.A. in Translation Studies by the University of Malta and the Post-Graduate Certificate in Laws (Distinction) by the University of London. He served as a member of the State Board of Co-Operative Societies, Honorary Secretary to the national Notarial Council, Honorary Consul of Latvia, and Barbados Deputy Ships Registrar. He has published numerous articles as well as *A Short History of Latvia* (Malta, 2004). He has co-authored *Law, Morality and Reason* with former European Court of Human Rights Judge Professor Giuseppe Mifsud Bonnici (Malta, 2008), and has contributed to *The Mediterranean: Different Perspectives, Common Objectives* (Centre for Higher Defence Studies, Defence Ministry, Italy, 2010).

# ACKNOWLEDGEMENTS

This book would not have been possible without the help given by the following (in alphabetical order):

Professor David J. Attard
His Excellency former President Professor Guido de Marco
Mr Andrew Griffin
His Lordship former Chief Judge Professor Giuseppe Mifsud Bonnici
Professor Jeanne Mifsud Bonnici
Ms Roberta Padovano
Dott. Paolo Quercia
the late Mr Barry Rose
Dr Joseph H. Sciriha

and, needless to say, my parents.

I am also indebted toward the staff at The Hague Academy of International Law, The Hague, and at the Max Planck Institute, Heidelberg.

# *Foreword*

## by H.E. Professor Guido de Marco (1931-2010)

President 45th General Assembly, United Nations
President Emeritus, Republic of Malta

Dr. Mark A. Sammut has made a valid contribution to legal aspects of Consular Relations. In spite of his quotation from Eric Clarke that "Consuls are the Cinderellas of the diplomatic service", this study shows through a historical evolution, the relevance of Consuls through their structure, competence, privileges and immunities. Dr Sammut gives a detailed approach to the functions of the Consul and chapter 4 dealing with the subject, is basic to the whole structure of the book.

The reference to the *travaux préparatoires* leading to the Vienna Convention on Consular Relations, reflects the considerable research work that Dr. Sammut has gone into. His analysis on the State's duty to protect consular officials and to treat them with due respect befitting their official position, is carried out with mastery of the subject.

I found most thought provoking the study which Dr. Sammut makes of the four cases before the International Court of Justice dealing with Consular Assistance. In particular, the analysis of the points of law in the *LaGrand* case, reflect new frontiers of law. Here, the main issue lies in that "inter-state rights and obligations can no longer be insulated from individual rights, and that the interlocking of Human Rights Law with other areas of Public International Law, corresponds to the reality of contemporary International Law". The annotations and the footnotes are illuminating and provide exhaustive points of reference. Equally relevant is the excellent bibliography attached to Dr. Sammut's study.

A very interesting Chapter is that dealing with the institution of Honorary Consuls. Quoting from various journals, Dr. Sammut maintains that since the duties of Honorary Consuls do not involve the handling of political or security measures, there is no cause for concern about conflicts of loyalty. However, Dr. Sammut adds that some countries expect that Honorary Consuls should be involved in forging relations between the two States. Dr. Sammut believes that the institution of Honorary Consuls ought to be reevaluated and the facilities, privileges and immunities accorded to such Consuls, reviewed. He maintains that, "the world is [...] still riddled with poverty, and poor countries can only maintain worldwide consular networks if manned by honorary consuls. Even if poverty were ever to be eradicated, the international polity will be made up of large, medium-sized, and small Nation States. The last two will never have enough human resources to man worldwide consular networks with career consuls."

In conclusion, Dr. Sammut provides interesting comments on the Vienna Convention on Consular Relations. He does not fail to mention the debate on whether Consular Law is separate from International Law. Dr. Sammut believes that the relationship between Consular Law and Public International Law is very much akin to that between so-called "family law" and civil law.

In Dr. Sammut's view, the Vienna Convention on Consular Relations points towards, "the ever evolving role of the Consul in International Law perceived as a necessary function of the co-existence of diverse human societies coping with the various environmental (understood in the widest sense) concerns and priorities."

Dr. Sammut has provided us with a dignified study on the role of the Consul in the first years of the twenty-first century.

# *Table of Cases*

# *Table of Authorities*

# AN INTERNATIONAL LAW STUDY IN A NEO-VICTORIAN ERA

This work is based on a dissertation submitted to the Faculty of Laws of the University of Malta. When collecting materials for this work, particularly at the libraries of the Peace Palace, at The Hague, and the Max Planck Institute, at Heidelberg, intuition told the present writer that the coming into being of the process of the Conventions on Diplomatic Relations and Consular Relations was somehow related to the process of decolonization and *de jure* dismantling of empires. In reality, this was perceived by the author as a political consideration extraneous to a discussion on international law. Yet, it would not be intellectually honest to put aside this intuition. After all, Professor Chittharanjan F. Chittharanjan's words on Diplomatic Protection can be extended to cover fully the entire contents of the two Conventions: "it cannot be suggested that because diplomatic protection grew up in a colonial climate and that most states currently members of international society were not party to its creation and development, it cannot be regarded as an institution which is relevant to and covers the post colonial independent States."[1] The suggestion has been put forward that Diplomatic Protection has indeed become the key to the understanding of the "new Consular Law" which rests on four pillars: human rights, migrations and refugees, and humanitarian law.[2] These could very well be the symptoms of post-colonialism. And yet it has been said that "the Third World argued that all international law [...] was part of an international law which they had played no role in formulating and which was not, therefore binding on them."[3]

---

[1] Amerasinghe, C.F. (2008): *Diplomatic Protection*, Oxford University Press, United Kingdom, p. 6.

[2] Herrada, Z.R.M. (2006): "*El Surgumiento de un Nuevo Derecho Consular Internacional (Política Exterior, Migraciones, Derechos Humanos y Relaciones Consulares en el Contexto de la Globalización)*" in *Revista Peruana de Derecho Internacional*, N° 132, July - September 2006, Peruvian International Law Society, Peru, pp. 51-70.

[3] Anghie, A. (2004): *Imperialism, Sovereignty and the Making of International Law*, United States, p. 210.

When setting out to write this work, the aim of the present writer was not to argue that the Conventions were drafted on the eve of the creation of so many new non-European States in order to set the scenario in which future international relations would take place, and to set it within strict European or Western cultural parameters. Neither was it to argue that Western supremacy was being given a new, more subtle semblance. Was not all this too much political, and too little legal? Yet, "decolonization," writes Professor Martti Koskenniemi, "effectively universalized the European State as the only form of government that would provide equal status in the organized international community. The first generation of political leaders in the Third World in the 1950s and the 1960s may have disagreed about whether to aim for independence by devolution or revolution. But it had thoroughly integrated Western ideas about the State form as the only viable shell within which to develop into modernity."[4]

Koskenniemi is not proposing here that Western supremacy is given subtler hues. Actually, what the present writer had perceived as Western imposition, Koskenniemi argues was a spontaneous act from the non-Westerners.

Still, Professor Chantal Thomas draws on the work of David Kennedy, Antony Anghie, Martti Koskenniemi, Annelise Riles, and others, to identify four "Victorian values": "(1) the preeminent importance of international *order* and the aspiration towards an international *rule of law*, (2) *optimism* both about the plausibility of an international order and about the consequences of free trade, (3) *conquest, or the colonial* impulse, and (4) a belief in the *civilizing mission* of the North and by extension, of Northern trade with the South." The current is "*neo*-Victorian" (emphasis added), says Thomas, "due to the following two contrasts with Victorianism: (1) it is no longer legitimate to assert explicitly a colonial impulse or a civilizing mission, so that these values have become at least partially submerged in international trade discourse, and (2) whereas trade relations stood outside the heart of international law in the Victorian era, the contemporary order features an elaborate system designed specifically to manage global trade."[5]

The nineteenth century was also characterized by the appearance of another "breed" of international law: Latin American international law. The Latin Americans were most anxious to "build a capacity to signify Spanish Americans as civilized (i.e., Latin American States as having a right to be

[4] Koskenniemi, M. (2001): *The Gentle Civilizer of Nations – The Rise and Fall of International Law 1870 – 1960*, United Kingdom, p. 175.
[5] Thomas, Ch. (2000): "Neo-Victorianism and the Ideology of Globalization" in *The Hague Yearbook of International Law*, pp. 121-122.

accepted in the community of the civilized nations)."[6] The preoccupation for the Latin Americans was the diversity of races making up their States: in 1815, Simón Bolívar, perhaps the most important of South American independence leaders, said (in words which today sound profoundly offensive): "Of the Indians, Africans, Spanish and Mestizos in America, certainly the minority is white, but it is also true that whites possess the intellectual qualities which give us relative numerical equality and an important influence in the moral and physical characteristics which will be apparent to those who judge us."[7] The preoccupation with the Latin Americans was the emergence of the Creole lawyers who, as Bolívar had predicted, represented those nascent nations in the world, and the fact that said Creoles included a large degree of miscegenation. The Latin Americans gave considerable importance to the consular institution, and the number of publications originating from that region is witness to this.

It is also significant that in 1999, Jared Diamond's *Guns, Germs, and Steel*[8] won a Pulitzer Prize. Professor Diamond discusses the geophysical and ecological factors which gave rise to societies which are more politically complex than others.[9] His work confirms the notion that some collectives are less politically developed than others, even though the individual members of the less politically developed collectives are not in any way biologically inferior to the individual members of the more politically developed collectives, whether such collectives are a tribe of hunter-gatherers, a chiefdom, or a State (possibly in the sense Weber assigned to the term). Diamond purifies political evolutionism argumentations of their racist over- or undertones, while supplying environmental (i.e., non-human) reasons to explain the disparities in the different political developments of different world regions.

In particular, Diamond claims that the east-west axis of the Eurasian continental mass accounts for the quick spread of agricultural innovations

[6] Obregón, L.: "The Forgotten 19th Century: A New History of a 'Latin American' International Law" in *The Hague Yearbook of International Law*, 2000, pp. 27-32.
[7] Simón Bolívar (1815): "*Carta al editor de la Gaceta Real de Jamaica*" in *Simón Bolívar, Escritos Políticos* (1990), Spain, p. 85.
[8] Diamond, J. (1999): *Guns, Germs, and Steel – The Fates of Human Societies*, United States.
[9] Professor Diamond's work (which also includes a study of the role of religion in the creation of complex societies) would seem to be a further answer to Max Weber's question: "Through what concatenation of circumstances did it come about that precisely, and only, in the Western world certain cultural phenomena emerged which, as at least we like to think, represent a direction of development of universal significance and validity?"

(namely the domestication of new species of flora and fauna) which were at the base of the increasing complexity of highly-complex societies. The north-south axis of Africa and the Americas precluded a similar development, for these continents are characterized by diverse environmental conditions within the same landmass. For instance, Africa has two areas with a Mediterranean climate (the northernmost part and the southernmost part) with a desert and a tropical belt in between. Any agricultural progress made in the north could never reach the south because the physical environment of the desert and the rain forests would nullify any advantage of newly-domesticated animal or plant species, making transit all but impossible.

The gist of Diamond's work is that the varying degrees of "civilization" of different human societies is due to environmental reasons not to inherent shortcomings or inherent superior qualities in any particular race of the human species.

This work will discuss the role of the consul as another *dramatis persona* on the stage of a globalized world, a world with a neo-Victorian *Weltanschauung*. This awareness will however serve only as a sort of historical – understood in the sense of history of ideas – backdrop to the more mundane functions of the consul, on which this work shall exclusively concentrate. The present writer does not subscribe to any notion that research exists *in vacuo*. This Introduction serves to register what he understands to be the particular *Zeitgeist* in which this work has been researched and written out.

The present writer is aware he may be in breach of what has been claimed to be one of the fundamental laws of writing,[10] and for this an apology is proffered. Reference is made to the unwritten contract which the writer stipulates with the reader at the beginning of the work, whereby the writer

---

[10] Reference is here being made both to the style and the content of the present work which, needless to say, will be different from this Introduction. In his *Testaments Betrayed* (trans. Linda Asher), 1993, Faber and Faber, United Kingdom, p. 4, the Franco-Czech novelist Milan Kundera, speaking of the opening scene of Salman Rushdie's *The Satanic Verses* [mentioned *en passant* in this work in the context of Anglo-Iranian relations], opines: "The novel opens with that scene, for, like Rabelais, Rushdie knows that *the contract between the novelist and the reader must be established from the outset; it must be clear: the story being told here is not serious, even though it is about the most dreadful things*" (emphasis added). Kundera's words may be applied, *mutatis mutandis*, to non-fiction too. In the case of the present work, the contract is being broken in the sense that the rest of the work will not be as abstract or interdisciplinary or both as the Introduction. Also, the themes raised in the Introduction will hardly feature throughout the rest of the work.

raises the expectations of the reader. No attempt shall be made in anything but a rendition of the law and the practice. Perhaps a remedy to this shortcoming might be found in declaring from the outset that this Introduction is – if the reader will pardon the use of such a comparison in a work of a scientific nature – like Rossini's overtures and the operas they introduce: with the exception of *William Tell*, they were not (necessarily) related.

**St. John's Day, 2009**

## Structure of the book

The book gives an overview of the history of consular relations, as well as the appointment, privileges and immunities and functions of consuls. It then gives a detailed analysis of consular assistance to co-nationals and the notarial function of consuls. The consular aspect of the protection of another State's interests and the figure of the honorary consul are treated fairly in detail.

# Chapter 1

# THE CONSUL THROUGH THE AGES

> *"The narrative of brilliant campaigns and heroic military achievements may, [...] at first glance, seem more attractive than the story of the reasons why battles have been fought [... yet] the plans and purposes and policies of nations are intrinsically more important than the march of armies and the carnage of military conflicts. It is the psychological factor in moments of creative action that gives history its highest instructive value and its most lasting social utility."* David J, Hill, 1906.

## 1.1 Ancient times to the early centuries of the Middle Ages

The term "consul" derives from the Latin "*consulendo*" or "*consulo*" denoting persons whose task was "*consulare*", that is "to counsel, to judge, to determine, to assist, to oversee...". The title was given on an annual basis to two magistrates of the ancient Roman Republic starting in 508 BC. Its functions had nothing in common with those of the modern consul.

Writing in 1925, Alberto M. Candioti gave an idealistically inspiring account of the institution's origins.[1] "I reckon that this institution has its distant origins in humanity's noblest sentiments: hospitality and protection to the foreigner [...] the Greek *Proxenia*, as the incontestable and unmistakable origin of the institution under review, which proceeded, through Roman patronage, to [acquire] a wider meaning in the Middle Ages in a shape externally different, but analogous in its principle. [...] Hospitality had, among some peoples, special magistrates and institutions meant to receive and assist those coming from foreign countries. It is the purest and most admirable sentiment among the ancient peoples before which the various forms of hatred engendered by war were vanquished; it is the first dawn of

---

[1] Candioti, A.M. (1925): *Historia de la Institution Consular en la Antigüedad y en la Edad Media*, Argentina, p. xi and p. 3.

human brotherhood. Hospitality inspired very important institutions like the Greek *proxenia* and the Roman patronage, which in their time, were the authentic and honourable, certain and clear origins of our consulates".[2]

The *praetor peregrinus* was another embodiment of this institution. He looked after the protection of foreigners who were outside the *jus civile*.[3]

The history of the Far East too suggests that similar laudable ideas of hospitality towards foreigners and readiness to offer them comfort as if they were co-nationals obtained even during times of war.

## 1.2 The Middle Ages to the Early Days of the Modern Era

The Græco-Roman notions prevailed for several centuries after the dismemberment of the Western Roman Empire. It was only in the beginning of the 12th century that the title "Consul" was attributed to special magistrates responsible for the protection of persons and commercial interests of their fellow citizens in certain cities of Italy like Venice, Pisa, and Genoa as well as the port-cities of the Levant.

In Ancient Germany, the foreigner (*Wargeneus*) was outside the law. In order to enjoy some protection he had to obtain the patronage of a free German by spending three consecutive nights under his roof. If this patron was a tribal chieftain, his *protégés* could even engage in commerce and be judged according to the laws of their country of origin. This custom of bestowing protection on foreigners by means of special official persons was retained along the Mediterranean littoral right into the first centuries of the Middle Ages. In the Communes, these officials were accorded the title of "*Consoli di*

---

[2] Translated by the present writer from the original in Spanish: "*Considero que esta Institución tiene sus remotos orígenes en los más nobles sentimientos de la humanidad: la hospitalidad y la protección al extranjero [...] la* Proxenia *Griega, como el origen cierto y evidente de la institución que me ocupa, que pasó, a través del Patronato Romano, a generalizarse en la Edad Media en una forma exteriormente diversa, pero análoga en su principio. [...] La hospitalidad, tuvo, en algunos pueblos, magistraturas e instituciones especiales destinadas a ofrecer acogida y amparo a los que llegaban de extraños países. Es el más puro y bello sentimiento de los pueblos antiguos, ante el que se rendían, vencidos, los odios engendrados por la guerra; es la primera alborada de la confraternidad humana. La hospitalidad inspiró instituciones tan importantes como la* proxenia *griega y el patronato romano, las que, a su vez, son los honrosos y dignos orígenes ciertos, evidentes, de nuestros consulados.*"

[3] Theoretically, the *praetor peregrinus* had the function to say how the law stood between citizens and foreigners as well as between foreigners in Rome. In reality, however, his function was to decide each case on its own merits by equity, for there was not really any *ius* between Romans and foreigners.

*Mare*", "*Consuli marinaiorum et mercantorum.*" Their decisions were compiled in the "*Consolato del Mare.*"

The term "*juges consuls*" or "*consuls marchands*" was also used in the Middle Ages to denote the magistrates appointed to settle commercial disputes between foreigners and the magistrates' own countrymen and among foreigners themselves. In those days, other designations like "*consuls d'outre-mer*" or "*consuls à l'étranger*" were used to indicate an officer in an independent city who was charged with protecting the commercial interests of his country and to pass judgment on the litigations of his countrymen residing in a port of a foreign country.

These consuls were *electi*, and flourished during the times of the Crusades, in the autonomous commercial establishments which Venice, Amalfi, Pisa, Marseille, Barcelona, and other rich maritime cities founded in Asia Minor and along the coast of the Levant. The same system spread with the bankers of the North Sea and the Baltic, under different denominations. England alone kept disregarding these *consuli electi* for a long time.

### 1.3 From the Emergence of the Great States to the Peace of Westphalia

The 15$^{th}$ century marks the setting up of permanent legations and diplomacy as a normal instrument of international relations. The fall of Byzantium, the invention of the printing press and gunpowder, the discovery of the Americas, the renaissance of art and letters, all went to produce an international upheaval which stressed the need of continual negotiations among States. The example set by Venice was imitated by Florence and other independent Italian city-states.

The practice was diffused all over Western and Central Europe, guided by Machiavellism as founded in the principle Machiavelli propagated in *The Prince* of 1532.

Machiavellian thought, concerned solely with the immediate interests of each State, justified all the means that were useful to the Prince's ends. According to Machiavelli, "A prudent ruler cannot, and should not, honour his word when it places him at disadvantage and when the reasons for which he made his promise no longer exist".[4]

---

[4] Machiavelli, N. (trans. George Bull, 1971): *The Prince*, United Kingdom, pp. 99-100. The *rebus sic stantibus* exception to the *pacta sunt servanda* principle will be discussed in the section dealing with the US withdrawal from the Optional Protocol of the Vienna Convention on Consular Relations.

Calvo ascribes to Richelieu the paternity of permanent legations. Others opine that the Venetian *bailo* (the Venetian Ambassador residing in Constantinople) was the first permanent representative, whereas others still are of the view that the Holy See accredited an *apocrisario*[5] in Constantinople before Venice established its *bailo*. However the case may have been, permanent legations became a regular feature of international affairs following the Treaty of Westphalia of 1648.

The consul assumed the characters of a civil servant of the State whose interests he protected with the privileges pertaining to a Public Minister. This was the era of the *consuli missi* endowed with political, commercial, and judicial attributes. It transpired that the *consuli electi*, delegated as they were by mercantile bodies, were no longer looking after the needs of the State: since they had no other powers than those conferred upon them by private citizens and were not sufficiently covered by the local sovereign – all of which placed them in an awkward and dangerous position particularly in the Muslim countries where foreigners embracing a different religion were considered inferior beings.

Official intervention made its first appearance in the so-called "Capitulations" (from the Latin "*capitula*", meaning "chapters"), treaties which various European nations concluded with the Barbary Coast States, the Sultan of Constantinople, the Viceroy of Egypt and other princes of the Orient. Through these agreements they regulated the establishment, rights, and privileges of the Christian Consuls.

In the rest of the countries, the *consuli electi* were gradually replaced by the *consuli missi* who performed all types of functions, by virtue of which the Legations still maintained a transitory nature.

The practice of the Capitulations persisted for more than three centuries and was discontinued only in the first half of the 20th century. Certain characteristics of foreign protection under the Capitulations that could be compared with contemporary practices are worth noting:[6]

(a) The general protection of Westerners regardless of nationality by the diplomatic and consular representatives in the Levant of various European powers (particularly France in the early days) was predicated

[5] Among the Greeks of the Low Empire, the officer charged with conveying the replies of the Emperor.

[6] See Franklin, W.M. (1946, 2005): *Protection of Foreign Interests: A Study in Diplomatic and Consular Practice*, United States.

on the absence, or inadequate extent, of representation within the Ottoman Empire of those European States whose nationals sought foreign protection.[7]

(b) This protection was based on the consent of the local sovereign, expressed and repeatedly confirmed in the Capitulations.

(c) A feeling of Christian humanitarianism and of common opposition to the arbitrary imposition of power on the individual person, regardless of his nationality, was discernible in this practice.

(d) The protection of foreigners under the Capitulations did not take the form of an official protection by one European power of the interests of another European power. It was essentially a bilateral agreement between the local power (the Ottoman Empire) and the protecting power, which in turn dealt with its foreign *protégés* of various nationalities on an individual basis and customarily without reference to their respective home governments or sovereigns.

## 1.4 From the Peace of Westphalia to the French Revolution

The Peace of Westphalia was Europe's political and diplomatic code down to the French Revolution of 1789. It recognized the equality of all States regardless of their religious creed, exhibited a precocious appreciation of the value of international conferences in deliberating over matters of common interests, and consolidated the theory of the balance of political power. The Treaty of Westphalia had the virtue of creating among nations laudable maxims and forms and of establishing a degree of human respect among governments. The preservation of the new order among nations necessitated more than ever the institution of permanent legations abroad. Down the centuries one would equally come across the evolution of the traditional terminology including "consular representative", "consular agent", "consular office", "consular authority", as well as "commercial agent."

This dispensation was shaken like almost every other sphere of life in Europe by the intellectually devastating French Revolution. Among other matters, the Revolution, at least in its initial phases, overturned the management of foreign policy. The triumph of the principle of popular sovereignty ended the

---

[7] The exercise of this "right" in Turkey was one of the contributing causes of the Crimean War: the Western Powers protected "Western" Christians, while Russia looked after the interests of the Orthodox Christians. See Mariot, J.A.R. (1971): *The Eastern Question*, United Kingdom, pp. 229-236.

confusion between the interests of the monarchy and those of the nation. The king was now obliged to consult with the people's representatives on international matters of major significance.

## 1.5 From the Congress of Vienna to the 20th Century

Napoleon greatly increased the power of France stretching its frontiers to the central lands of Germany and a good part of Italy, founding around them a series of States governed by the Bonaparte family. This disproportionate expansion by France overturned the scenario established by the Peace of Westphalia in turn causing a reaction from the rest of the powers who formed a coalition against France. After Napoleon's abdication, there arose again the need to establish a new international order and a new balance of power. This was the mission of the 1815 Congress of Vienna which was realized in a less than equitable manner.

From the point of view of the history of diplomacy, the Congress of Vienna approved the *Règlement* concerning the rank of Diplomatic Agents; further points were settled in the 1818 Congress of Aix-la-Chapelle. The result was that diplomatic representatives were divided into four distinct classes, namely: ambassadors, nuncios, and papal legates; envoys extraordinary, ministers plenipotentiary, and other ministers accredited directly to the sovereign; ministers resident; and *chargés d'affaires.*

In certain decisions emanating from French courts in the following years, one may notice the view gaining ground that the consul does not have a "public ministry" – "*minister public*". The 14 August 1823 *Cour d'Aix* pronouncement is an example.[8] "One would not accord the nature of public minister to the consul who is but the protector, the man in charge of the operations or the difficulties of his countrymen, in brief, the man of the law of the country whose mandatary he is, rather than that of his sovereign."[9] On the 25 July 1849, the *Cour de Renner* held[10] that "Consuls are only charged with protecting the commercial interests of persons of their nation."[11]

---

[8] Sirey, 1830, 2, 190.

[9] Translated by the present writer from the original in French: "*On ne saurait pas donner le caractère de minister public au consul qui n'est pas que le protecteur, le régulateur des operations ou des difficultés de ses nationaux, l'homme, enfin, de la loi du pays dont il est le mandataire, plutôt que celui de son souverain.*"

[10] Sirey, 1850, 2, 34.

[11] Translated by the present writer from the original in French: "*Les consuls sont seulment chargés de protéger les interêts commerciaux des personnes de leur nation*".

During the 19th century, certain authors defended the idea that consuls were "public ministers."[12] One could mention Engelhardt who, in his proposal of the regulations on consular immunities submitted at the Geneva session of the Institute of International Law in 1892, took a firm position in favour of the abovementioned view. While underlining the notion that the "consuls' functions are not exclusively of an economic order, the domain of their observations and official correspondence encompasses also issues that are essentially political"; he further added that "consuls abroad have the quality of public ministers ..."[13] This view was not shared by the members of the Institute who did not actually pronounce themselves on the nature of the consuls' status.

For some time during the 19th century, consuls were actually considered "public ministers", but not for long. This was no longer the case in the 20th century. The theory was abandoned and neither the doctrine nor international practice recognized the consuls' claim to the designation of diplomatic agents.[14] This despite the fact that the Consul Institution garnered prestige on account of the increased economic, commercial, and migratory activities which took place over the preceding two centuries.

The controversy may be summed up by listing the following main theories:

(a) For some, consuls had no political quality at all. This theory was held by Bynkershoeck, Wicquefort, and other writers of the 18th century. Bynkershoeck held that, generally speaking, consuls were merchants who were sent not to represent the Prince before a foreign power, but to protect his subjects in matters of commerce, and to become acquainted with and decide upon any difference that might arise between them for

[12] Cfr. De Cussy, F. (1846): *Dictionnaire ou Manuel-Lexique du Diplomate et du Consul*, Leipzig, pp. 181-182; Heffter, A.G. (1857): *Le Droit International Publique de l'Europe, traduction de la 3e édition allemande par Bergson*, Paris-Berlin, p. 463; Clercque & De Vallat (1898): *Guide Pratique des Consuls, 5e édition* (cited by Žourek, J. (1963): *Journal du droit international*, No. 1, Paris, p. 40); Steck (1790): *Essai sur les Consuls*, p. 18 (cited by Bonfils, H. (1914): *Droit International Publique*, France, p. 503).

[13] *Annuaire de l'Institut de Droit International*, vol. XVII, 1892-1894, p. 281. See also Engelhardt's report in the same series, vol. VIII, pp. 179-187; Žourek, J. "Quelques problèmes théoriques du droit consulaire", in *Journal du Droit International*, No. 1, France, 1963, p. 42.

[14] See Oppenheim (1955): *International Law and Practice*, Vol. 1, p. 840; Irrizarry, Y. (1937): *Traité sur les Functions Internationales des Consuls*, pp. 15-16; Lee, L.T. (1961): *Consular Law and Practice*, Oxford, p. 223.

business reasons.[15] Wicquefort wrote in a similar vein arguing that consuls are merchants who, though being trusted with the task of resolving disputes between their countrymen, did not demur from promoting their own business concerns nor from submitting themselves to local laws.[16]

(b) For others, consuls, though having a public character, were not Public Ministers. This notion was held by Vattel and Klüher. Vattel opined that previously these agents were a kind of Public Ministers. In his day, however, this appointment was flourishing as the title of Consul was being granted at increasing speed to simple agents of the Prince to look after his private affairs. These were quite often subjects of the country where they resided. Therefore, Vattel concluded, they were not Public Ministers.[17] Klüher expressed himself in the sense that consuls, though vested with a public character, do not belong with the number of Public Ministers.[18] This opinion was shared by Wheaton.[19]

(c) Others opined that consuls were Public Ministers but had neither a representative nor a diplomatic character. G.F. de Martens wrote in 1788 that though being under the protection of the Law of Nations, and being able to consider themselves, in a general sense, as Public Ministers of the State which appoints them, inasmuch as that State puts them in charge of commercial affairs, it is however impossible to view them as Ministers or even as Officers in charge of business in the light of their prerogatives.

(d) Still others affirmed consuls were not Public Ministers: they had a representative character, but not a diplomatic one. This theory was upheld by J.-J. G. Foelix who wrote in 1866 that like Public Ministers, consuls receive their commission directly from the sovereign but the two commissions do not have the same character and from this difference emanates the diversity of their positions: the consul does not represent his Sovereign; he is simply an agent charged with protecting the commercial interests of his countrymen in the country where he is established.[20]

---

[15] Bynkershoeck (1721): *De Foro Legatorum*, Chapter X, paras. 5, 6.
[16] Wicquefort (1766): *L'Ambassadeur et ses Fonctions*, Book 1, Section 5, p. 63.
[17] Vattel (1758): *Le Droit des Gens*, Tome II, para. 75.
[18] Klüher, K.L. (1819, 1861): *Droit des gens moderns de l'Europe*, para. 173.
[19] Wheaton, H. (1884): *Éléments de Droit International*, Tome I, p. 223.
[20] Foelix (1866): *Traité de Droit International*, Tome I, para. 215.

Alfred Chrétien supported this theory when he said that on a par with diplomatic agents, consuls were representatives that a State sends with a permanent duty to a foreign land. But between the former and the latter there was a fundamental difference: diplomatic agents represented, under all aspects, in any manner and in absolute fashion, the State which accredited them, and on its behalf, might deal and negotiate with the foreign government, whereas consuls had a much more restricted mandate. They must secure the respect and development of economic and intellectual interests that a State or its nationals might have in a foreign country, and exercise privately and by special delegation the duty of providing their co-nationals with protection. This was their quasi-exclusive brief. Consuls were, therefore, not really diplomatic agents, as their mission was more commercial than political.[21]

(e) The literature gives prominence to Oppenheim's opinion that consuls are State agents residing in another State for various purposes, but particularly with the aim of monitoring the former State's commercial and shipping interests.[22] In general, they have nothing to do with State-State relations, they are not diplomatic representatives because they do not represent that State that accredited them in its bilateral relations except for some business matters. P.L.E. Pradier-Fodéré held a similar view.[23] The doctrine which denied consuls a diplomatic nature and the pretence to be considered as Public Ministers was to his mind more defensible and more justified than other theories; this was because the writer viewed Public Ministers as primarily political whereas consuls were above all commercial agents designated to perform determined functions in the locality of their residence. Pradier-Fodéré cites the Congress of Vienna of 1815 with regard to the post of Diplomatic Agents and the Conference at Aix-la-Chapelle regarding Resident Ministers and points out that the post of consul does not feature at all. These ideas were shared by other authorities like Aspiazu, Bello, Bevilaqua, Bonfils, Bry, Casanova, Despagnet and Boek, Dudley-Field, Foignet, Halleck, Jordan, Mérignhac, Pomeroy, Planas Suarez, Taylor, and Twiss.

(f) In contrast with the foregoing emerged the view that consuls are Public Ministers or Diplomatic Agents of a lower order. This thesis

---

[21] Chrétien (1893): *Principes de Droit International Publique*, p. 499.
[22] Oppenheim (1912): *International law, a treatise*, 2 ed., Vol. I, para. 410 and para. 434, pp. 484 and 493.
[23] Pradier-Fodéré (1885-1886): *Traité de Droit International Public Européen et Américain*, Tome IV, nos. 2110 and 2111.

originally advanced by Steck was defended by Pinheiro-Ferreira, Heffter, Moser, Espersen, and Carnazza Amari. Steck held that it was a futile discussion to deny this quality to such State representatives: anybody who was charged by his superiors to look after the State business and national interests should be considered a Public Minister.[24] Pinheiro-Ferreira defended this thesis in a note he appends to Baltic-Russian G.F. de Martens' *œuvre* by arguing that the distinction between Ministers and Consuls was based only on a misunderstanding.[25] Diplomatic Ministers were Public Agents accredited to foreign governments; if Consuls fulfilled the same tasks they should be deemed also as such. De Martens pointed out that consuls were originally agents whose designation was drawn up by merchants with the object of protecting the commercial interests of the latter in foreign countries. In this quality, they could not be considered Public Agents or Ministers since they did not receive their mandate from the State but only from a somewhat sizeable fraction thereof. However, when these Agents were subsequently transformed into representatives of the national commerce, and the country's authorities rather than the commercial corporations started nominating them to protect the interests of the State itself, not those of individuals wishing to employ their go-between services, these consuls should have been considered as Public Agents or Diplomatic Agents accredited to foreign governments even if of a lower order than Public Ministers (or ambassadors); for this reason, they should not be excluded from the Diplomatic Corps. Heffter too maintained that consuls formed a special class of Diplomatic Agents.[26] Of the same opinion were Esperson[27] and Carnazza-Amari. The latter maintained that in view of the common functions they shared in a certain manner with Diplomatic Agents, consuls could be considered Public Ministers of a lower order though with a character distinct from the State's representatives.

(g) Various authors held that consuls *missi* should have the diplomatic character. The difference between the *missi* and the *electi* was advanced by Cussy, Bluntschili, Clerq and Vallat, Engelhardt, Lehr, Laigue and Trajano Mera. Baron de Cussy opined that the nature of their service and relations with the government which accredits them and the different attributions of their responsibilities demonstrate in a positive

[24] Steck (1790): *Essai sur les Consuls*, Section V, p. 18.
[25] Pinheiro-Ferreira's note to paragraph 147, de Martens, G.F. (1883, trans. Alfred Leo), *Traité de Droit International Public*, Tome II, pp. 307 and 309.
[26] Heffter, A.G., *op. cit.*, para. 246. p. 559.
[27] Esperson (1874): *Diritto Diplomatico e Giurisdizione Internazionale Marittima*, Tome II, p. 15.

way that consuls *missi* should not be denied the double quality of Public Agents and Diplomatic Agents. Cussy explained further the reasons why, to his understanding, their government deprived them of this character. In the beginning, consuls were elected by their countrymen; accustomed to consider them as mere traders, the early jurists accepted along with Wicquefort the principle that consuls are commercial agents. This theory was continued by later authors who, without investigating the changes that took place in the consular institution, accepted the received wisdom which did not, however, reflect the realities of the day. In actual fact, some countries were already engaging in their consular service traders who, without abandoning their commercial concerns, served as mediums of information and unsalaried correspondents. Against such background it was natural for authors as well as governments to resist attaching the endowment of Public Ministers to all these functionaries. This notwithstanding, jurists and governments were obliged to install the former in their armies and the latter in their acts to wit: the non-trading consuls *missi*, but political and diplomatic agents of the Prince who employs them who form part of the consular career devoting their whole time to their work after being prepared in this wise with special studies; and the simple consuls – commercial agents – with whatever honorific title they may be invested. Cussy argued that the former doubtlessly deserved the endowment of Public Minister and only they should receive the Letters Patent signed by the Sovereign. The designation of Public Minister should not be attributed to the latter because these were neither independent nor State civil servants. These latter consuls or commercial agents should only receive a *diploma* granted by the Legation or the Consulate General. Cussy concluded that it is indispensable in the interests of the service and in that of the consular institution and of its success, that the most powerful maritime States set an example and establish the principle by including in their future treaties that the non-trading consuls *missi* shall have the designation of Public Ministers in their quality as political and diplomatic agents.[28] Bluntschli, De Clerq, Vallat, and Engelhardt upheld this classification of consular functionaries. In the project Engelhardt presented to the *Institut de Droit International* in 1889, he stated that consuls had the quality of Public Ministers, assuming that consuls meant the *missi* type.[29] Lehr supported this thesis arguing that the underlying division between some members

---

[28] Baron de Cussy, F. (1851): *Réglements Consulaires des Principaux États Maritimes de l'Europe et de l'Amerique*, Leipzig, pp. 16, 75, 87 and 88; *Dictionnaire de Diplomate et du Consul*, *op. cit.*, pp. 190 and 193.

[29] *Annuaire de l'Institut de Droit International*, Tome II, 1889-1892, Germany, pp. 347 and 394.

of the Diplomatic Corps and Career Consuls in various countries and under distinct aspects did not appear as totally arbitrary as before. Consuls must be subordinate to the Chief of Mission in the same way that a Sub-prefect is subordinate to a Prefect or a District Director under the Governor of the Province, but they have similar functions and both have the quality of Public Ministers.[30] Laigue argued that the consuls *missi* are Public Ministers who come after Officers in charge of commerce.[31] Trajano Mera saw basic differences between a Minister and a Career Consul. He asks whether the consul is but an agent sent by a government to a government of another nation. Is the consul not granted various functions of a political nature? Does the consul not have several attributes and obligations which enter the sphere of those properly known as diplomatic ones and which are exercised by both in turn?[32]

(h) Finally, it was held that the consuls *missi* did not have a diplomatic nature nor that of Public Ministers, yet they had to be conceded greater prerogatives than the *electi*. This was the doctrine adopted by the *Institut de Droit International* and had also the support of Calvo, Halleck, Fiore, and Nys, among other authorities. The Regulation on Consular Immunities, approved by the *Institut* on 26 September 1896 in its Venice session, stated that only consuls *missi* were entitled to the title of Consul, while the rest of the consular officers the appellation "Consular Agents": the former were entitled to much wider prerogatives than those pertaining to the latter.

## 1.6 The Vienna Consular Convention of 1963

In his first report on consular relations redacted in 1957, Professor Žourek chose the term "consular representative."[33] In 1960, the special rapporteur to the International Law Commission used the simple term "consul"[34] but the following year used "consular official" to designate every person, including the mail officer, connected with the consul's functions inside a consulate.[35]

---

[30] Lehr, E.: "*De quelques modifications à apporter à l'organisation du corps consulaire et de la création d'agents commerciaux*" in *Revue de Droit International et de Législation Comparée*, Tome XXII, 1890, pp. 438-454.

[31] Laigue, "*L'institution consulaire*" in *Revue d'Histoire Diplomatique*, IV year, no. 4.

[32] Mera, J.T. (1910): *Cónsules y Consulados*, Ecuador, pp. 199 and 204.

[33] Article 3, Document A/CN 3/108, *Annuaire de la Commission du Droit International*, 1957, vol. II, p. 97.

[34] Document A/CN.4/L.86, *Annuaire de la Commission du Droit International*, 1960, vol. II, p. 96.

[35] Article 1(d). Document A/4843, *Annuaire de la Commission du Droit International*, 1961, vol. II, p. 96.

"Consular officer" was the term adopted by the Vienna Convention on Consular Relations of 1963.[36]

The choice of the term "consular officer" is nowadays deemed as the best in order to eliminate all confusing notions that might mar somewhat the substantial significance of the institution. It was adopted in the regulations and conventions of the United Kingdom, the Netherlands, and the United States and the (unratified) European Convention on Consular Functions of 1964.

Notable individual experts too have commented on this matter. Paul Fauchille amplifies.[37] "Consuls are official agents a State establishes in cities or ports of a foreign State with the mission to protect its commercial interests, to provide assistance, and to render protection to its nationals – traders or legal persons –, to police its merchant navy, to supervise the implementation of commercial and maritime treaties, to supply report on the agricultural produce and industrial production, and on the commercial activities of foreign countries, etc."[38]

A definition which may be considered quite complete was the one forwarded by Professor Guggenheim.[39] "Consuls are official representatives of the State, however lacking a diplomatic nature. They must perform the functions assigned to them by the domestic law of the State they represent and which are frequently mentioned also in consular conventions. It is not seldom for local customs to determine some of their consular functions."[40]

---

[36] Article 1(d). Doc. Off. A/Conf. 25/16 Add. 1, "*Conférence des Nations Unies sur les relations consulaires*", Vienna, United Nations, 4 March-22 April 1963, vol. II, p. 179.

[37] Fauchille, P. (1921-26): *Traité de Droit International Publique*, (8 ed.), *Tome 1, Part III*, pp. 109-111.

[38] Translated by the present writer from the original in French: "*Les consuls sont des agents officials qu'un État établit dans des villes ou dans des ports du pays étranger, avec la mission de veiller à ses interêts commerciaux, de preter assistance et d'accorder protection à ses nationaux, commerçants ou judiciares, d'exercer la police de sa marine marchande, de surveiller l'exécution des traités de commerce et de navigation, de fournir des renseignements sur les productions agricoles et industrielles et sur le movement commercial des pays étrangers, etc.*".

[39] Guggenheim, P. (1953): *Traité de Droit International Publique*, Switzerland, p. 512.

[40] Translated by the present writer from the original in French: "*Les consuls sont des représentants officials de l'État mais sans caractère diplomatique. Ils doivent exercer les functions que leur attribute le droit national de l'État qu'ils représentent et qui se trouvent souvent mentionées aussi dans les conventions consulaires. Il n'est pas rare non plus que l'usage local determine certaines des fonctions consulaires*".

The Harvard Law School provides this definition: "Consul is a person entitled to exercise consular functions as an agent of a State in the territory of another State."[41]

The abovementioned definitions of "consul" may be summed up under four points:

(a) he/she is an official agent designated by a government to exercise consular functions in a foreign State;

(b) he/she does not have a diplomatic make-up meaning s/he does not enjoy all the privileges enjoyed by a diplomat;

(c) his/her functions are generally speaking of a commercial nature; this was the case at the beginning of the 20th century but this role has noticeably changed since then;

(d) there is a marked difference between *missi* and *electi*, the latter being afforded less prerogatives than the former.

Most modern authors nevertheless seem to concur on the following definition: the consul, after being appointed in the capacity of official representative by a State with the consent of another State, is sent to exercise, within the territory of the latter, certain functions of an economic, administrative, cultural, and judicial order, as well as other functions, in conformity with the rules of international law.

It is nowadays the general sentiment that the ultimate objective of international law, and indeed, of all law is human welfare.[42] This objective seems to define the new trends in consular law which have emerged not only due to globalization and the movements of great masses of peoples[43] but also

[41] Harvard Law School (1932): "Legal Position and Function of Consuls", in *Research in International Law*, art. 1(a), p. 193.

[42] Mani, V.S. (1999): "The Right to Consular Assistance as a Basic Human Right of Aliens – A Review of the ICJ Order dated 3 March 1999" in *The Indian Journal of International Law*, Vol. 39, July- September 1999, India, p. 442.

[43] According to Zlotnik, H. (2002): *International migration trends since 1980*, Population Division, Department of Economic and Social Affairs, United Nations, p. 13, from 1980 to 2000 there was a 2.8% yearly increase in international migrants, with numbers rising from 100 million to 175 million. According to certain estimates, in 2008 the number of persons residing legally in another country surpassed 200 million, equivalent to approximately 3% of world population – Quercia, P.

to the "humanization" of the protection of nationals[44] particularly in the aftermath of the three cases decided by the International Court of Justice, which will be discussed in detail in Chapter Five.

(ed.)(2009): *Fare Italia nel mondo: le sfide post-globali delle nuove relazioni internazionali*, Italy, p. 36.

[44] See Mennecke, M. (2001): "Towards the humanization of the Vienna Convention of Consular Rights – The *LaGrand* Case Before the International Court" in *The German Yearbook of Internaitonal Law*, Vol. 44, Berlin, Germany, pp. 430-468; Pergantis, V. (2006): "Towards a 'humanization' of Diplomatic Protection?' in *66 Zeitschrift für Ausländisches Offentliches Recht und Völkerrecht*, Germany, pp. 351-397; Cançado Trindade, A.A. (2007): "The Humanization of Consular Law: The Impact of Advisory Opinion No. 16 (1999) of the Inter-American Court of Human Rights on International Case-law and Practice" in *Chinese Journal of International Law*, Vol. 6, No. 1, pp. 1-16.

# Chapter 2

# THE APPOINTMENT OF CONSULS

> *"Consul. In American politics, a person who having failed to secure an office from the people is given one by the Administration on condition that he leave the country."* Ambrose Bierce, 1906.

## 2.1 The Consular Commission

There are no rules in international law which regulate the choice and appointment of heads of consular posts. It is the domestic legislation of each State which determines the necessary conditions for the appointment of such office. Such appointments are done by the sending State, but have to be admitted by the receiving State.[1]

After having been freely chosen and designated by the sending State, the head of consular post must be given, by his government, a certificate (*lettre patente*) providing details of the commission. This *lettre patente* usually carries the name and surname of the appointee, the category and calls, and the district wherein the consular functions are to be exercised. This letter is transmitted through diplomatic or other channels to the government of the State in whose territory the consular functions will be exercised. The notification must contain the same indications as a letter of commission.[2]

## 2.2 The *Exequatur*

Having been appointed and commissioned by the sending State, the head of consular post must be recognized by the receiving State to exercise his functions.

By admitting the head of post, it is understood that the receiving State is also admitting the consular staff working under the direction and responsibility of the same head of post. The admission of the head of post to the free exercise of consular duties within the consular district as well as to his official character is called the *exequatur*.

---

[1] Art. 10, *Vienna Convention on Consular Relations*, 1963 (hereinafter referred to as VCCR).

[2] Art. 11, VCCR.

Which is the competent authority to deliver the *exequatur*? This usually depends on the domestic legislation of the receiving State; however, generally speaking, it is delivered by the Minister of Foreign Affairs. With regard to the form of the *exequatur*, once again this is wholly dependent on domestic legislation.

The International Law Commission found that the most common forms of the *exequatur* are the following:

> (a) an ordinance of the Head of State, signed by him and countersigned by the Minister of Foreign Affairs, the original whereof is delivered to the head of consular post;
>
> (b) an ordinance signed as aforesaid, but only a copy of which is delivered to the head of consular post, the authenticity of the copy being certified by the Minister of Foreign Affairs;
>
> (c) a transcription of the letter of commission, which transcription can take various forms;
>
> (d) a notification through diplomatic channels delivered to the sending State.

A proposal to have other less formal forms of authorization recognized was not accepted by the Conference on the Vienna Convention on Consular Relations (hereinafter referred to as VCCR).

### 2.3 Refusal of *Exequatur*

The receiving State may, as a function of its sovereignty, refuse the *exequatur* to a foreign consul. State practice is somewhat inconsistent with regard to whether a reason has to be provided for a refusal. Some old conventions, such as the 1867 Diplomatic and Consular Convention signed between the Latin American countries, and domestic legislations, imposed on the receiving State a duty to give the reason for a refusal. Žourek, however, claimed that "conventions prescribing the communication of reasons constitute an exception."[3]

The VCCR, upon an amendment brought forward by Argentina and India, does not include the giving of reasons as a requirement for a refusal.

---

[3] Žourek, J. (1957): *International Law Commission Yearbook*, vol. II, p. 102.

The history of consular relations offers some examples where the *exequatur* was refused. For instance, Žourek says that in 1830 Austria refused the *exequatur* to Stendahl as French consul in Trieste, on account of quarrels which Stendahl had had with the Austrian police.[4] In 1869, the British government refused the *exequatur* to Major Haggerty, a naturalized American citizen of Irish descent, as United States consul in Glasgow (Scotland) because of the part he had taken in the Fenian revolt.[5]

The receiving State has also the right to withdraw the *exequatur* if the consul violates the receiving State's domestic laws or interferes in the receiving State's internal affairs. This measure may terminate the official role of the consul in the receiving State upon the withdrawal of the *exequatur.* In 1856, the United States withdrew the *exequatur* of the British consuls in New York, Philadelphia, and Cincinnati, because they had tried to recruit American residents in the British army occupied in the Crimean war, thereby violating the law on neutrality. In 1948, the United States withdrew the *exequatur* of the Soviet consul in New York, because he was abusing of his privileges and immunities.[6]

Once again the question arises whether the receiving State is bound to offer reasons for the withdrawal of an *exequatur.* There is no uniform practice, as each Convention has its own peculiar regime. Žourek's opinion is that reasons are obligatory only in the case of a refusal of *exequatur.*[7] Article 23 VCCR confirms this view. It does not impose on States the obligation of supplying reasons when a consul becomes *persona non grata.* The wisdom of this position cannot be discounted, for it avoids the possibility of conflict between States caused by the behaviour of a single person.

### 2.4 Provisional exercise of functions pending delivery of *exequatur*

It is generally accepted that until the *exequatur* is issued, a head of consular post can be authorized to exercise his consular functions on a provisional basis. The VCCR has recognized the practical usefulness of this rule in Article 13.

### 2.5 Rupture of Diplomatic Relations, Implications

The rupture of diplomatic relations between States does not necessarily bring in its wake a similar rupture in consular relations. Nonetheless, consular

[4] *Op. cit.*, pp. 101 and 102.
[5] Irizarry, Y. (trans. Schlegel, 1937): *Traité sur les fonctions internationales des consuls*, France, p. 62.
[6] *Revue générale de droit international public*, 1958, no. 2, p. 262.
[7] *Op. cit.*, p. 108.

relations may still be severed. Positive international law is not well-equipped for such situations.

When consular relations are terminated, it is first of all important to determine the moment of termination and the reasons for it. The practical consequences of this lie in the validity of official acts performed by the consul. The VCCR regulates this contingency in Article 25. However, this provision is not exhaustive for it only mentions the more frequent cases when consular functions are terminated. State practice and doctrine have identified other causes: the decease of a consular official or employee, the closing down of the consulate, the severance of consular relations, the extinction of the sending State or the incorporation of the consular district within another State, or if the two States enter a state of war.

## 2.6 The Demise of a Consular Officer

It is evident that when a consular officer dies, his consular functions and status cease automatically. However, despite the demise of the consul, his family members keep enjoying consular privileges and immunities until the moment they leave the receiving State or until the expiry of a reasonable lapse of time since the consul's death.

In the case of the decease of a member of a consulate or a member of his family, the receiving State is bound (a) to allow the exportation of the movables belonging to the deceased, with the exception of those acquired in the receiving State and are the object of a rule forbidding their exportation at the moment of the death; (b) not to charge succession duties on the movables which are in the receiving State only because the deceased consular officer was posted in that State, or because the deceased was in that place because of his being a member of the family of the consular officer.

## 2.7 Closing Down of Consular Post

A sending State may take the decision to close down, whether temporarily or permanently, the consular post within the territory of the receiving State. Such decisions may be due to budgetary reasons, not necessarily political ones.

Article 27(2) VCCR provides for the temporary closing down of one consular post in the territory of the receiving State when the sending State has other consular posts within the same territory. In this case, the latter consular post may assume the continuation of the functions of the former, and may also assume the responsibility (with all the privileges and immunities relating thereto) for the former's archives.

## 2.8 Extinction of States: Implications

The official status of a consul is constituted by two States, and it necessarily follows that the disappearance of one of them brings in its wake the *ipso facto* cessation of consular relations. However, a distinction is to be made if it is the receiving State which has become extinct. In this case, if the consul is to continue exercising his functions, he must demand a new *exequatur* or at least a provisional authorization from the State which has absorbed the State of residence. Following the Italian military conquest of Ethiopia in 1936, for instance, it was only upon British *de facto* recognition of Italian sovereignty on Ethiopia that the British consul-general at Addis Ababa was granted the *exequatur* by the Italian government.

When the sending State loses its sovereignty, upon annexation, it is not always the case that consular functions will terminate, particularly if the receiving State does not recognize the annexation. For instance, the United States never recognized the annexation of the Baltic States to the Union of Soviet Socialist Republics. However, maintaining consular relations with States that lack international juridical personality is not sustainable under international law. The American-Baltic experience brought to the fore a series of problems not all of which were of a legal nature. For instance, there was a dilemma regarding how to maintain the missions once the representative appointed prior to the 1940 annexation died. Actually, it was very rare for Baltic diplomats to retire during this period (even when faced with failing health) because of the desire to avoid losing any members of a dwindling staff.[8] Whereas the British government saw the natural development of affairs as "heralding an end to an awkward situation," the United States recognized the children of Baltic diplomats within the United States as "the legal successors [...] to the diplomatic powers and privileges their parents had continued to enjoy after the 1940 annexation of their respective countries. [...] Yet the extension of diplomatic credentials solely by authority of a diplomatic mission, with no government available to authorize it, was a clear departure from the conventions and letter of international law."[9]

## 2.9 War between the Two States, Implications

In the case of proper war between States (as opposed to the Cold War between the United States and the Soviet Union), there is no doubt that the cessation of all possible relations between the warring States causes the

[8] McHugh, J.T. & Pacy, J.S. (2001): *Diplomacy Without a Country – Baltic Diplomacy, International Law, and the Cold War*, United States, p. 88, fn. 38. This book gives a detailed account and analysis of this peculiar experience.
[9] *Ibid.*, p. 81.

rupture of diplomatic and consular relations between the two States. The maintenance of consular relations depends on peaceful relations between the two States. During wartime, the sending State can entrust its consular functions to a third State acceptable to the receiving State.[10]

[10] This is will discussed in more detail in Chapter Seven, dealing with the protection of foreign interests.

# *Chapter 3*

# CONSULAR PRIVILEGES AND IMMUNITIES

> *"The inviolability of ambassadors is sacred and acknowledged as such by all civilized peoples."* Julius Caesar.

In the *Case Concerning Diplomatic and Consular Staff in Tehran (United States of America* v. *Iran)*, the International Court of Justice (ICJ) stated that "there is no more fundamental prerequisite for the conduct of relations between States than the inviolability of diplomatic envoys and embassies, so that throughout history nations of all creeds and cultures have observed reciprocal obligations for that purpose; and [...] the obligations thus assumed, notably those for assuring the personal safety of diplomats and their freedom from prosecution are essential, unqualified, and inherent in their representative character and their diplomatic function. [T]he unimpeded conduct of consular relations, which have also been established between peoples since ancient times, is no less important in the context of present-day international law, in promoting the development of friendly relations among nations, and ensuring protection and assistance for aliens resident in territories of other States. [...T]herefore the privileges and immunities of consular officers and consular employees, and the inviolability of consular premises and archives, are similarly principles deep-rooted in international law."[1]

In his Separate Opinion to the same Judgment, Judge Lachs underlined that "the principles and rules of diplomatic privileges and immunities are not – and this cannot be over-stressed – the invention or device of one group of nations, of one continent or one circle of culture, but have been established for centuries and are shared by nations of all races and all civilizations. [...The two Vienna Conventions] reflect the law as approved by all regions of the globe, and by peoples belonging to both North and South, East and West alike. The laws in question are the common property of the international community and were confirmed in the interest of all."[2]

---

[1] *Request for the Indication of Provisional Measures, Order of the 15 December 1979*, pp. 16-17.
[2] *I.C.J. Reports* 1980, pp. 48-49.

In his Dissenting Opinion to the same Judgment, Judge Morozov reiterated that the "long-established rules of general international law relating to the privileges, inviolabilities and immunities of diplomatic and consular personnel are among those which are particularly important for the implementation of such basic principles of contemporary international law as the peaceful coexistence of countries with different political, social and economic structures. These rules are reflected in the [...] Vienna Convention of 24 April 1963 on Consular Relations."[3]

### 3.1 Nomenclature

Due to the divergent terminology used in various States, it is necessary, first of all, to make a few remarks on the nomenclature to be used in this Chapter. "Privileges and immunities" is a common term used to designate the legal status of the members of permanent diplomatic missions, of consular posts, and of special missions. Many attempts have been made in the international legal literature to differentiate between a "privilege" and an "immunity."

Some define as a "privilege" the legal capacity to do or to ask for what others are not entitled to, and as "immunity" the legal capacity not to do what others are obliged to do.[4] By the term "immunities," other authors understand the exemption from the jurisdiction of the receiving State, and by the term "privileges," other prerogatives not covered by the term "immunities."[5] Others argue that the term "privilege" may be used in a much wider sense that the term "immunity" and that in fact the latter is only a specific type of "privilege."[6]

In this Chapter, references to honorary consuls will be deliberately omitted given that the privileges and immunities of that class will be discussed in Chapter Eight.

### 3.2 The Rationale behind Privileges and Immunities

The matter of privileges and immunities reflects the fundamental distinction between diplomatic representatives and consular officers. Whereas the observance of diplomatic immunities was guaranteed by international law, consular privileges and immunities were based on provisions of treaties and practice of States. States had been generally reluctant to accord diplomatic privileges to consular officers. Indeed, the extent of consular privileges and immunities varied considerably depending on the terms of respective treaties

[3] *I.C.J. Reports* 1980, p. 51.
[4] Libera, K. (1960): *Principles of International Consular Law*, Poland, p. 265.
[5] See do Nascimento e Silva, G.E. (1972): *Dictionary in International Law*, the Netherlands, p. 89.
[6] Verdross, A. (1957) in *Yearbook of the International Law Commission*, 1957, vol. 1, p. 52.

and municipal legislation. Proof of this lies in the fact that only two immunities a consul may claim are universally recognized: the inviolability of consular archives and non-liability for acts performed in official capacity.[7]

Several authors (Oppenheim, Hyde, Hackworth, for instance) have maintained, however, that consuls should be accorded those privileges and immunities that are essential to the discharge of their functions by virtue of their being agents of the appointing State and on account of their being recipients of *exequaturs* from the receiving State; otherwise, the admission of these representatives would serve no useful purpose.

The old distinction between diplomatic agents and consuls has been questioned by some of the recent authors (e.g. Luke T. Lee) who assert that consular officers at important posts have to assume greater responsibilities than the chief of a mission in smaller countries. Perhaps the distinction might be removed altogether by the amalgamation of diplomatic and consular services in most countries.

Giuliano, Scovazzi, and Treves[8] put it thus: "The establishment of consular relations among States, followed by the effective opening of the consular post/s of one State in the territory of the other, engenders the subjective right of one State to exercise, without hindrances, the totality of consular functions in the territory of the other State. It also engenders the latter State's relative obligation not to hinder said exercise. This is yet another example of the consequences of a general rule of international law linked directly and with immediacy to the establishment of consular relations between States. It follows that the bases of said rule need not be sought in the implicit or presumed consent of the State which had already given its consent to the opening on its territory of another State's consular offices."[9]

The VCCR contains the indispensable minimum of privileges and their scope is being constantly extended in bilateral consular conventions.

---

[7] Beckett, W.E. (1944): "Consular Immunities" in *British Yearbook of International Law*, XXI, pp. 34 and 37.

[8] Giuliano, M., Scovazzi, T., & Treves, T. (1983): *Diritto Internazionale, II Gli Aspetti Giuridici della Coesistenza degli Stati*, Italy, pp. 382-383.

[9] Translated by the present writer from the original in Italian: "*Dallo stabilimento di relazioni consolari tra Stati, seguito dalla effettiva instaurazione di uffici consolari di uno Stato nel territorio dell'altro, discende il diritto soggettivo di uno Stato di svolgere senza intralci l'insieme delle funzioni consolari nel territorio dell'altro Stato; e correlativamente l'obbligo di questo ultimo di non intralciarne l'esercizio. Si tratta, anche qui, di una conseguenza che una regola internazionale generale riallaccia direttamente e immediatamente al fatto dell'instaurazione di relazioni consolari tra Stati; e il cui fondamento non ha pertanto bisogno di essere ricercato nel consenso implicito o presunto dello Stato che ha consentito allo stabilimento nel suo territorio di uffici consolari di un altro Stato.*"

### 3.3 States' Duty to Protect

There seems to be universal agreement that the receiving State is under an obligation to accord special protection to consular officials, treating them with due respect befitting their official position. This obligation, regarded as forming part of customary international law, stems from the fact that the consul is an official representative of his government in the receiving State, and is charged with official functions on behalf of the sending State within the consular district. This duty of protection is deemed *sine qua non* for the consul to carry out his official duties properly. Failure to afford that degree of extra care may render the receiving State answerable in international law. In the case of career consular officers, the State is obliged to ensure the prevention of any attack on their persons, freedom or dignity. When such attacks do take place, the presumption has always been that the receiving State has failed in its duty to provide protection and it is that State's duty to prosecute the perpetrators and to apologize to the sending State. Foreign governments expect receiving States to be vigilant in respect of the safety and security of their representatives.[10]

In the *Case Concerning Diplomatic and Consular Staff in Tehran*, the ICJ held that any "feeling of offence could not affect the imperative character of the legal obligations incumbent upon the [receiving State] which is not altered by a state of diplomatic tension between the two countries."[11] In other words, privileges and immunities are to be upheld no matter what the circumstances.

### 3.4 Immunity from Judicial Proceedings

Unlike diplomatic agents, consular officers do not enjoy immunity from the jurisdiction of local civil and criminal courts. Any exemptions from local judicial jurisdiction depend on treaty provisions, reciprocity, and courtesy, as well as the national law, regulations and policy of the receiving State. Exemption from local jurisdiction does apply to acts consuls perform in the course of their official functions, as they would be acting in representation of the sending State and for States to be sued for their sovereign acts their consent is required. This position is reflected in Article 43(1) VCCR. Article 43(2), however, provides that if a consular officer or a consular employee does not contract, expressly or implicitly, as an agent of the sending State then he shall not enjoy immunity from jurisdiction in civil actions arising out of such contract. There are two exceptions to the foregoing: (1) a consular officer is exempt from jurisdiction in respect of all his acts, irrespective of

---

[10] Sen, B. (1988): *A Diplomat's Handbook of International Law and Practice*, 3rd Revised Ed., the Netherlands, p. 289.
[11] *I.C.J. Reports* 1980, p. 42.

whether they are done in a private capacity or in the exercise of official functions, if and only if the officer is accorded the same immunities as a diplomatic agent; and (2) if in his official capacity the consular officer enters into a contract the subject-matter which is of a commercial nature, then if the receiving State applies the doctrine of sovereign immunity restrictively, the dispute may be subjected to local jurisdiction.[12]

In order to establish the orbit within which consular immunity from judicial proceedings is operative, Yoram Dinstein argues that it is essential to determine the theoretical foundation upon which such immunity is grounded and from which it emanates.[13] Dinstein criticizes the view that without immunity consuls would be unable to exercise their functions with the necessary independence. He points out that the view was espoused by Section 69 of the Tentative Draft Restatement of the Foreign Relations Laws of the United States, formulated in 1958 under the auspices of the American Law Institute, and is upheld by Beckett, Fodéré, and Starke.

Dinstein's objective is based on his assertion that if a consul is to enjoy such immunity in order not to be hindered from attending the duties of his office, surely this consideration must lead us to the conclusion that the consul be conceded a comprehensive immunity from judicial process applicable *ratione personae* (as long as his mission lasts), regardless of the nature of his acts.

Dinstein asks, "If [the consul] is anyhow amenable to local proceedings – if in any event he can sit behind bolt and bar, rather than behind his desk; or he may have to devote his time, energy, and financial resources to defend himself against litigious persons, instead of concentrating on carrying out the important assignments allotted to him – what is the virtue of affording him partial immunity, in respect of merely some of his acts?" Dinstein concludes that "such a limited protection seems to be too inadequate for comfort."[14]

Dinstein can still see the argument cropping up that "consular immunity is designed to gratify the consul's psychological demand for self-confidence by extinguishing his fears of an ultimate day of reckoning in court insofar as the exercise of his functions is concerned; fears that could result in his refraining from the doing of acts of consequence in the line of duty on account of their possible legal repercussions in the future." In reply to such argumentation, Dinstein retorts "[...] that self-confidence is in any case illusory where the immunity covers not the whole canvas of activity of the consul but only a

---

[12] Sen, B., *op. cit.*, p. 290.
[13] Dinstein, Y. (1966): *Consular Immunity from Judicial Process*, Israel, pp. 21-22.
[14] *Ibid.*, p. 22.

segment of it. So long as the immunity is applicable *ratione materiae*, rather than *ratione personae*, the consul with uneasy anticipations of a latter-day lawsuit must check all his contemplated actions, to distinguish between acts that are sheltered by it and those that are not, and often will find it difficult to separate the wheat from the straw." Dinstein's conclusion: "It follows that, consular immunity from judicial process notwithstanding, the jurisdictional sword of Damocles continues to hang over the consul's head in an interminably threatening manner. The concern for the proper performance of consular functions cannot, then, explain, why the immunity relates to certain acts, to the exclusion of others."[15]

The rationale of consular immunity from proceedings is, and must be, impressed in the special nature of the particular acts to which it pertains. As the Harvard Research on the Legal Position and Functions of Consuls set forth:

> "This exemption is not based directly on the principle of insuring the unimpeded functioning of the consular office [...]; it is a consequence of the rule of general international law regarding the recognized public acts of one State in the territory of another."[16]

In the sequel, the *Research* declares that consular immunity applies to "official acts." In trying to define when an "official act" is, one may suggest that an act is official if performed under the authority and on behalf of a State by one of its organs. This means that consular immunity from judicial process is based on, and derived from, the official nature of acts that are performed by a foreign consul in his capacity as an arm of a mouthpiece of the sending State, because such acts should be ascribed to that State and regarded as its own. As Lauterpacht puts it: "The immunity of consuls constitutes, upon analysis, one aspect of the jurisdictional immunity of States on whose behalf they act."[17]

Many other authoritative writers agree that it is the official nature of the acts carried out by a consul, and the need to attribute them to his sending State, that lie at the root of consular exemption from proceedings.[18] This is also the rational foundation of Article 43(1) VCCR, as unequivocally demonstrated by its *travaux préparatoires.* Thus, in its first Report submitted by Special

[15] *Ibid.*, p. 23.
[16] *Harvard Research* (Comment), pp. 338-339.
[17] Lauterpacht-Oppenheim, *International Law*, vol. 1, United Kingdom, p. 841, n.2.
[18] Foremost among them: Accioly, Carnazza-Amari, Chrétien, Despagnet, Fauchille, O'Connell, Panhuys, Puente, Žourek.

Rapporteur Žourek to the International Law Commission, the following explanation was given:

> "The immunity from jurisdiction enjoyed by consular officers (consular representatives and members of their staff) with regard to acts performed by them in the discharge of their functions is based on the respect due the sovereign of the foreign State whose organs they are. It is therefore not a personal immunity but an immunity attaching to every act of a sovereign State."[19]

The Second Report reiterated this point even more emphatically:

> "The immunity accorded to consuls in respect of official acts is not *strictu sensu* a personal immunity of the consul, but an immunity on the part of the receiving State in respect of the official acts of a sovereign State."[20]

It emerges that the rationale of consular immunity from judicial process, whether under customary or under conventional international law, is one and the same: the imputation of certain acts performed by a consul to his home State, and their character as acts of State, are the groundwork of the immunity. The conclusion that its applicability is confined to official acts is contestable. It is for this reason that the literature defines immunity as "attaching to 'official acts' or to 'acts performed in the official capacity' or 'character' of the consul, or to 'acts done under the authority and direction'" of his Government, etc.

Unofficial acts include purely personal ones performed by consuls without their having anything to do with official assignments. Between the realm of official acts and that of personal acts there is, however, a buffer zone, a sort of limbo, of intermediate acts that cannot be labelled as official because not imputable to the sending State, but are not entirely personal either. They may be called, for the purpose of this argument, "semi-official" acts.

One category of "semi-official" acts would comprise ordinary non-official acts performed in the course of executing the consul's official duties or in connection with such duties. One outstanding example is that of "a consul who, provoked by some remarks made in the course of an official conversation, killed the speaker."[21] In common practice, however, the most

---

[19] Žourek, *First Report*, p. 99.
[20] Žourek, *Second Report*, p. 10.
[21] See *International Law Commission Yearbook*, 1961, vol. 1, p. 119.

typical are less dramatic, like traffic accidents occurring during the discharge of an official assignment and in connection with it. Most of the cases end by being, *ex hypothesi* and automatically, excluded from its sphere of incidence. The question now arises whether the terminology used in the formulation of Article 43(1) VCCR (constituting substantially a codification of existing customary international law relative to the subject of consular immunity from jurisdiction) is in conformity with that conclusion. An answer to this question may be deduced from an in-depth probe of the *travaux préparatoires* of the article and a close examination of all the phases of its legislative *iter*.

In the *First Report* of 1957, Special Rapporteur Žourek wrote: "Consular representatives and members of consular staff shall not be amenable to the jurisdiction or administrative authorities of their State of residence in respect of acts performed in the discharge of their functions."[22] In the *Second Report* of 1960, when referring to his initial proposal in the matter, he observed that, as established in it, and in accordance with general international law, consuls are granted immunity "in respect of acts performed in the exercise of their functions (official acts)."[23] Dinstein's analysis: "From the interesting use of the brackets in the (latter) quotation, it may be inferred that the Special Rapporteur did not distinguish between the two formulas of 'acts performed in the exercise of their functions' and 'official acts', considering them to be synonymous or interchangeable."[24]

Furthermore, "this inference is reinforced when one recalls the statements made by Žourek in the two Reports in expounding the rationale of consular immunity, namely, that the immunity is founded on the 'respect due the sovereignty of the foreign State' and that it affects the 'official acts of a sovereign State'."[25]

Dinstein underlines the fact that whereas Žourek, in 1960, adhered to the essence of the provision of Draft Article 27 which had not yet been reviewed by the Commission as a whole, he did insert some minor modifications in it. At the commencement of the Article – whose number was changed to 34(1) – the expression "consular representatives and members of consular staff" was replaced as a result of a change in definitions, by "members of the consular staff"; in the middle, the phrase "their State of residence" was substituted by

[22] Žourek, *First Report*, p. 99.
[23] Žourek, *Second Report*, p. 10.
[24] Dinstein, Y., *op. cit.*, p. 28.
[25] *Idem.*

"the receiving State"; and, towards the end, in lieu of "discharge", the term "exercise" was preferred.

Article 34(1) of Žourek's *Second Report* reads: "Members of the consular staff shall not be amenable to the jurisdiction of the judicial or administrative authorities of the receiving State in respect of acts performed in the exercise of their functions." In this Report, too, Žourek, for the first time, proposed to add a new Article, numbered 42(1), dealing with the special case of immunity from jurisdiction on the part of a foreign consul who happens to be a national of the receiving State, such immunity being also applicable to "acts performed in the exercise of his functions."[26]

When Article 34 came up for discussion by the Commission, later in 1960, one of the its members (François, of the Netherlands), adduced Žourek's observations with regard to the rationale of consular immunity, and suggested that the term "official acts" be used in the Article, since "that was an apt way of qualifying the concept 'acts performed in the exercise of their functions' which was too sweeping. Thus, a traffic offence committed in the course of official functions would not itself be an official act."[27]

One might have expected that at this juncture, Žourek, or another Commission member, would retort that the amendment proposed by the Dutch member was redundant, it being anyhow plain, on the basis of the commentary to the Draft Article as well as the very nature of the immunity, that only acts imputed to the State are exempt from jurisdiction. In other words, the answer could have been anticipated that Article 34 was inapplicable to traffic offences and similar acts, which are not those "of a sovereign State" and the "respect due the sovereignty of the foreign State" does not oblige, or justify, immunity in their case.

Curiously enough, it was assumed that Article 34 necessitated an amendment because it curtailed the exemption to purely official acts. In addition to this assumption, the view prevailed that it was expedient to broaden consular immunity to "semi-official" acts, and as a result, they favoured retention of the original language of the article and were opposed to its alternative in line with the Dutch proposal.

The British member, Fitzmaurice, made comments which proved to be a reflection of his colleagues' typical attitude. "If a consul drove too fast when going to visit a national (i.e., in the performance of his functions), that might

[26] Žourek, *Second Report*, pp. 28 and 38.
[27] *International Law Yearbook*, 1960, vol. 1, p. 75.

be deplorable, but he should be personally immune from process."[28] Fitzmaurice lay particular emphasis on the view that immunity in such an instance falls within the precise ambit of Article 34.[29] The member from Italy, Ago, argued against qualifying the word "acts" in the article by the limitative adjective "official", lest such a change severely impair the scope of application of consular immunity.[30] Žourek voiced objection to the use of the expression "official" in Article 34.[31] Before this matter was brought to finality by the Commission, Article 42 was thoroughly dissected and discussed concerning the immunity of consuls who are nationals of the receiving State. The proposal was raised by the Austrian member, Verdross, to revise the wording of the article by having recourse to the term "official acts" in the delimitation of the immunity.[32] The proposal carried the day after gaining support from other members, like Žourek, who had rejected the same measure insofar as the general provision of Article 34 was involved.[33]

In order to eliminate the dissimilarity in terminology, and to make it clear that exemption under both articles pertained to official acts exclusively, Verdross put forward the proposal to replace the last words in each article by a uniform new formula: "in respect of [the] acts within the scope of their functions."[34]

Article 43 VCCR as finally adopted by the Conference, lays down, in its entirety, as follows:

> 1.Consular officers and consular employees shall not be amenable to the jurisdiction of the judicial or administrative authorities of the receiving State in respect of acts performed in the exercise of consular functions.
>
> 2.The provisions of paragraph 1 of this article shall not, however, apply in respect of a civil action either:
> (*a*) arising out of a contract concluded by a consular officer or a consular employee in which he did not contract expressly or impliedly as an agent of the sending State; or

[28] *Ibid.*, p. 106.
[29] *Ibid.*, p. 82.
[30] *Ibid.*, p.83. Cfr. also, *ibid.*, p. 106.
[31] *Ibid.*, p. 106.
[32] *International Law Commission*, 1960, vol. 1, p. 104.
[33] *Ibid.*, pp. 104-107, 309.
[34] *Ibid.*, pp. 307, 309-310.

(*b*) by a third party for damage arising from an accident in the receiving State caused by a vehicle, vessel or aircraft.

**3.5 Giving of Evidence**

The VCCR provides that consular officials and other members of a consulate are not exempted from liability to attend as witnesses in courts of law or in the course of administrative proceedings. Nevertheless, State practice shows that the evidence should be recorded, wherever possible, at the consulate or at the consul's official residence. In some countries, the law even permits acceptance of a written declaration by the consul as admissible evidence. There is also general agreement among authors that consular privileges include giving of oral or written testimony on consular premises instead of in court, except perhaps in criminal cases.[35]

The *Harvard Research Draft* succinctly put the practice thus:

> "A receiving State shall exempt a consul from attendance as a witness at a trial of a civil case; it may require a consul to give testimony orally or in writing at his residence or office or to attend as a witness at the trial of a criminal case, but such requirements shall be enforced with due regard for the dignity of the consul and his convenience in the exercise of his functions."

The VCCR provides that if a consular official should decline to give evidence, no coercive measures or penalty may be applied to him.[36] In other words, no warrant can be issued for his arrest and compulsion to give evidence, nor can he be convicted for contempt of court if he does not follow the directions of the court to give evidence.[37]

Whereas none of all these exemptions applies to honorary consuls or to consular employees, members of a consulate may be summoned as witnesses. However, there is no obligation to give evidence concerning matters connected with the exercise of their functions or to produce official correspondence and documents relating thereto. The consul's prerogative to choose not to produce official correspondence and documents in judicial and administrative proceedings is a logical extension of the principle of inviolability of consular archives and documents. This applies both to career consular officers and to honorary consuls as well as to consular employees.

---

[35] Oppenheim, *op. cit.*, p. 843.
[36] Art. 44(1).
[37] Sen, B., *op. cit.*, p. 296.

Consuls may also decline to give evidence as expert witness with regard to the law of the sending State.[38]

Any conversation that a consular officer or employee may have with any individual in the course of his official acts, such as an interview before granting a visa, is privileged.[39]

### 3.6.1 Liability of Consuls

A consul is liable for his acts which are not wholly unconnected with his official duties. Proceedings may be instituted under the laws of the receiving State for such acts, unless the provisions of a specific treaty endow the consul with full diplomatic entity.[40]

An act can be established to fall within the official functions of the consul by considering the following criteria:

a. (subjective) – who the privileges refer to;
b. (objective) – which spheres of the functions of consular officers and their personnel are covered by privileges;
c. (temporal) – duration of privileges;
d. (territorial) – territory where privileges are operative.

### 3.6.2 Espionage Activities

Needless to say, acts of espionage carried out by a consul would be for the benefit and in the interests of his government. Yet, international law does not consider espionage as being one of the consular functions, and a consular officer, unless covered by full diplomatic immunity, may be prosecuted in the receiving State for subversive and espionage activities as defined by the laws of the receiving State.[41]

In the *Case Concerning Diplomatic and Consular Staff in Tehran*, the ICJ expressed the principle thus:

> "The Vienna Conventions of 1961 and 1963 contain express provisions to meet the case when members of an embassy staff, under the cover of diplomatic privileges and immunities, engage in such abuses of their functions as espionage or interference in the internal affairs of the receiving State. It is precisely with the possibility of such abuses in

[38] Art. 44(3) VCCR.
[39] Sen, B., *op. cit.*, p. 296.
[40] *Ibid.*, p. 291.
[41] *Ibid.*, p. 292.

contemplation that [...] Article 55, paragraph 1, of the Vienna Convention on Consular Relations, provide[s] "Without prejudice to their privileges and immunities, it is the duty of all persons enjoying such privileges and immunities to respect the laws and regulations of the receiving State. They also have a duty not to interfere in the internal affairs of that State." Paragraph 3 of Article 41 of the 1961 Convention further States: "The premises of the mission must not be used in any manner incompatible with the functions of the missions ... "; an analogous provision, with respect to consular premises is to be found in Article 55, paragraph 2, of the 1963 Convention.

Thus, it is for the very purpose of providing a remedy for such possible abuses of diplomatic functions that Article 9 of the 1961 Convention on Diplomatic Relations stipulates : "1. The receiving State may at any time and without having to explain its decision, notify the sending State that the head of the mission or any member of the diplomatic staff of the mission is *persona non grata* or that any other member of the staff of the mission is not acceptable. In any such case, the sending State shall, as appropriate, either recall the person concerned or terminate his functions with the mission. A person may be declared *non grata* or not acceptable before arriving in the territory of the receiving State. If the sending State refuses or fails within a reasonable period to carry out its obligations under paragraph 1 of this Article, the receiving State may refuse to recognize the person concerned as a member of the mission." The 1963 Convention contains, in Article 23, paragraphs 1 and 4, analogous provisions in respect of consular officers and consular staff. Paragraph 1 of Article 9 of the 1961 Convention, and paragraph 4 of Article 23 of the 1963 Convention, take account of the difficulty that may be experienced in practice of proving such abuses in every case or, indeed, of determining exactly when exercise of the diplomatic function, expressly recognized in Article 3 (1) (d) of the 1961 Convention, of "ascertaining by all lawful means conditions and developments in the receiving State" may be considered as involving such acts as "espionage" or "interference in internal affairs". The way in which Article 9, paragraph 1, takes account of any such difficulty is by providing expressly in its opening sentence that the receiving State may "at any time and without having to explain its decision" notify the sending State that any particular member of its diplomatic mission is "*persona non grata*" or "not acceptable" (and similarly Article 23, paragraph 4, of the 1963 Convention provides that "the receiving State is not obliged to give to the sending State reasons for its decision"). Beyond that remedy for dealing with abuses of the diplomatic function by individual members of a mission, a receiving State has in its hands a more radical remedy if abuses of their functions by members of a mission reach serious proportions. This is the power which every receiving State has, at its own discretion, to break off diplomatic relations with a sending State and to call for the immediate closure of the offending mission.

The rules of diplomatic law, in short, constitute a self-contained régime which, on the one hand, lays down the receiving State's obligations regarding the facilities, privileges and immunities to be accorded to diplomatic missions and, on the other, foresees their possible abuse by members of the mission and specifies the means at the disposal of the receiving State to counter any such abuse. These means are, by their nature, entirely efficacious, for unless the sending State recalls the member of the mission objected to forthwith, the prospect of the almost immediate loss of consular privileges and immunities, because of the withdrawal by the receiving State of his recognition as a member of the mission, will in practice compel that person, in his own interest, to depart at once. But the principle of the inviolability of the persons of diplomatic agents and the premises of diplomatic missions is one of the very foundations of this long-established régime..."[42]

### 3.6.3 Traffic Accidents

An exception which is generally made to the rule of immunity from jurisdiction in respect of official acts lies in the case of actions concerning traffic accidents. Receiving states generally require consular motor vehicles to be adequately insured against third party risks. Consuls cannot disclaim liability from third party actions for damages arising out of traffic accidents.[43]

### 3.7.1 Inviolability of Consular Premises

The principle of inviolability of consular premises is widely recognized, although there could be specific exceptions. Certain conventions allow police or other executive authorities to enter the premises in certain circumstances, such as a court order or in the case of fire, other disaster, or crime. Other conventions, however, contemplate no exception whatsoever. On the other hand, certain States give no immunity to foreign consular offices, although it has been suggested that if the office is used solely for consular purposes then the receiving State shall prevent the invasion of the office by its agent of any character.[44]

---

[42] *I.C.J. Reports* 1980, pp. 39-40.
[43] Art. 43(2) VCCR.
[44] Sen, B., *op. cit.*, p. 247.

It has been argued whether the term "disaster" can also include a *cyber disaster*, such as the spread of cyber bombs or computer viruses.[45] Won-Mog Choi sums up the position with regard to internet and the inviolability of consular premises under the VCCR in this table.[46]

| | **Cyber Crime inside Premises** | **Cyber Disaster affecting Premises** |
|---|---|---|
| Condition of entry | Entry with consent of the head of consular post; or<br>Entry without consent of the head if (i) entry into parts used for non-consular functions; (ii) there is consent of his designee or ambassador. | Entry without consent is possible. |
| Possible Action | Expropriation with compensation | Only protective action |

### 3.7.2 Taxation of Consular Premises: Exemption

There is now universal agreement that premises for consular purposes, like premises of diplomatic missions, are exempt from national, regional and municipal taxation in the receiving State, on the basis that these premises are used for the public purposes of a foreign sovereign State. The person contracting with the sending State is not exempt from taxation, and services rendered to the sending State, such as electricity and water rates, are also not exempt.[47]

## 3.8 Freedom of Movement

Subject to its laws and regulations concerning zones entry into which is prohibited or regulated for reasons of national security, the receiving State shall ensure freedom of movement and travel in its territory to all members of the consular post.[48] Whereas it is self-evident that this freedom is fully

---

[45] Choi, W.-M. (2006): "Diplomatic and Consular Law in the Internet Age" in *Singapore Yearbook of International Law and Contributors*, Singapore, (2006) 10 p.122.

[46] *Ibid.*, p. 126.

[47] Art. 32 VCCR.

[48] Art. 34 VCCR.

justified with regard to the consular district, as the consul has to have unhindered access to his co-nationals in his district, there remain doubts as to whether this freedom extends beyond the confines of the consular district to the rest of the territories of the receiving State.[49]

### 3.9.1 Communication with Home Government

The need to make reports and receive instructions renders frequent communication with the home government and its diplomatic mission a priority for consuls. This need serves as the basis for the privilege of free communication with own Government and with its diplomatic or consular representatives within the domain of the receiving State.[50] In this respect, consular officers act as much in the interest of the sending State as a diplomatic agent.[51] In communicating with the home government and other diplomatic missions, the VCCR allows the consular post to use all appropriate means, which include diplomatic or consular couriers and the diplomatic or consular bag (*valise*). The normal practice is for consulates to make use of the diplomatic courier service, and the consular bag at times forms part of the diplomatic bag.[52] The provisions of the VCCR on the inviolability of consular correspondence are to be read in the light of the need markedly felt by consular posts in remote locations which need to communicate with the diplomatic mission, or by consular posts which need to communicate with the sending State particularly if the latter has no diplomatic mission in the sending State.[53] Only if the competent authorities of the receiving State have serious reason to believe that the bag contains something other than correspondence, documents or articles intended exclusively for official use, may they request that the bag be opened, and then by a representative of a sending State. If this is refused, the bag may be returned to the sending State.[54]

Although freedom of communication includes messages in cipher or code, a consulate does not have the right to install and use a wireless transmitter without the consent of the receiving State, and in times of war or national emergency, it is permissible for States to restrict this freedom on grounds of security.[55]

---

49 Ben, S., *op. cit.*, p. 297.
50 *Idem.*
51 This is reflected in Art. 35 VCCR.
52 Sen, B., *op. cit.*, p. 298.
53 *Idem.*
54 Art. 35 (3) VCCR.
55 Sen B., *op. cit.*, p. 298.

In this internet age, the use of cipher and code has become less frequent. Instead, emails are the more usual mode of communication, and these too are inviolable. However, if e-mail or internet connections are made through a wireless transmitter, such connections and the installation of such transmitter must be made only "with the consent of the receiving State."[56]

### 3.9.2 Communication with Co-Nationals

This freedom applies equally to career and honorary consuls. It is dealt in detail in Chapter Five.

## 3.10 Consular Fees

Consular fees are levied for various services rendered by consular offices, such as notarial services and estate administration. The fees for specific services are usually regulated by the sending State's national legislation, whereas customarily, for estate administration a percentage of the valuation of the estate is charged. The moneys collected belong to the sending State, and are as such exempt from all taxes and dues in the receiving State.[57]

## 3.11 Immunity in Mission Disputes

It is not uncommon for diplomatic and consular establishments to employ staff from among nationals or residents of the receiving State. It would seem that the current customary international law position is that the sending State's absolute immunity with regard to matters involving such staff is being viewed restrictively. The sending State's immunity is upheld only in the context of unfair dismissal actions by employees in positions of trust and confidence, a distinction being made between senior staff and subordinate employees.[58]

## 3.12 The Consular Corps

Consular status implies, apart from the other privileges and immunities, the *de facto* membership of the "consular corps," an entity made up of individuals not to be confused with the diplomatic corps, which is an entity made up of States. It usually happens that career consuls living in the same city, though rarely meeting with each other while carrying out their functions, tend to face the same problems. Besides, it is a precise duty to entertain cordial relations with other consuls. Furthermore, these consuls

---

[56] Choi, W.-M., *op. cit.*, p. 125.
[57] Art. 39 VCCR.
[58] Garnett, R. (2005): "The precarious position of embassy and consular employees in the United Kingdom" in *The International and Comparative Law Quarterly*, 54 (2005) 3, pp. 714-715.

tend to encounter honorary consuls who, though representing foreign States, are residents of the same city. This natural encounter of all accredited consuls in the same particular moment in the same jurisdiction brings about the existence of an entity called "*corps consulaire*" (*CC*). The VCCR's silence on this entity further strengthens the notion that this is a *de facto* entity. Although it has been held that this entity has no autonomous powers and lacks juridical origins,[59] Article 16 VCCR has been construed as implying some sort of acknowledgement.[60]

Even if the consuls were to form a legal entity according to the domestic law of the receiving State, one could never speak of a juridical framework for the consular corps, as the only source would be international law which, on this point, is silent.[61]

### 3.13 The Political Context

The scope and nature of consular privileges and immunities point towards the principle enunciated in the Preamble of the VCCR. It reflects the spirit of both conventional and customary conferment of such privileges and immunities, namely that they are meant "not to benefit individuals but to ensure the efficient performance of functions by consular posts on behalf of their respective States."

The same Preamble considers the codification of the rules relating to consular privileges and immunities as a further contribution to "the development of friendly relations among nations, irrespective of their differing constitutional and social systems." This enunciation merits attention for it conveys the delicate, volatile nature of foreign relations, in the sense that the presence of foreigners representing their country of origin while sharing the same social sphere of nationals of the receiving State could in particular political situations create tensions. This fact was acknowledged by the international community in the VCCR Preamble and the obligations contained in the Convention which "are of cardinal importance for the maintenance of good relations between States in the interdependent world of today."[62]

---

[59] Biscottini, G. (1969): *Manuale di Diritto Consolare*, Italy, p. 33.
[60] Maresca, A. (1984): *Convenzione di Vienna sulle relazioni consolari*, Italy, p. 20.
[61] Fragola, M. (2004): *Nozioni di Diritto Diplomatico e Consolare – Tecnica, Pryassi, Esperienza*, Italy, pp. 127-129.
[62] *I.C.J. Reports*, 1980, p. 43. (*Case Concerning Diplomatic and Consular Staff in Tehran.*)

# Chapter 4

## FUNCTIONS OF CONSULS

*"The powers of [consular officers] are infinitely varied. They are in a position of exercising throughout the extent of their district the functions of judge, arbitrator, and conciliator for their compatriots; often, they are officers charged with vital statistics; they carry out the tasks of notaries, and sometimes those of shipping administrator; they survey and note health conditions. It is they who, through their regular reports, can give a true and complete idea of the state of commerce, of navigation and of the characteristic industry of the country in which they reside"* Talleyrand

### 4.1 Introduction

Gian-Carlo Menotti's opera *The Consul* (1950) portrays the consul as a heartless bureaucrat.[1] This might have been a criticism for all bureaucrats or just for the consular one.[2] Indeed modern Foreign Ministries perceive themselves as public service organizations. As such, they are under a moral obligation to perform their functions with a sense of humaneness, inspired by the ancient dictum that rules are made for human beings and not the other way round. Career diplomat William S. Shepard's autobiographical *Consul Tales* takes this point of departure for granted. He considers consular work as that area where "the human stories of diplomacy" all happen.[3]

---

[1] Both libretto and score were written by Menotti himself. The opera premiered in Philadelphia, United States, on March 1, 1950. See Herz, M.F. (ed.) (1983): *The Consular Dimension of Diplomacy*, United States, p. 26, for a context to the opera's portrayal of the consul as a heartless bureaucrat.

[2] See *infra* on the doctrine of consular absolutism.

[3] Shepard, W.S. (2001): *Consular Tales*, United States.

Concrete historical necessities have probably brought about the transformation of consular functions. This explains why, although the consular office has maintained its typical structure, relative functions have been expanded with additions that were perhaps unthinkable or unforeseeable in the past, and yet without trespassing into the diplomatic sphere.[4]

Consular functions may indeed be performed by a diplomatic mission apart from a consular post, as laid down in Article 70 VCCR. In those cases in which a single person performs both diplomatic and consular functions, the status of such official depends on his formal accreditation. However, if an official has been accredited as a diplomatic representative, but then performs consular functions, the receiving State may protest and declare such person *non grata*. If this is not done, then the receiving State is bound to extend diplomatic status to that official.[5] Article 17 VCCR allows consular officers to perform diplomatic acts but denies such consular officers "any right to claim diplomatic privileges and immunities."

Professor G.R. Berridge puts it thus:

> While there may have been a considerable degree of administrative unification, the distinction between diplomatic and consular work is still widely acknowledged and is reflected in international law. Indeed, diplomatic and consular agents operate under different legal regimes.[6]

This Chapter will focus on consular functions proper, whether performed by consuls or other officials of the sending State.

### 4.2 Sources of Consular Functions

Consular functions are, on the one hand, defined by custom, usages, and international conventions (e.g. the function to assist nationals of the sending State, the function to promote commerce and navigation); on the other hand, they are determined by the laws of the sending State (e.g. the issuance of passports and visas). Generally speaking, contemporary international law does not exhaustively determine consular functions.[7]

---

[4] Fragola, M. (2004): *Nozioni di Diritto Diplomatico e Consolare – Tecnica Prassi Esperienza*, Italy, p. 88.
[5] Vignali, H.A. (1992): *Lecciónes de Derecho Diplomatico y Consular, Tomo I*, Uruguay, pp. 77-78.
[6] Berridge, G.R. (2002): *Diplomacy – Theory and Practice*, United Kingdom, p. 20.
[7] Ahmad, M.A. (1973): *L'institution consulaire et le droit international*, France, p. 83.

## 4.3 Functions as carried in the Vienna Consular Convention, 1963

The functions as enumerated by Article 5 VCCR were the subject of long discussions during the Vienna Conference, particularly because of the choice between a general definition and an enumerative one.

Explaining the rationale behind Article 5, Rapporteur Žourek argued that State practice was so varied that it was not possible for the Commission to draft a general definition.[8] The Conference decided to pronounce itself on whether to choose a succinct definition of a general nature or a longer definition of an enumerative, albeit not exhaustive, nature. At the end, by 42 votes against 26 and 8 abstentions, the principle of a general definition was not approved by the Conference.[9] The majority of those in favour were the new States that lacked an own consular code of regulations.

The classification of consular relations carried in this chapter does not follow precisely the order set by Article 5 VCCR.[10]

## 4.4 Protection of the Rights and Interests of the Sending State and its Nationals

The consul has the function to protect in the receiving State the interests of the sending State and of its nationals (Article 5(a) VCCR). He is bound to safeguard the possibility of all his co-nationals to make use of all rights accorded them by the domestic law of the receiving State, on the one hand, and by international law, on the other. If nationals of the sending State are subjected to vexatious or arbitrary measures by the local authorities, then the consul has the right to intervene to obtain justice for his co-nationals.[11] The term "nationals" includes both natural and juridical persons.

The 1959 session of the International Law Commission was the scene of a controversy concerning the existence of the consul's right to defend the rights and interests of the sending State. Two points of view prevailed during that session. Their arguments could be summarized as follows:

---

[8] A/Conf.25/C.1/SR 8, vol 1, pp. 143-44.

[9] *Idem*, p. 148.

[10] The *European Convention on Consular Functions*, though an important development, is being deliberately ignored owing both to the fact that to date it has not been ratified and to its regional nature which is necessarily dwarfed by the universal nature of the VCCR.

[11] Žourek, J. (1962): "*Le statut et les fonctions des consuls*" in *Receuil des Cours de l'Academie du Droit International, Tome 106, 1962-II*, pp. 387-391.

A. The consular officer cannot protect the rights and interests of the sending State for the following reasons:

(a) it is the competence of the diplomatic agent accredited to the sending State;

(b) the diplomatic agent performs his acts as a representative of the sending State; the consular officer performs only "administrative acts";

(c) whereas a diplomatic agent intervenes on behalf of the sending State on the international plane, the consular officer intervenes on the local plane.

B. For the subscribers to the second stance, the consular officer in reality defends the rights and interests of the sending State; this he does by:

(a) defending the interests of his co-nationals;

(b) drawing the attention of local authorities to the provisions of obtaining conventions;

(c) within the ambit of some functions, seeing to the needs of state-owned merchants ships, like examining the vessels' papers, delivering passports and visas;

(d) developing the economic interests of his country.

The words of former Consul General Smith Simpson probably best flesh out the tension between the two schools of thought:

> Consular functions are not, and have never been, simply "consular" functions. They have always been an affirmation of the political, economic and other social interests and objectives of governments. For democratic societies in contemporary times they possess not only an overseas but [...] a domestic aspect of political import.
>
> Consular posts are in reality political, economic and cultural outposts, adding to a government's observation, listening, intelligence-gathering, crisis-alerting, trade promotion, cultural and public relations opportunities. They are often in touch with whole regions of a country with which embassies in capitals are not. In the case of

> some sending governments, they also add to espionage and subversion capabilities.
>
> [...]
>
> The category of what is called "special consular services" includes a wide variety of services relating to the whereabouts and welfare of citizens, relaying emergency messages to citizens resident or travelling abroad, child custody issues and child abuse, the arrest and trial of citizens and the like. These are of a basic political nature. [...] They tend to be called "consular" simply because they have been delegated to consular officers. This does not make them "consular" as distinct from political or diplomatic.[12]

## 4.5 Protection of Interests of Persons Lacking Full Capacity

The consul is bound to safeguard, within the limits imposed by the laws and regulations of the receiving State, the interests of minors and other persons lacking full capacity who are nationals of the sending State, particularly where an guardianship or trusteeship[13] is required with respect to such persons (Article 5(h) VCCR).

The tutorship of minors is regulated by their national law. However, when domestic law does not provide for minors who are abroad, then it is incumbent on diplomatic representatives and consular officers to intervene in order to regulate the tutorship, unless the receiving State opposes. The same applies to curatorship of persons other than minors who lack full legal capacity.

This provision has been construed as to empower the consul to officiate adoptions, as adoption might in certain circumstances prove a better option than tutorship, particularly in those countries which do not recognize this latter institution or where there are prohibitions for adoption procedures in the case of foreigners.[14]

Also falling in this category is the consular function to safeguard the interests of nationals, both individuals and bodies corporate, of the sending State in cases of succession *mortis causa* in the territory of the receiving State, in

---

[12] Simpson, S. (1983): "Political Functions of Consuls and Consulates" in Herz, M.F. (ed.), *op. cit.*, pp. 14 and 17.

[13] One might use "tutorship" and "curatorship"; in French: "*tutelle*", "*curatelle*".

[14] Agüeras, J.M.P. (1990): *La Adopción Consular*, Ministry of Foreign Affairs, Spain, pp. 17-18.

accordance with the laws and regulations of the receiving State (Article 5(g) VCCR). The consul has the right to intervene with local authorities to ascertain the truthfulness of the inventory of the deceased's estate, and to participate personally, or through an intermediary, in the choice of an administrator charged with the conservation or liquidation of said estate.

Whereas a consul may accord protection to nationals who are simultaneously nationals of the receiving State, this he cannot do for stateless persons, and for nationals of a third country.[15]

### 4.6 Development of Economic, Cultural, and Scientific Relations

An age-old function of the consul is that of furthering the development of commercial, economic, cultural, and scientific relations between the sending State and the receiving State and otherwise promoting friendly relations between them (Article 5(b) VCCR), on the one hand, and of ascertaining by all lawful means conditions and developments in the commercial, economic, cultural and scientific life of the receiving State, reporting thereon to the Government of the sending State and giving information to persons interested (Article 5(c) VCCR), on the other.

Consuls may be called upon to participate in the organization of fairs and commercial expositions in the receiving State. Consuls must be capable of giving useful information on the addresses and reputation of importers and other businessmen, to initiate business relations with banks, insurance companies, and the press to obtain from them useful information.[16]

Consuls have a similar role in the cultural and scientific fields, by organizing and encouraging the exhibitions of the works of artists, the projection of documentaries on their country, conferences, student and lecturer exchanges, sports manifestations, and so on.

Lastly, it is admitted in international law that the exercise of consular functions impliedly includes the right to oversee the application of commercial treaties and other such agreements in existence between the sending State and the receiving State.[17]

---

[15] See Žourek, J., *op. cit.*, pp. 422-424.
[16] Heyking, A. (1930): "*La théorie et la pratique des services consulaires*" in *Recueil des Cours de l'Académie du Droit International, Tome 34, 1930-IV*, p. 871.
[17] Scelle, G. (1943): *Manuel élémentaire de droit international public*, France, pp. 440-441.

### 4.7.1 Functions of an Administrative Nature

Article 5(f) VCCR allows consuls to perform functions of an administrative nature, provided that there is nothing contrary thereto in the laws and regulations of the receiving State. These functions include:

(a) enrolling nationals residing within the consular district on the appropriate register of the consulate;

(b) delivering and extending the validity of passports and other travel documents of nationals of the sending State (Article 5(d) VCCR);

(c) issuing visas and other information necessary and required by persons wishing to travel to the sending State (Article 5(d));

(d) confirming certificates issued abroad attesting the State of origin or the provenance of merchandise, as well as commercial invoices and other similar documents;

(e) accepting the remittance of moneys or indemnities due to nationals of the sending State if the beneficiary is outside the receiving State and no other method of effecting payment between the two States is available;

(f) conveying to nationals residing in the receiving State payments for services rendered, moneys or indemnities allowed to right-holders in conformity with the laws of the sending State and with international conventions then in force, particularly in the sector of social security.[18]

### 4.7.2 The Doctrine of Consular Absolutism

This common law doctrine holds that consular decisions relative to the granting or denial of visas are not subject to judicial review. The doctrine is usually justified on the basis that, being "inherent in sovereignty" and political in nature, it belongs to the realm of non-justiciable political decisions.[19] This is based on the necessity to have univocal Government views in foreign affairs[20] as well as on the notion, expressed by a United States Senate subcommittee, that no right is being infringed given that aliens *ab initio* do not have a right to enter the United States and bring their case

---

[18] Žourek, J. (1961): "*Quelques problèmes théoriques du droit consulaire*" in *Journal du Droit International*, no. 1, p. 28.

[19] *Roberto Saavedra Bruno, et al., v. Madeleine K. Albright, Secretary of State, et al, 1999*, 197 F3d, 1158.

[20] Nafziger, J.A.R. (1991): "Review of Visa Denials by Consular Officers" in *Washington Law Review*, Vol. 66, No. 1, United States, pp. 47-48.

before that country's courts for judicial review of consular decisions.[21] There is also a countercurrent arguing that if consular discretion in visa matters is exercised as a "duty to act," then it is outside judicial review; if it is a "duty to adjudicate," then, in theory, consular officers' act become justiciable.[22]

## 4.8 Civil Status

Consular functions include the power to act as civil registrar, by registering the births and deaths of nationals of the sending State.

Consuls can also celebrate marriages between nationals of the sending State and between a national of the sending State and a national of a third country, if the laws of the sending State so permit and the law and regulations of the receiving State do not oppose. They can also register the dissolution of a marriage decided by a tribunal and regarding nationals of the sending State. Such nationals are, however, bound to have their status registered also in terms of the applicable laws and regulations of the receiving State with the apposite State organs.

The function of solemnizing marriages was attributed to consuls concomitantly with the secularization of the institution of marriage. This non-religious celebrative form was for this historical reason given the name "consular marriage". But this has created a question of semantics. Not all consular marriages are celebrated by the consular authority. In fact, Article 5 VCCR confers the authority to celebrate such marriages not only to the consul but also to certain diplomatic officials.[23]

The consular function relating to the termination of marriages raises a thorny issue with reference to the validity of Muslim *talaq* divorces decreed before foreign consuls. It would seem that although divorce legislation in many Muslim countries allows citizens to obtain divorce through the services of a foreign consul, such consular divorces would not be recognized as valid unless the receiving State grants the necessary authority to the foreign consul. On the other hand, if the consul of a Muslim sending State merely transmits the *talaq* divorce declaration to a tribunal in the sending State, then the

---

[21] S. Rep. No. 1515, 81st Cong., 2nd Sess. (1950), p. 622.
[22] Zas, M. (2004): "Consular Absolutism: The Need for Judicial Review in the Adjudication of Immigrant Visas for Permanent Residence" in *The John Marshall Law Review*, Vol. 37, No. 2., United States, p. 593, referring to the (U.S.) Immigration and Nationality Act.
[23] Montero, R.A. (1991): *El Matrimonio Consular*, Spain, p. 20.

ultimate divorce will be valid if it satisfies all the other requirements of private international law.[24]

### 4.9 Notarial and Judicial Functions

Chapter Six will deal with notarial functions.

Judicial functions have changed significantly since the end of the Capitulations. Under the Capitulations, Westerns living, mostly to carry out business, in Oriental and African countries preferred to resort to courts with a Western set-up. This led to the concept of extraterritoriality, whereby a foreign Sovereign relinquished authority within his own State over Western nationals who would then be subject to their consular judicial authority.

The VCCR (Article 5 (i) and (j)) provides for two kinds of consular interventions in judicial matters: representation and transmission.

(a) Function to represent

Subject to the laws and regulations in force in the receiving State, consular officers are authorized to represent or arrange appropriate representation for nationals of the sending State before the tribunals and other authorities of the receiving State, for the purpose of obtaining, in accordance with the laws and regulations of the receiving State, provisional measures for the preservation of the rights and interests of these nationals, where, because of absence or any other reason, such nationals are unable at the proper time to assume the defence of their rights and interests (Article 5 (i) VCCR). This provision provides the legal basis for consuls to intervene before tribunals or other competent organs in favour of absent co-nationals or those who are in the impossibility of doing so personally or of being represented by a lawyer, it being understood that this is all subject to the proviso that the law on civil or criminal procedure of the receiving State does not oppose such practice, and that such consular practice is permitted by the consular regulations of the sending State.

(b) Function to transmit

Consular officers may transmit judicial and extrajudicial documents or execute letters rogatory or commissions to take evidence for the courts of the sending State in accordance with international agreements in force or in the absence of such international agreements, in any other manner compatible with the laws and regulations of the receiving State (Article 5 (j) VCCR).

---

[24] Bleimaier, J.K. (1980): "Recognition to be accorded the Quasi-Judicial acts of foreign consul" in *Annuaire de l'A.A.A.*, 1979/1980, vol. 49-50, the Netherlands, pp. 131 *et seq.*

### 4.10 Navigation and Aviation

Consuls may exercise rights of supervision and inspection provided for in the laws and regulations of the sending State in respect of vessels having the nationality of the sending State, and of aircraft registered in that State and in respect of their crews (Article 5 (k) VCCR).

Not only is the consul empowered to supervise and inspect vessels and aircraft belonging to the sending State, but also to ensure order and discipline on board vessels and aircraft of his nationality found in the harbour(s) or airport(s) situated within his consular district.[25] However, State practice retains that in cases of contentions between the captain and crew, the consul is enabled only to reconcile them.[26]

Consuls may extend assistance to such vessels and aircraft, and to their crews, taking statements regarding the voyage of a vessel, examining and stamping the ship's papers and, without prejudice to the authorities of the receiving State, conducting investigations into any incidents which occurred during the voyage, and settling disputes of any kind between the master, the officers and the seamen in so far as this may be authorized by the laws and regulations of the sending State (Article 5 (l) VCCR).

The consul's role with regard to seamen is still rather important, despite modern developments. Consuls can take all necessary steps to ensure medical assistance for seamen, including the hospitalization of the captain and crew of ships of the sending State. Consuls are also bound to take the necessary steps for the repatriation of such seamen and to provide for their urgent needs.[27] Subject to the laws of the receiving State, the consular officer can also conduct inquiries relating to incidents taking place on board during a voyage.[28]

Consuls also play an important role in maritime successions, that is successions which relate not to the entire patrimony but to the movables and other personal effects which the seamen or passenger had with him at the moment of his demise. The captain is bound to deposit with the consul all the personal effects and salaries due to the deceased as well as all

---

[25] Ahmad, M.A., *op. cit.*, p. 100.

[26] Allary-Valentin, J. (1980): "*Consuls et Navigation Maritime*" in *Annuaire de l'A.A.A.*, 1979/1980, vol. 49-50, the Netherlands, p. 148.

[27] *Ibid.*, p. 150.

[28] Ahmad, M.A., *op. cit.*, p. 101.

information capable of facilitating the search for the successors with a view to deliver the objects to them.[29]

Consuls are bound to extend assistance to the captain and crew of fishing boats. This role has been rendered more important in the wake of the creation of exclusive economic zones and, more precisely, fishing zones.[30]

### 4.11 Other functions not mentioned by the Vienna Convention

The enumerative definition provided by the VCCR is not exhaustive. Article 5 (m) VCCR, in fact, states that the consul can perform any other functions entrusted to the consular post by the sending State which are not prohibited by the laws and regulations of the receiving State or to which no objection is taken by the receiving State or which are referred to in the international agreements in force between the sending State and the receiving State.

Among such functions may be mentioned the following:

(a) The role of the consul as arbiter or as mediator in conflicts which may arise between nationals of the sending State and which may be submitted to him.[31] However, there are doubts as to the validity of the consul's decision stemming from the following considerations: (i) the foreign consulate is not a forum and is not in a position to enforce its own quasi-judicial decisions; (ii) the consular decision is not a domestic judgment of the sending State as it does not emanate from its judiciary and was not rendered within its own territory; (iii) from the perspective of the receiving State it would be a foreign judgment, because given by an officer of a foreign State. Thus the party pleading the decision's validity has to prove it is pursuant to the rules of private international law.[32] With regard to disputes arising on vessels of the sending State, consular quasi-judicial decisions are valid and enforceable and entitled to recognition only if given in accordance with and on the basis of the specific authorization of the receiving State.[33]

(b) The consul may apply the provisions on the supervision of military service due by the nationals of the sending State residing in the receiving State, and the receipt of taxes relating to exemption from military service.

---

[29] Allary-Valentin, *op. cit.*, p. 151.
[30] *Ibid.*, p. 152.
[31] Žourek, J., *op. cit. supra* n. 17, p .34.
[32] Bleimaier, J.K., *op. cit.*, p. 128.
[33] *Ibid.*, p. 130.

(c) Article 17 (2) VCCR envisages the case in which a consular officer acts as a representative of the sending State at international organizations. When so acting, the consular officer is entitled to enjoy any privileges and immunities accorded to such a representative by customary international law or by international agreements. This is also confirmed by Article 75 of the Vienna Convention on the Representation of States in their Relations with International Organizations of a Universal Character of 1975 which lays down that when members of a permanent diplomatic mission or of a consular post in the host State are included in a mission, a delegation or an observer delegation, they shall retain their privileges and immunities as members of their permanent diplomatic mission or consular post in addition to the privileges and immunities accorded by the Convention.

## 4.12 "Jack of all trades"

Because of the vastness of the services they may render to co-nationals and to the sending State, consuls have been also referred to as "*Maître Jacques*"[34] – "Jack of all trades." The majority of these functions seem to point to the nature of the consular office being overwhelmingly related to the *micro*-level of diplomacy, which could be political in certain ways, but is clearly distinguishable from the *macro*-level of diplomacy. Despite calls by authors to amalgamate the two levels, it would still seem that the neat line of demarcation should be retained, particularly due to the geopolitical landscape of the new, post-Cold War international community, where large-scale migrations, and related issued of human rights law, humanitarian international law, and international refugee law, are making consular assistance an increasingly important aspect of international relations.

• Ahmad, M.A., *op. cit.*, p. 101.

## *Chapter 5*

# ASSISTANCE TO NATIONALS

> *"It is the duty of a Consular officer to go immediately to any [citizen] who from having been arrested or for any other difficulty in which he may find himself with the local Authorities, may request his aid; and such Consular officer is not performing his duties when he rests satisfied with the statements made to him by the Authorities who have arrested a [citizen] as to the grounds on which they have done so; and who neglects to go and hear from the accused himself what he may have to say on his own behalf. A [citizen] may be unjustly accused by the Officers of the Police. And a ... Consular officer would very imperfectly perform his duty by sending him the name of a lawyer to be employed, instead of enquiring into the case and giving such assistance as might appear expedient and proper."* Palmerston, 1840.

### 5.1 The Distinction between Diplomatic Protection and Consular Protection

Diplomatic *and* consular protection? Diplomatic *or* consular protection? Texts and authors seem to confuse the two terms. It would seem that in both cases it is "consular protection" exercised by diplomatic authorities. Nevertheless, one must be careful, as there is a "false symmetry" between diplomatic and consular protection.[1] "Consular protection" may be equated to "consular assistance."[2]

---

[1] Decaux, E. (2006): "*La Protection Consulaire et Les Droits de l'Homme*" in *La Protection Consulaire* (S. Doumbe-Bille & H. Gherari, eds.), France, p. 51.
[2] *Ibid.*, p. 52.

Traditionally, when a "State committed a wrong against an individual who was an alien, then that wrong, if unredressed, was translated into a wrong against the alien's State of nationality. Once two States were involved, traditional international law handled the issue through its normal mechanisms (diplomacy, arbitration, and even war)."[3]

### 5.1.1 Diplomatic Protection

Article 1 of the Draft Articles on Diplomatic Protection, 2006, states that for the purposes of those Articles, diplomatic protection consists of the invocation by a State, through diplomatic action or other means of peaceful settlement, of the responsibility of another State for an injury caused by an internationally wrongful act of that State to a natural or legal person that is a national of the former State with a view to the implementation of such responsibility.

According to Special Rapporteur Dugard:

> In the *Panevezys-Saldutiskis Railway* case, the Permanent Court of International Justice appeared to distinguish between "diplomatic action" and "judicial proceedings" – a distinction repeated by the International Court of Justice in the *Nottebohm* case and by the Iran-United States Claims Tribunal in *Case No. A/18*. In contrast, legal scholars draw no such distinction and use the term "diplomatic protection" to embrace consular action, negotiation, mediation, judicial and arbitral proceedings, reprisals, retorsion, severance of diplomatic relations, economic pressure and, the final resort, the use of force.[4]

Denza provides an example of this: "[i]n determining the legal rules applicable to members of a diplomatic mission exercising consular functions, it must be borne in mind that there is no clear dividing line between diplomatic and consular functions."[5]

The fact that a consul is assisting nationals of the sending State is not tantamount to the exercise of diplomatic protection by the sending State.[6] Such a situation is "usually neither directed against the other State nor based

---

[3] Lillich, R.B. (1984): *The Human Rights of Aliens in Contemporary International Law*, United States, p. 1.

[4] Dugard, J.R. (2000): *First Report on Diplomatic Protection*, International Law Commission, 52nd session, A/C.N.4/506, paras. 42-43.

[5] Denza, E. (1998): *Diplomatic Law, a Commentary on the Vienna Convention on Diplomatic Relations*, United Kingdom, p. 33.

[6] Amerasinghe, C.F. (2008): *Diplomatic Protection*, United Kingdom, p. 45.

on a real or alleged violation of international law."[7] Consular assistance is of a preventive nature, whereas diplomatic protection is of a remedial nature.[8] An injured State would exercise its right of diplomatic protection against a delinquent State if the latter failed to allow consular assistance to the nationals of the former. In the cases discussed hereunder the merits of the cases concerned the exercise of consular assistance while the mechanism used to bring the cases before the International Court of Justice, the exercise of diplomatic protection.[9]

### 5.1.2 Consular Assistance

As a *sous-directeur* responsible for consular matters in the French Foreign Ministry once put it, consular assistance is incontestably the most diversified field of consular activity. It is that which most puts the consul to the test in the most varied of human situations, the most unexpected, and often the most complex. Their solution frequently depends on the good relations which the consul entertains with local authorities, and on whether he is endowed with *sang froid*, experience, human qualities, ability to adapt, common sense and imagination as well as a profound knowledge of local laws.[10]

Consuls have the function to protect in the receiving State the interests of the sending State and of its nationals, both individuals and bodies corporate, within the limits permitted by international law; to help and assist nationals, both individuals and bodies corporate, of the sending State; and subject to the practices and procedures obtaining in the receiving State, to represent or arrange appropriate representation for nationals of the sending State before the tribunals and other authorities of the receiving State, for the purpose of obtaining, in accordance with the laws and regulations of the receiving State, provisional measures for the preservation of the rights and interests of these

[7] Geck, W.K. (1992): "Diplomatic Protection" in *Encyclopedia of Public International Law*, the Netherlands, p. 1046.

[8] Künzli, A. (2006): "Exercising Diplomatic Protection: The fine line between Litigation, Demarches and Consular Assistance" in *Zeitschrift für ausländisches öffentliches Recht und Völkerrecht* (*Heildelberg Journal of International Law*), Vol. 66, No. 2, Germany, p. 332. Elsewhere (Künzli, A. (2005): "Case Concerning Mexican Nationals" in *Leiden Journal of International Law*, Vol. 18, No. 1, the Netherlands, p. 64), the same author argued that by turning the *Avena* case, *infra*, "into an example of diplomatic protection in disguise," by "putting the veil of direct injury over it" there was a reopening of "the Pandora's box [of past abuses of diplomatic protection by Western powers in the nineteenth and even early twentieth centuries] that it took so long to close."

[9] Künzli (2006), *op. cit.*, p. 337.

[10] Mucetti, S. (2006): "*Communication*" in *La Protection Consulaire* (*op. cit*, p. 161.)

nationals, where, because of absence or any other reason, such nationals are unable at the proper time to assume the defence of their rights and interests.[11]

Consular protection has rarely been regarded in the same way as diplomatic protection. It has been rediscovered thanks to the cases recently filed with the International Court of Justice (ICJ) against the United States of America.[12]

### 5.2.1 Consular Assistance in Criminal Matters[13]

States' treatment of aliens arrested and tried in their jurisdiction might be discriminatory, non-discriminatory, or preferential, when compared to the treatment of own nationals. Elihu Root captured the essence of this trichotomy thus:

> Each country is bound to give to the nationals of another country in its territory the benefit of the same laws, the same administration, the same protection, and the same redress for injury which it gives to its own citizens, and neither more nor less; provided that the protection which the country gives to its own citizens conforms to the established standards of civilization.[14]

The non-discrimination of aliens seems to depend on the "cultural bridge" provided by Article 36 VCCR to address the disadvantages of the arrested or detained foreign national. Without measures that recognize and remove these disadvantages, "existing rights become merely nominal rights."[15]

When, on November 17, 1997, Mexico requested an Advisory Opinion on the right to information on consular assistance in the framework of the guarantees to the due process of law from the Inter-American Court of Human Rights, it described this type of consular assistance thus:

---

[11] VCCR Article 5 (1)(a), (e) and (i).

[12] Gherari, H. (2006): "*L'Institution Consulaire Entre Tradition et Modernité*" in *La Protection Consulaire* (*op. cit.*, p. 9).

[13] Consular assistance is also applicable to civil matters, such as, for instance, when governments undertake custody or control of foreign children or dependent adults, due to deaths of foreign nationals in plane crashes or shipwrecks; see Kemp Parker, P. (2001): "When a Foreign Child Comes Into Care: Has the Consul Been Notified?" in *Child Law Practice*, Vol. 19, United States, p. 177 *et seq.*

[14] Root, E. (1910): "The Basis of Protection to Citizens Residing Abroad" in *American Journal of International Law*, Vol. 4, United States, p. 521.

[15] Aceves, W.J. (1998): "International Decisions" in *American Journal of International Law*, Vol. 92, No. 3, United States, p. 523.

> The consular assistance granted from the moment of the arrest guarantees, *inter alia*, that a detained alien is made aware, in his own language and in an accessible manner, of his constitutional and legal rights in the country in which he is apprehended; that he is provided without delay with adequate legal assistance; that he is made aware of the possible legal consequences [...] of the crime of which he stands accused; that the manner in which the legal system functions in the country in which he is detained is explained to him and, particularly that he is informed of his right not to incriminate himself and not to make any statement or confession before he has been provided with adequate legal counsel. [...]
>
> Consular agents take measures to ensure that the defendant or convicted person receives adequate legal defense throughout the proceedings; for instance, *via* bar associations or private law firms that possess the human and material resources to ensure thorough performance of the task. [...]
>
> There is also the need for professional interpreters when aliens are involved. Nationals of the receiving State do not find themselves at this disadvantage, which may be attenuated in the case of aliens by the timely intervention of consular agents.
>
> Consular agents can assist the defense in obtaining evidence, including evidence that attests mitigating circumstances. [...]
>
> In particular, consular assistance can facilitate: the hiring and payment of investigators by the Government of [the sending State] should it be necessary, to help the defense attorneys accurately establish the facts on which the outcome of the proceedings depends. [...]
>
> Consular agents can keep other interested authorities and bodies of the State of origin [...] informed of the development of the case. These, in turn, can undertake whatever measures they deem appropriate within their respective spheres of competence, such as supporting the gathering of evidence referred above.

### 5.2.2 The Purpose and Scope of Consular Assistance

When a foreign national is arrested or detained, he is unlikely to be familiar with the criminal justice system of the arresting State. He is a "stranger in a strange land." He might not be conversant with the arresting State's way of doing things, police practices, or criminal procedure. There might be language-related problems,[16] or other problems stemming from a lack of resources, ignorance, and discrimination based on the foreigner's origin. There could be difficulties in obtaining witnesses or evidence from the country of origin.[17]

Cultural differences not only have far-reaching consequences, but are also hard to presuppose. In the *Breard* case (*infra*), it would seem the accused was under the false impression that by doing what is apparently usually done in his home country, that is confess with a view to obtaining the mercy of the Court, he would actually be helping himself rather than assisting his prosecutors in securing his conviction, and ultimately bringing his own death unto himself. In Russia, it would seem that due to fear of physical force, it is not uncommon for suspects to give statements to the police, even though the prosecution would then use those statements against them if they opt not to give testimony in court. It can therefore only be expected of a Russian immigrant arrested abroad to believe he would be beaten up, irrespective of assurances to the contrary given by the police or his lawyer. He would thus make a statement even if it would not be in his best interests. In the *Avena and other Mexican Nationals* case (*infra*), one of the Mexican nationals made a confession because he feared that back in Mexico, police, known for their brutality, would beat up his relatives whom they had detained. He might have not confessed had he been informed of his right to contact consul, as the Consul would have probably set his mind at rest that the implied threats would not take place or he would have immediately procured the release of the parents from their illegal detention.[18]

---

[16] "Even if both lawyer and client speak the same language, thought patterns may be different in the creation of the message [...] Many other variables may also cause problems in the intercultural exchange between lawyer and client. Nonverbal communication aspects such as differences in the use of personal space, and differences in the use of the value of time, are examples. Beliefs, attitudes, and values, roles, [...] the environment or setting in which the interaction takes place, and the worldview of those involved are all other intercultural variables that might produce barriers affecting the intercultural exchange. [...] Other factors may cause problems in intercultural interaction. Lack of empathy, lack of trust, stereotyping, and especially ethnocentrism, or judging another culture according to one's own cultural values, may lead to communication problems." – Kessler, J.B. (1988): "Perspective: The Lawyer's Intercultural Communication Problems with Clients of Diverse Cultures" in *North Western Journal of International Law and Business*, Vol. 9, No. 1, United States, p. 76.

[17] Chin, D.C. (1994): "The Cultural Defense: Beyond Exclusion, Assimilation, and Guilty Liberalism" in *California Law Review*, Vol. 82, United States, p. 1053.

[18] Springrose, L.J. (1999): "Strangers in a Strange Land: the Rights of Non-Citizens under article 36 of the Vienna Convention on Consular Relations" in *Georgetown Immigration Law Review*, Vol. 14, No. 1, United States, pp. 185-213.

Irrespective of the form consular assistance for detained nationals takes, each intervention would be satisfying three needs. (i) Humanitarian: Through consuls, detained foreigners have "an essential and reliable link to the outside world"[19] (e.g., communicating with family and friends). Consuls ensure that detained co-nationals do not lack any basic necessity while incarcerated. The presence of an authority from the detainee's country of citizenship assuages the anguish and anxiety of the detainee. (ii) Protective: Regular consular visits might serve to avert the ill-treatment of detainees. In cases where detainees allege mistreatment, the consul may intervene on their behalf with the prison authorities. (iii) Legal assistance: Consuls do not act as lawyers, and their role is not to replace the defence counsel. Nevertheless, they can supplement the role of the detainee's lawyer in that they can explain the local legal system to the detainee and suggest possible lawyers to engage. Whereas consular assistance is not meant to offer foreign nationals immunity from local law, consuls can take measures necessary for the fair and equal treatment of their nationals under the laws of the arresting State.[20] Furthermore, consuls may also help the defence lawyer to understand any cultural[21] differences between the society of the arresting State and the society of the national's State on such matters as motivations, premeditation, provocation, heat of passion, and understanding and perception[22] of circumstances before and after indictment.

## 5.3 The Triptych in Article 36 VCCR

Dupuy[23] defines this triptych thus: "communication-notification-assistance."[24]

---

[19] The experience is described with these precise words by Billy Hayes, author of the novel *Midnight Express*, who spent five years in a Turkish prison during the 1970s. See Brief *Amicus Curiae* of Ambassador L. Bruce Laingen and Lieutenant Colonel John J. Swift, *et al.*, in support of Petitioner (2005) in the *José Ernesto Medellín v. Doug Dretke, Director, Texas Department of Criminal Justice, Correctional Institutions Division Case*, Supreme Court of the United States, No. 04-5928, p.3.

[20] James, A. & Warren, M. (2002) : *Equal Protection: Assistance and Criminal Justice Procedures in the USA, An Introductory Guide for Consulates*, United States, p. 10.

[21] Culture could be defined as "special populations which share the same worldview or tend to make the same assumptions about their environment" – Kessler, J.B., *op. cit.*, pp. 64-67.

[22] "Perception is the 'internal process by which we select, evaluate, and organize stimuli from the external environment.' It is a key component of any communication, and especially of the intercultural exchange.'" – Kessler, J.B., *op. cit.*, pp. 64-67.

[23] Pierre-Marie Dupuy appeared on behalf of Mexico in the *Avena* case (*infra*).

[24] Dupuy, P.-M. (2006): "*La Protection Consulaire sous les Feux de la Jurisprudence Internationale*" in *La Protection Consulaire* (*op. cit.*, p. 42).

The declared aim of Article 36 (1) is to facilitate "the exercise of consular functions relating to nationals of the sending State." Paragraph (a) establishes the consular officer's freedom to communicate with his co-nationals and the freedom of the latter to communicate with him:

> (*a*) consular officers shall be free to communicate with nationals of the sending State and to have access to them. Nationals of the sending State shall have the same freedom with respect to communication with and access to consular officers of the sending State;

Paragraph (b) lays down *(1)* that notification of the right to communication and assistance has to be made to the sending State's national and *(2)* the circumstances in which the sending State is to be notified by the receiving State of the deprivation of liberty. The collocation "without delay" is used thrice in this subparagraph. This is significant because diplomatic language rarely makes use of redundancies.[25]

> (*b*) if he so requests, the competent authorities of the receiving State shall, without delay, inform the consular post of the sending State if, within its consular district, a national of that State is arrested or committed to prison or to custody pending trial or is detained in any other manner. Any communication addressed to the consular post by the person arrested, in prison, custody or detention shall be forwarded by the said authorities without delay. The said authorities shall inform the person concerned without delay of his rights under this subparagraph;

Paragraph (c) lays down how consular assistance may be given:

> (*c*) consular officers shall have the right to visit a national of the sending State who is in prison, custody or detention, to converse and correspond with him and to arrange for his legal representation.
>
> They shall also have the right to visit any national of the sending State who is in prison, custody or detention in their district in pursuance of a judgement. Nevertheless, consular officers shall refrain from taking action on behalf of a national who is in prison, custody or detention if he expressly opposes such action.

[25] *Ibid.*, pp. 42-43.

Finally, the context for the exercise of the aforesaid rights:

> 2. The rights referred to in paragraph 1 of this article shall be exercised in conformity with the laws and regulations of the receiving State, subject to the proviso, however, that the said laws and regulations must enable full effect to be given to the purposes for which the rights accorded under this article are intended.

This Article of the VCCR is not at all lengthy, and with reason. Concrete fact situations may be so diverse that it is impossible to provide for them in detail without risking to compromise possible future developments in the field. A general approach in fact allows future evolution of consular protection and avoids limiting it to the State practice as it was prior to the VCCR.[26]

### 5.4.1 Consular Assistance as a Right of the Foreign National

Prior to the VCCR, no general treaty specifying protection of nationals or other consular functions existed.[27] In this respect, the codified rules considered in Article 36 VCCR would therefore seem to be novel.

Courts and commentators have suggested that individual persons gain derivative rights under treaties.[28] A treaty conferring such private rights is often termed "self-executing", although the term could be misleading because "self-executing" is sometimes also used to describe a treaty that does not require any implementing legislation to take effect.[29]

The interpretation of treaties is governed by the Vienna Convention on the Law of Treaties. Article 31 provides the general rules of interpretation, and Article 32 provides for supplementary means of interpretation. The point of departure is good faith interpretation of the meaning of the text of the treaty, based on the twin principles of *pacta sunt servanda* and that the interpretation of the treaty should not lead to results which are manifestly absurd or unreasonable. The text must be read as a whole, in context, in the

---

[26] Gherari, H. (2006), *op. cit.*, p. 27.

[27] The only exception was a regional treaty concluded in 1911 between Bolivia, Colombia, Ecuador, Peru, and Venezuela. – Shank, S.A., and Quigley, J., (1995): "Foreigners on Texas' Death Row and the Right to Access to a Consul" in *St. Mary's Law Journal*, Vol. 26, no. 3, United States, pp. 719-753.

[28] Kadish, M.J. (1997): "Article 36 of the Vienna Convention on Consular Relations: A Search for the Right to Consul" in *Michigan Journal of International Law*, Vol. 18, issue 4, United States, pp. 565-613.

[29] Deek, J.A. (1998): "A New Miranda" in *Vanderbilt Journal of Transnational Law*, Vol. 31, United States, p. 1004.

light of the object and the purpose of the treaty,[30] in consideration of relevant rules of international law,[31] and subsequent agreements and practices regarding interpretation or application of the treaty provisions. The *travaux préparatoires* of the treaty may supplement the textual interpretation, however the plain meaning of treaty terms holds sway unless it would render a result inconsistent with the intent or expectations of its signatories.

Article 36 (1)(b) unequivocally states that "the person concerned" has "rights under this subparagraph." Admittedly, Article 36 VCCR is "an awkward place to enumerate the rights of an individual national."[32] There have been arguments forwarded that the location of a provision in a statute influences its meaning.[33] The purpose of the VCCR, as set forth in the Preamble, is not to benefit individuals but to enable the efficient performance of consular functions. This seems to militate against an interpretation that the VCCR confers an individual right. Yet the Preamble's reference to the benefit which may accrue to individuals can be easily understood to mean that consular privileges and immunities are granted to individuals who serve as consuls, not as a personal entitlement but because of their office, to enable them to carry out their consular functions. The 1961 Vienna Convention on Diplomatic Relations uses almost identical language, and it has been construed in the same way; likewise the Vienna Convention on the Privileges and Immunities of the United Nations. It would thus seem that the VCCR Preamble cannot support the categorical preclusion that the VCCR does not grant rights to individual persons, although the Preamble by itself would allow only the interpretation that the VCCR does grant rights but only to individuals holding a consular office. The *travaux préparatoires*, however, seem to indicate that Article 36 VCCR was indeed intended to confer individual rights to nationals other than consuls. There was insistence on the automatic notification to consuls in case of arrest or detention of nationals, but concern for the free will of the arrested or detained national prevailed. Paragraph 2 was subjected to the criticism that it would accord privileged status to aliens. During the counterarguments, which won the day, the point was raised that Article 36 was concerned with aliens and their rights. The importance of paragraph (1)(b) was highlighted by referring to the "fundamental and indispensable rights of the individual" and to "the right of nationals of a sending State to communicate with and have access to the consulate and consular officials of their own country [as being] one of the

[30] That is, "the search for the common intentions of the parties who drew up the Treaty" – Sinclair, I. (1984): *The Vienna Convention on the Law of Treaties*, United Kingdom, p. 78.

[31] That is, "whether convention or customary" – *idem*.

[32] Kadish, M.J., *op. cit.*, p. 593.

[33] Haitian Courts Council, 969 F.2d at 1359-60, cited by Kadish, *op. cit.*, pp. 565-613.

most sacred rights of foreign residents in a country."[34] In its Pleadings before the ICJ in the *Case Concerning United States Diplomatic and Consular Staff in Tehran*, the United States contended that "Article 36 establishes rights not only for the consular officer, but, perhaps more importantly, for the nationals of the sending state."[35]

An individual person has the option – not the obligation – to appeal to his State for protection,[36] but he may not "sign away" the right to such protection, as this would diminish the rights of his own State under international law,[37] even though in the case of consular assistance the sending State is bound not to offer consular assistance if the national expressly opposes it.[38] The sending State's right to offer consular assistance can be exercised only if the national requests it;[39] however, Nava argued that in Italy (unlike Switzerland and the United States, but similarly to the United Kingdom) whereas the consul's duty to protect his co-nationals is by law, this duty does not translate into a right of the national to be protected. The rule, he argued, says that "consuls assist and protect co-nationals," and it can be converted into "nationals are assisted and protected by consuls." But it cannot be converted into "nationals have a right to be assisted and protected by consuls."[40] In other words, the national would seem not to have the right to sue the sending State if it fails to give him consular assistance.[41] This question would seem to fall within the ambit of the dichotomy between utopian and apologetic visions of International Law. Nava would be proposing the positivist, or apologetic (about State practice), position. On the other hand, it has been argued that the instrumentalist analysis ("the law of diplomatic protection as an instrument for the promotion of human rights") is a "utopian vision of international law inspired by humanistic ideals which are not directly transposable into the institution of diplomatic protection."[42] This second position would raise a further consideration. If consular assistance is considered a human right, not just a treaty right, then

[34] *Ibid.*

[35] *I.C.J. Pleadings* 1980 (United States Memorial), 174.

[36] Shank, S.A., and Quigley, J. , *op. cit.*, pp. 719-753.

[37] Svarlien, O. (1955): *An Introduction to the Law of Nations*, United States, p. 419.

[38] Article 36 (1) VCCR.

[39] Article 36 (1)(b) VCCR. See Uribe, V.M. (1997): "Consuls at Work: Universal Instruments of Human Rights and Consular Protection in the Context of Criminal Justice" in *Houston Journal of International Law*, Vol. 19, United States, p. 390.

[40] Nava, S. (1956): *Corso di Diritto di legazione e consolare*, Italy, p. 139.

[41] It would seem that neither Article 46 of the Charter of the Fundamental Rights of the European Union nor (at least to date) Article 23 of the Treaty on the Functioning of the European Union affect this position.

[42] Pergantis, V. (2006): "Towards a 'Humanization' of Diplomatic Protection?" in *Heildelberg Journal of International Law*, Vol. 66, No. 2, Germany, p. 353 *et seq.*

would not the position of the sending State change? Would not providing assistance to the national abroad cease to lie within its discretion and assume an obligatory nature?[43]

### 5.4.2 The Nature of the Right to Consular Assistance

"Wrongfully to deprive human beings of their freedom and to subject them to physical constraint is in itself manifestly incompatible with the principles of the [United Nations] Charter 'as well as with the fundamental principles enunciated in the Universal Declaration of Human Rights'," observes Shabtai Rosenne referring to the *United States Diplomatic and Consular Staff in Tehran* case.[44] Yet in the *LaGrand* case, he goes on, the ICJ "found it unnecessary to consider a contention that a provision in the Consular Relations Convention of 1963 requiring notification to the consul of the arrest of a person of foreign nationality was a human right."[45] It has been argued that the ICJ's attempts in *LaGrand* "to differentiate between Article 36 as an individual and as a human right seem artificial and short-sighted."[46] In the *Avena* case, the ICJ hinted that it does not consider consular notification to be a human right.[47]

The Inter-American Court on Human Rights did decide that the right created by Article 36 VCCR is a human right.[48] In his Concurring Opinion, the President of this Court, Judge Cançado Trindade held that "the subjective individual right to information on consular assistance of which are *titulaires* all human beings who are in the need to exercise it, has crystallized" in "the confluence of [consular relations] with human rights" and that "such individual right [is now] inserted into the conceptual universe of human rights."[49] In 2000, the United Nations General Assembly passed a resolution underlining the importance of human rights of migrants. In this context, it referred in particular to the assistance and protection provided for in the

---

[43] Cerna, C.M. (2008): "The right to consular notification as a human right" in *Suffolk Transnational Law Review*, Vol. 31, No. 2, United States, pp. 415 and 431.

[44] Rosenne is here paraphrasing. See *United States Diplomatic and Consular Staff in Tehran (U.S. v. Iran)*, 1980 *I.C.J. Reports*, para. 91.

[45] Rosenne, Sh. (2004): *The Perplexities of Modern International Law*, the Netherlands, p. 215.

[46] Mennecke, M. (2001): "Toward the Humanization of the Vienna Convention of Consular Rights - The *LaGrand* Case before the International Court of Justice" in *German Yearbook of International Law*, Vol. 44, Germany, p. 453.

[47] *Avena and Other Mexican Nationals (Mexico* v. *United States)*, 2004, *I.C.J. Reports* para. 124.

[48] Cerna, C.M. (2008): *op. cit., passim.*

[49] *The Right to Information on Consular Assistance, Advisory Opinion*, OC-16/99, Inter-Am. Ct. H.R. (ser. A.) No. 16 ¶ 35 (October 1999) (Trindade, J., concurring).

VCCR.[50] In 2001, the United Nations Commission on Human Rights urged all States that still maintain the death penalty "to observe the Safeguards guaranteeing protection of the rights of those facing the death penalty and to comply fully with their international obligations, in particular with those under the Vienna Convention on Consular Relations."[51]

Nevertheless, as was pointed out in one US case,[52] a Mexican national had been living in the United States since the age of three and had elected never to become a US citizen. Why should an individual in such circumstances be entitled to a remedy if his Article 36 right is violated? Perhaps entitlement should not depend on the nationality carried in the passport, but on an individual's cultural link with the arresting State. The principle of the "sufficiently close link," which allows the application of European Union law to European Union citizens who are on the territory of a third State, could serve as an inspiration.[53]

### 5.4.3 No Right Exists Without a Remedy

It would seem from national court decisions that the national of the sending State does not have a right to judicial remedy by the receiving State if the latter State fails to notify him that he has the right to inform his State and thereby putting in motion the mechanism leading to the possibility of consular assistance. An Australian case and an Italian case could serve as illustrations.[54] Both dealt with failure to notify a foreign national of right to contact consul, and in both cases, the Courts refused to overturn convictions on the basis of said failure. The Italian Court held that rights pursuant to the VCCR are of a "complementary and subsidiary nature, and do not replace the right of the accused to make his own arrangements for his own defence." United States Courts are split on this issue, with instances[55] in which the

---

[50] UN Doc. A/RES/54/166, 24 February, 2000, item 4.

[51] UN Voc. E/CN.4/RES/2001/68, 25 April 2001; UN Doc. E/CN.4/RES/2000/65, 27 April 2000.

[52] See Judge Hervey's opinion in *Ex Parte* Medellín, 223 S.W.3d 315, 357-358 (Tex. Crim. App. 2006) (Hervey, J., concurring).

[53] See also Misson, P.L., Berthe E., Delree C, and Kaëns L. (2007): *La protection diplomatique et consulaire est-elle un droit fondamental?*, Belgium, http://ec.europa.eu/justice_home/news/consulting_public/consular_protection/contributions/contribution_mission_fr.pdf, pp. 4-5. Also, for a fuller discussion on the determination of nationality, see Doumbe-Bille, S. (2006): "*L'Assistance Consulaire*" in *La Protection Consulaire* (*op. cit.*, p. 123 and *passim*).

[54] Cited by Springrose, L.J., *op. cit.*, pp. 185-213.

[55] E.g., *U.S. v. Nai Fook Li* (1st Circuit, 206 F.3d 56, 60, 62, February 29, 2000); U.S. v. Chaparro-Alcantara (7th Circuit, 226 F.3d 616, August 21, 2000); *U.S. v. Lombera-Camorlinga* (9th Circuit, 206 F.3d 882, 885 En Banc March 6, 2000); *Mir Aimal Kasi v. Commonwealth of Virginia* (Supreme Court of Virginia, 256 Va. 407; 508 S.E.2d

Courts held that the VCCR "created no rights enforceable by defendants as individuals" (to borrow from *U.S. v. Cordoba-Mosquera*[56]) against the receiving State,[57] and cases in which the United States Courts did recognize the existence of an individual right.[58] Also, the implementation of Article 36 VCCR in the United States has to be analyzed from the federal viewpoint, particularly in view of the state immunity rule developed by *New York v. United States* and *Printz v. United States.*[59] There have also been cases in the United States of a civil remedy being sought for matters relating to consular assistance.[60]

The other remedy available is through the sending State's exercise of the right of diplomatic protection.[61] A scansion of the *travaux préparatoires* of

57, November 6, 1998); *Rocha v. State of Texas* (Texas, 16 S.W.3d 1, 21, Court of Criminal Appeals), *Felix Rocha v. State of Texas* (Court of Criminal Appeals of Texas, 16 S.W. 3d 1, April 21, 2000), *U.S. v. Emuegbunam* (6th Circuit, 268 F.3d 377, 2001) and *U.S. v. Jimenez-Nava* (5th Circuit, 243 F.3d 192, 2001). See also: Wooster, A.K. (2002): "Constructions and Application of Vienna Convention on Consular Relations, Requiring that Foreign Consulate be Notified when One of its Nationals is Arrested" in 175 *A.L.R. Fed* 243, for more United States domestic cases dealing with failure to notify as per Article 36 VCCR.

[56] 11th Circuit, 212, F.3d 1194, 1195-1996, May 23, 2000.

[57] This view is shared by some authors, e.g., Vadnais, M. (1999): "A Diplomatic Morass: An Argument Against Judicial Involvement in Article 36 of the Vienna Convention on Consular Relations" in *UCLA Law Review*, Vol. 47, no. 1, United States, pp. 25-33, who argues that in ratifying the VCCR, the United States did not intend to confer a private right of action to foreign criminal defendants.

[58] E.g., *U.S. v. Calderon-Medina* (9th Circuit, 591 F.2d 529, 1979).

[59] Thornberry, C. (1999): "Federalism v. Foreign Affairs: How the United States can administer Article 36 of the Vienna Convention on Consular Relations within the States" in *McGeorge Law Review*, Vol. 31, No. 1, United States, pp. 107-145. Deek, J.A., *op. cit.*, p. 1002, however warns that "if the United States government does not have the constitutional power to bind state governments to the obligations of the treaty, then other countries might avoid the provisions of the treaty on somewhat analogous grounds."

[60] A civil action may be brought based on 42 United States Code § 1983, e.g. *Sorensen v. City of New York* (No. 98 Civ. 3356 (HB), 2000) and *Standt v. City of New York* (153 F. Supp. 2d 417, 2001). See Deck Harrill, E. (2004): "Exorcising the Ghost: Finding a Right and a Remedy in Article 36 of the Vienna Convention on Consular Relations" in *South Carolina Law Review*, Vol. 55, United States, pp. 587-589.

[61] It has been argued that some States are too politically or economically weak to resort to the exercise of diplomatic protection against stronger States (like the United States) on whose political and economic goodwill they might depend. For more elaboration see Weinman, J.L. (2002): "The Clash between U.S. Criminal Procedure and the Vienna Convention on Consular Relations: An Analysis of the International Court of Justice Decision in the *LaGrand Case*" in *American University International Law Review*, Vol 17, No 4, United States, p. 900. See also Aeschleman, N.L. (2005): "The Vienna Convention on Consular Relations: Quo Vadis America?" in *Santa*

the VCCR and a reading of Article 36 in particular reveal no indication as to the consequences of a violation of the rights mentioned therein. However, this is fundamental to the proper guarantee of the effective protection of said rights.[62] It has been argued that since the VCCR gives no remedy, there is no right to consular notification.[63] This argument was quashed by the ICJ.

#### 5.4.3.2 State Responsibility

State responsibility is regulated by customary law; the Draft Articles on State Responsibility for Internationally Wrongful Acts (DASRIW) have paved the way for a better understanding of it.[64] A very succinct review of the more essential elements of State responsibility will prove useful to this end.

The characterization of an act of a State as internationally wrongful is governed by international law and such characterization is not affected by the characterization of the same act as lawful by internal law.[65] The responsible State is under an obligation to make full reparation for the injury (which includes any damage, whether material or moral) caused by the internationally wrongful act.[66]

The obligations of the responsible State may be owed to, among others, another State. This is without prejudice to any right, arising from the international responsibility of a State, which may accrue directly to any person or entity other than a State.[67]

---

*Clara Law Review*, 45 (2005), United States, 4, p. 974, on the realpolitik element in this context. There seems also to have been a case which was never brought before the ICJ: the 1999 *Saldaño* case. An Argentine, Victor Hugo Saldaño, was sentenced to death in the United States; his mother sued Argentina before the Inter-American Commission on Human Rights alleging Argentina did not fully pursue all redress against the United States for his scheduled execution. Argentina also did not take the United States to the ICJ because of the possibility of forfeiting financial aid at a time of economic woes. (See Mendenhall, M. (2002): "A Case for Consular Notification: Treaty Obligation as a Matter of Life and Death" in *Southwestern University Journal of Law and Trade in the Americas*, Vol. 8, United States, p. 343.)

[62] Iovane, M. (1990): *La riparazione nella teoria e nella prassi dell'illecito internazionale*, Italy, pp. 263-264.

[63] Argument submitted by the United States in the *LaGrand* case. See Weinman, J.L., *op. cit.*, pp. 877 *et seq.* for further elaboration.

[64] The 1996 Draft Articles were cited by the ICJ in the *Gab íkovo-Nagyamaros Project (Hungary/Slovakia)* case.

[65] Article 3 DASRIW. Article 32 spells it out: the responsible State may not rely on the provisions of its internal law as justification for failure to comply with its obligations under this Part.

[66] Article 31 DASRIW.

[67] Article 33 DASRIW.

Full reparation for the injury caused by the internationally wrongful act shall take the form of restitution, compensation and satisfaction.[68] Cessation of the wrongful act and assurances and guarantees of non-repetition may also be claimed.[69]

Restitution in kind (or *restitutio in integrum*), which restores the *status quo ante*[70] (i.e., it re-establishes the situation which existed before the wrongful act was committed), must be materially possible, and not involve a burden out of all proportion to the benefit deriving from restitution instead of compensation.[71] A disagreement as to the proper remedy on the merits of a case can affect the argument on the appropriate provisional measures.[72] However, in the *Passage Through The Great Belt Case*, in which Finland sought an order that Denmark should not undertake any construction of the planned bridge over the Great Belt strait as it would interfere with international navigation, the ICJ held that though they might be "excessively onerous," if it were "established that the construction of works involves an infringement of a legal right, the possibility cannot and should not be excluded *a priori* of a judicial finding that such works must not be continued or must be modified or dismantled."[73]

### 5.5 Cases before the ICJ

All the cases dealt with involve the United States.

Denied consular assistance was the subject-matter of the very first proceeding initiated by the United States at the ICJ. It was in 1954, nine years before the conclusion of the VCCR. In its pleadings in the *Treatment in Hungary of Aircraft and Crew of United States of America Case (U.S.* v. *Hungary*; *U.S.* v. *U.S.S.R.*), the United States claimed that the failure by the Hungarian and Soviet authorities to allow consular access and assistance had deprived the United States and its citizens of their respective right to provide and receive consular assistance. "International law," the United States observed, "recognizes the right of the government [...] to act on behalf of its nationals and is applied in Hungarian judicial practice."[74]

---

[68] Article 34 DASRIW.
[69] Article 30 DASRIW.
[70] See *Factory at Chorzów (Merits)* case *(Germany* v. *Poland)*, Permanent Court of International Justice, 1928, No. 17.
[71] Article 35 DASRIW.
[72] Gray, C. (1999): "The Choice between Restitution and Compensation" in *European Journal of International Law*, 10, Italy, p. 415.
[73] *Passage Through the Great Belt (Finland* v. *Denmark)*, Order 29 VII 1991, p. 19.
[74] Application Instituting Proceedings and Pleadings (*United States* v. *Hungary*; *United States* v. *Union of Soviet Socialist Republics*), 1953 ICJ Pleadings (*Treatment in*

The facts of the case were as follows. On November 19, 1951, a United States Air Force cargo aircraft carrying four American airmen was making a routine flight from Germany to Belgrade, Yugoslavia, during which it accidentally crossed into Hungarian airspace, was brought down by Soviet authorities in Hungary and subsequently turned over with its crew to Hungarian authorities. Despite repeated requests, Hungarian officials would not allow American officials to speak with the airmen. Secretary of State Dean Acheson claimed that Hungary failed to "live up to the accepted standards of international practice with regard to the right of consular officers to exercise protective functions on behalf of nationals of their country."[75]

Both Hungary and the Soviet Union refused to accept the jurisdiction of the ICJ and the cases could not proceed.

### 5.5.1 Case Concerning the Vienna Convention on Consular Relations (*Paraguay* v. *United States of America*), 1998

The Court was thus composed: President, Schwebel; Vice-President and (since the President was a United States citizen) Acting President, Weeramantry; Judges, Oda, Bedjaoui, Guillaume, Ranjeva, Herczegh, Shi, Fleischhauer, Koroma, Verschchetin, Higgins, Parra-Aranguren, Kooijmans, and Rezek.

#### 5.5.1.1 Facts

Born in Argentina, Angel Francisco Breard was sexually assaulted by a soldier when he was 7 years old. Six years later, his family moved to Paraguay, and two years later, aged 15, Breard followed his father's example and began drinking heavily. In 1985, he sustained serious head injuries in a car accident, and seemed to have undergone a personality change which unleashed impulsive behaviour and difficulties with temper control. He moved to the USA in October 1986, learned English, found employment and married one of his English teachers. His drinking problem did not subside and his marriage fell apart after four months, following which he became severely depressed. His alcoholism worsened, jeopardizing his ability to find employment.

In 1992, Breard was arrested and charged with attempted rape and capital murder. He never denied his involvement in the homicide, although he claimed he committed it because of a Satanic curse put on him by his former

*Hungary of Aircraft and Crew of United States of America*) Annex 1, p. 36 (February 16, 1954).

[75] Press Release, United States Department of State, Statement by Secretary Acheson (December 28, 1951), in 26 Department of State Bulletin (1952), United States, p. 7.

father-in-law. Despite legal advice to the contrary, he laboured under the impression, based on his perception of trial procedures in his native countries, that he could expect leniency from the jury if he admitted and expressed his remorse.

The prosecution offered Breard the possibility of plea bargaining. Despite his own admission of guilt and legal advice, he refused and insisted on confessing, expecting a lenient jury that could even exculpate him because of the Satanic curse. Breard entered a plea of "not guilty"; his case went to trial in June of 1993. He was convicted of attempted rape and capital murder and sentenced to capital punishment.

At this very late stage, Breard sought to overturn the judgment basing his case on the failure to receive consular notification, arguing that had he spoken to a Paraguayan Consul he would have avoided the fatal mistakes in his defence strategy which lead to his predicament. The literature is vociferously unanimous in its disagreement with the Court, which in *Breard* v. *Greene* rejected his arguments. An example epitomizing the criticism levelled at the Court's reasoning: "In view of the fact that the *Breard* per curiam opinion was delivered most hurriedly and without full consideration of complex issues, the treaty-based claims of individual accused, consular officers and foreign States under the Vienna Consular Convention should be revisited by the Court at the earliest opportunity. If followed even partly abroad, the opinion could have serious consequences for U.S. nationals detained in foreign countries. In the meantime, state and federal judges should ensure that foreign accused are notified of their right to communicate with their consulate and that the consulate is properly notified of their arrest. [The Executive's] claims before our Courts portend miserable representations of U.S. citizens abroad."[76]

**5.5.1.2 History of the Proceedings**

On April 3, 1998, the Republic of Paraguay instituted as *ultima ratio* before the ICJ proceedings against the United States of America alleging violations of the VCCR. Paraguay asserted that, in charging, trying, convicting and sentencing to death Mr. Breard without informing him of his rights under Article 36(1)(b) VCCR, the United States had violated the VCCR. Paraguay argued that this violation had prevented it from exercising its consular functions under Articles 5 and 36 VCCR and had resulted in Mr. Breard making objectively unreasonable decisions which had led to the imposition

---

[76] Faust, J.P. (1998): "*Breard* and Treaty-Based Rights Under the Consular Convention" in *American Journal of International Law*, Vol. 92, United States, pp. 696-697.

of the death penalty. As such the United States was under an international legal obligation not to apply any municipal law doctrine that would preclude the exercise of rights under Article 36. Paraguay was thus entitled to *restitutio in integrum* and a guarantee of non-repetition of the illegal acts.

As the execution date had been set for April 14, Paraguay also submitted a request for the indication of provisional measures pending the Court's decision on the merits. It argued that measures were required urgently in order to prevent the execution of Mr. Breard, thus protecting Paraguay's rights and the possibility of restoration *quo ante* pending the Court's decision on the merits. In addition to its interest in the life and liberty of its nationals, Paraguay emphasized the importance of an individual human life as established in international law and as recognized by Article 6 of the International Covenant on Civil and Political Rights, 1966.

The United States, however, argued that such measures were inappropriate. Mr. Breard, whose guilt was well-established, had not been prejudiced by the non-notification of rights under Article 36 VCCR which had been unintentional. Neither was there support in the relevant provisions, their *travaux préparatoires* or State practice for a resultant automatic invalidation of domestic proceedings. A stay of execution depended exclusively on the United States Supreme Court and the Government of Virginia. An indication of provisional measures would be contrary to the interests of States Parties to the VCCR, the international community as a whole and the Court, and would seriously disrupt the criminal justice system of States Parties to the Convention given the risk of proliferation of cases.

### 5.5.1.3 Points of law

The Court held that on a request for the indication of provisional measures, it was not required fully to satisfy itself it had jurisdiction on the merits of the case but should not indicate such measures unless the provisions involved by the applicant appeared, *prima facie*, to afford a basis for jurisdiction.

The Court unanimously indicated the following measures: the United States should take all measures at its disposal to ensure that Mr. Breard was not executing pending the final decision in these proceedings, and should inform the Court of all the measures that it had taken in implementation of this Order. The Court was to remain seised of the matters which formed the subject-matter of this Order until it gave its final decision.

The declarations made by some members of the Court are worth noting. President Schwebel (himself a United States citizen):

> I have voted for the Order, but with disquiet. The sensitive issues it poses have been hastily, if ably, argued. The evidence introduced is bare. The Court's consideration of the issues of law and fact, in the circumstances imposed upon it, has been summary. The United States maintains that no State has ever before claimed as Paraguay now does that, because of lack of consular access under the Vienna Convention on Consular Relations, the result of a trial, conviction, and appeal should be voided. Not only has the United States apologized to Paraguay for the unintentional failure of notification to Paraguay's consul of the arrest and trial of the accused, but it has taken substantial steps to strengthen what appears to be a practice in the United States of variable compliance with the obligations imposed upon it by the Vienna Convention [...]
>
> I have so voted essentially for these reasons. There is an admitted failure by the Commonwealth of Virginia to have afforded Paraguay timely consular access, that is to say, there is an admitted breach of treaty. An apology and Federal provision for avoidance of future such lapses does not assist the accused, who Paraguay alleges was or may have been prejudiced by lack of consular access, a question which is for the merits. It is of obvious importance to the maintenance and development of a rule of law among States that the obligations imposed by treaties be complied with and that, where they are not, reparation be required. The mutuality of interest of States in the effective observance of the obligations of the Vienna Convention on Consular Relations is the greater in the intermixed global community of today and tomorrow (and the citizens of no State have a higher interest in the observance of those obligations than the peripatetic citizens of the United States). In my view, these considerations outweigh the serious difficulties which this Order imposes on the authorities of the United States and Virginia.

Judge Oda:

> I voted in favour of the Court's Order with great hesitation. I believed and I still believe that the request for the indication of provisional measures of protection submitted by Paraguay to the Court should have been dismissed. However, in the limited time – one or two days – given to the Court to deal with this matter, I have found it impossible to develop my point sufficiently to persuade my colleagues to alter their position.
>
> [...] I can, on humanitarian grounds, understand the plight of Mr. Breard and recognize that owing to the fact that Paraguay filed this

request on the 3 April 1998, his fate now, albeit unreasonably, lies in the hands of the Court. I would like to add, however, that, if Mr. Breard's rights as they relate to humanitarian issues are to be respected then, in parallel, the matter of the rights of victims of violent crime (a point which has often been overlooked) should be taken into consideration. It should also be noted that since his arrest, Mr. Breard has been treated fairly in all legal proceedings within the American judicial system governed by the rule of law.

The Court cannot act as a court of criminal appeal and cannot be petitioned for writs of *habeas corpus*. The Court does not have jurisdiction to decide matters relating to capital punishment and its execution, and should not intervene in such matters.[77]

As stated earlier, Paraguay's request was presented to the Court on 3 April 1998 in connection with and at the same time as its Application instituting proceedings against the United States for violations of the 1963 Vienna Convention on Consular Relations. Paraguay's Application was unilaterally submitted to the Court on the basis of the Optional Protocol. I very much doubt that, on the date of filing of the Application and the request, there was any "dispute[s] arising out of the interpretation or application of the [Vienna] Convention" (Optional Protocol, Article I).

If there was any dispute between Paraguay and the United States concerning the interpretation or application of the Vienna Convention, it could have been that the United States was presumed to have violated the Convention at the time of the arrest of Mr. Breard in 1992, as the United States did not inform the Paraguayan consul of that event.

This issue was raised by Paraguay when it became aware of Mr. Breard's situation. In 1996, negotiations took place between Paraguay and the United States concerning the consular function provided for under the Convention. In July 1997, the United States proceeded to remedy the violation by sending a letter to the Government of Paraguay apologizing for its failure to inform the consul of the events concerning Mr. Breard and giving an assurance

---

[77] See Stirling-Zanda, S. (2004): "Obtaining judicial enforcement of individual conventional rights: The Consular Convention at the ICJ and at the Inter-American Court" in *Archiv des Völkerrechts*, Vol. 42, No. 2, Germany, pp. 184-216, for a treatment of the hybrid nature of the *LaGrand* claim (*infra*).

> that this failure would not be repeated in future. In my view, the United States was thus released from its responsibility for violation of the Vienna Convention. [...]
>
> Paraguay requested *restitutio in integrum.* However, if consular contact had occurred at the time of Mr. Breard's arrest or detention, the judicial procedure in the United States domestic courts relating to his case would have been no different. This point was made clear in the pleadings of both Parties. [...]
>
> I reiterate [...] that I voted in favour of the Order, for humanitarian reasons, and in view of the fact that, if the execution were to be carried out on 14 April 1998, whatever findings the Court might have reached might be without object.

Judge Koroma:

> My decision to vote in favour of the Order granting the interim measures of protection in this matter was reached only after careful consideration and in the light of the urgency and exceptional circumstances of this case. Torn as I was between the need to observe the requirements for granting provisional measures of protection under Article 41 of the Statute of the Court, thereby ensuring that whatever decision the Court might reach should not be devoid of object, and the need for the Court to comply with its jurisdiction to settle disputes between States which, in my view, includes respect for the sovereignty of a State in relation to its criminal justice system.
>
> It was, therefore, both propitious and appropriate, for the Court to bear in mind its mission which is to decide disputes between States, and not to act as a universal supreme court of criminal appeal. On the other hand, it is equally true that the Court's function is to decide disputes between States which are submitted to it in accordance with international law, applying international conventions, etc. The Order, in my judgement, complies with these requirements.
>
> Paraguay's Application [...] requested the Court to grant provisional measures of protection under Article 41 of the Statute so as to protect its rights and the right of one of its nationals who had been convicted of a capital offence committed in the United States and sentenced to death.

> The purpose of a request for provisional measures is to preserve as well as to safeguard the rights of the parties that are in dispute, especially when such rights or subject matter of the dispute could be irretrievably or irreparably destroyed thereby rendering the Court's decision ineffective or without object. [...]
>
> When the facts presented were considered by the Court in the light of the Vienna Convention on Consular Relations, in particular in relation to its Articles 5 and 36, and Article I of the Optional Protocol concerning the Compulsory Settlement of Disputes of 24 April 1963, the Court reached the correct conclusion that a dispute existed and that its jurisdiction had been established prima facie.

The case was removed from the List by an Order of the Court of November 10, 1998, following discontinuance by the applicant Government in view of the fact that the Governor of Virginia refused a stay of execution. But the concerns expressed by the Judges were addressed in the two cases subsequently instituted against the United States by Germany and Mexico.

### 5.5.2 LaGrand (*Germany* v. *United States of America*), 2001

The Court was thus composed: (Provisional Measures Order) Vice-President Weeramantry, Acting President; President Schwebel; Judges Oda, Guillaume, Ranjeva, Herczegh, Shi, Fleischhauer, Koroma, Vereschchetin, Higgins, Parra-Aranguren, Kooijmans, and Rezek; (Judgment): *President* Guillaume; Vice-President Shi; *Judges* Oda, Bedjaoui, Ranjeva, Herczegh, Fleischhauer, Koroma, Vereshchetin, Higgins, Parra-Aranguren, Kooijmans, Rezek, Al-Khasawneh, and Buergenthal.

#### 5.5.2.1 Facts

Karl and Walter brothers LaGrand were German nationals but had lived in the United States since early childhood. In 1982, having just been released from prison for three supermarket robberies, they attempted to rob a bank in Marana, Arizona. The robbery foiled because the two staff members present at the Bank had only one-half of the vault combination. The course of events left the two brothers no choice but to escape empty-handed, not before murdering one bank employee and inflicting grievous bodily harm on the other, who survived. A third bank employee who was still outside the bank while the robbery was taking place, had taken note of the number plate of the car they used and a fingerprint of Karl was found at the bank premises. Upon arrest, Karl confessed to the crimes whereas Walter gave no statements. Following a trial by jury, they were found guilty on all counts. After considering all attenuating and aggravating circumstances, the Court handed down the death sentence to both. They appealed arguing that the failure by the State of Arizona to inform them of their right to consular assistance had effectively denied them the opportunity of preparing a proper defence. Their appeal was rejected by the United States Courts, and the sentence imposing capital punishment was not overturned. Karl LaGrand was the first German citizen to be executed in the United States ever since the founding of the Federal Republic of Germany way back in 1949. His brother Walter was executed despite the Order of the ICJ calling upon the United States to ensure the execution be stayed pending the Court's final decision in the matter.

### 5.5.2.2 History of the Proceedings

In the Application, Germany stated[78] that in 1982, the authorities of the State of Arizona detained two German nationals, Karl and Walter LaGrand; that these individuals were tried and sentenced to death, without having been informed, as was required under Article 36 (1)(b) VCCR, of their rights under that provision. Germany also alleged that the failure to provide the required notification precluded it from protecting its nationals' interests in the United States provided for by Articles 5 and 36 VCCR, at both the trial and the appeal level in the United States.

Germany stated that it had been, until only a short time before the case was entered, the contention of the authorities of the State of Arizona that they had been unaware of the fact that Karl and Walter LaGrand were nationals of Germany; and that it had accepted that contention as true. However, during the proceedings before the Arizona Mercy Committee of 23 February 1999, the State Attorney admitted that the State of Arizona had indeed been aware since 1982 that the two detainees were German nationals. Germany further stated that Karl and Walter LaGrand, finally with the assistance of German consular officers, did claim violations of the VCCR before the Federal Court of First Instance, which, applying the municipal doctrine of "procedural default" decided that, because the individuals in question had not asserted their rights under the VCCR in the previous legal proceedings at State level, they could not assert them in the Federal *habeas corpus* proceedings. The intermediate federal appellate Court, last means of legal recourse in the United States available to the LaGrands as of right, affirmed this decision.

Germany asked the Court to declare that the United States had violated its international obligations under Articles 5 and 36 VCCR; that Germany was entitled to reparation; that the United States was under an international obligation not to apply the "procedural default" doctrine or any other

[78] The facts were undisputed by the United States.

doctrine of national law so as to preclude the exercise of the rights under Article 36 VCCR; that the United States was under an international obligation to carry out in conformity with Article 36 VCCR any future detention of or criminal proceedings against German nationals on its territory. Germany asked the Court to adjudge that the criminal liability of the LaGrands had been in violation of international legal obligations and therefore recognized as void by United States legal authorities; that the United States should provide reparation, in the form of compensation and satisfaction, for the execution of Karl LaGrand which had already taken place; that the United States should restore the *status quo ante* in the case of Walter LaGrand; and that the United States should provide Germany a guarantee of the non-repetition of the illegal acts.

On March 2, 1999 Germany also submitted an urgent request for the indication of provisional measures, in the interests of Walter LaGrand, emphasizing that the "importance and sanctity of an individual human life are well-established in international law." Only a stay of execution, ordered by the ICJ's provisional measures, would avoid Germany being "deprived of the opportunity to have the *status quo ante* restored in the event of a judgment in its favour."

On March 3, the Court ordered the United States to take all measures at its disposal to ensure that Walter LaGrand would not be executed pending the final decision of the Court, and should inform the Court of all measures taken in implementation of this Order. Furthermore, the Court ordered the Government of the United States to transmit this Order to the Governor of the State of Arizona. The Court's Order was ignored; the second LaGrand brother was executed, provisional measures notwithstanding.

**5.5.2.3 Points of Law**

In the *LaGrand* judgment, the Court found that Article 36 VCCR creates individual rights; that such rights may be invoked before it by the national State of the detainee; and that the United States violated these rights in this case.

It has been argued that two conceptions of international law emerged from the arguments of the parties in this case. For the United States,

> international law consists of a myriad of watertight compartments: at the level of sources, treaty law and customary law have separate existence and thus one excludes the application of the other; at the level of rights and obligations, inter-state relations can be isolated from their bearing on individual rights; in respect of the different areas of public international law, they may not converge, human

> rights being like oil, never to mix with the water of consular relations or diplomatic protection.[79]

For Germany,

> a treaty-law provision is not self-sufficient but [...] it may interact with other norms and sources in its application; [...] inter-state rights and obligations can no longer be insulated from individual rights, and [...] the interlocking of human rights law with other areas of public international law corresponds to the reality of contemporary international law.[80]

For the United States, "norms can be neutrally applied regardless of context and circumstances," whereas for Germany, "context is important."[81]

Germany's reasoning would seem to stem from or lead to the mechanism called custom *praeter legem* whereby "customary law operat[es] alongside the codified rules, and fill[s] in the inevitable gaps which if they were not realised and intended at the time when the treaty was concluded, are bound to emerge in the course of the application of the treaty to the manifold circumstances of international relations."[82]

The United States held that the VCCR concerns only inter-State relations. Germany contended that the distinction between 'inter-State relations and

---

[79] Tinta, M.F. (2001): "Due process and the Right to Life in the Context of the Vienna Convention on Consular Relations: Arguing the *LaGrand case*" in *European Journal of International Law*, Vol. 12, no. 2, Italy, para. 2.

[80] *Ibid.*

[81] *Ibid.*

[82] Thrilway, H. (1972): *International Customary Law and Codification – An Examination of the Continuing Role of Custom in the Present Period of Codification of International Law*, p. 98. Judge Cançado Trindado put it thus: "The positivist-voluntarist trend, with its obsession with the autonomy of the will of the States, in seeking to crystallize the norms emanating therefrom in a given historical moment, came to the extreme of conceiving (positive) law *independently of time*: hence its manifest incapacity to accompany the constant changes of the social structures (at domestic as well as international levels), for not having foreseen the new factual assumptions, being thereby unable to respond to them; hence its incapacity to explain the historical formation of customary rules of international law. The very emergence and consolidation of the *corpus juris* of the International Law of Human Rights are due to the reaction of the *universal juridical conscience* to the recurrent abuses committed against human beings, often warranted by positive law: with that, the Law (*el Derecho*) came to the encounter of the human being, the ultimate addressee of its norms of protection." – Trindade, J. concurring, *op. cit.*, para. 4.

human rights does not correspond to the current stage of international law and international human rights law. Rather, human rights today are embodied in inter-State conventions and they are part and parcel of contemporary international relations.'[83]

Germany argued that the very text of Article 36 reveals that it not only establishes obligations for the receiving State in respect to the sentencing State but also in respect to the individual himself. Thus Article 36 on the one hand provides for the right of the detainee to information about his rights; on the other, it contains the right of the consulate to assist its nationals.

The crucial point for the whole mechanism to function effectively is that the authorities of the receiving State have to inform the detainee *without delay* of his right to contact the consulate. If this obligation of the receiving State is violated, the other rights contained in Article 36 (1) are rendered in practice meaningless.

The United States maintained that the German interpretation "turned Article 36 on its head."[84] The Convention does not purport to address the internal criminal justice systems of States Parties, or questions of individual rights in the criminal process. "The Preamble's only reference to rights that might be thought to benefit individuals in a judicial context – privileges and immunities – is immediately qualified by a statement that such privileges and immunities are intended not to benefit individuals but States."[85] Article 36 (1) opens with the phrase, "With a view to facilitating the exercise of consular functions relating to nationals of the sending State," thereby underlining that the article is meant to enable the sending State to perform its consular functions. The United States did concede that "the performance of consular functions inherently benefits individuals," but "the right to communication of the individual flows from the right of the sending State,"[86] for "it is the sending State that has the right to have its national informed."[87]

However the United States did acknowledge that Article 36 recognizes the rights of individuals:

> [The] United States and Germany agree with respect to two central matters in the case. First, we agree that the Consular Convention

[83] CR 2000/30, at 21, para. 7.
[84] CR 2000/28, at 57, para. 4.17.
[85] *Ibid.,* at 56, para. 4.14.
[86] *Ibid.,* at 58, para. 4.19.
[87] *Ibid.,* at 59, para. 4.21.

> required the competent authorities to inform Walter and Karl LaGrand without delay that each had a right to have those authorities notify German consular officials of the arrest. And second, we agree that the competent authorities did not inform either of the LaGrands of this right.[88]

In effect, Germany argued that a number of international instruments showed that subsequent to the conclusion of the VCCR in 1963, Article 36 assumed the character of a human right pertaining to foreigners. Article 10 of the 1985 Declaration on the Human Rights of Individuals who are not Nationals of the Country in Which They Live adopted by the General Assembly by consensus; Paragraph 16.2 of the Body of Principles for the Protection of All Persons Under Any Form of Detention or Imprisonment (adopted by the General Assembly, Resolution 43/173 of 9 December 1988); and Rule 65 of the Rules of Detention of the International Criminal Tribunal for Former Yugoslavia, all recognize the right to consular assistance as a human right.

The United States brought forward an argument on the human rights quality of Article 36 (1), revolving round the notion of reciprocity. Its argument can be reduced to the following syllogism: Whereas the principle of reciprocity is pivotal in consular law, it is an alien concept to human rights. Article 36 (1) is subject to the rules of reciprocity. Therefore, Article 36 (1) could not contain a human right. However, commentators have argued[89] that whereas it is true that reciprocity is alien to human rights, it is also true that the right found in Article 36 (1) is not merely convention-based. In the *Case Concerning United States Diplomatic and Consular Staff in Tehran*, the ICJ stated that "the obligations of the Iranian Government here in question are not merely contractual obligations established by the Vienna Conventions of 1961 and 1963, but also obligations under general international law."[90]

The Court deemed that Germany's requests did "not convert [it] into a court of appeal of national criminal proceedings."[91] It then concentrated on Article 36 VCCR, leaving aside considerations on Article 5 VCCR.[92] Most importantly for our discussion, the Court concluded that "Article 36, paragraph 1, creates individual rights which may be invoked in this Court by

[88] *Ibid.*, at 8, para. 1.6.
[89] Tinta, M.F., *op. cit.*, para. 4.
[90] I.C.J. Reports, 1980, para. 62.
[91] *LaGrand* Judgment, para. 52.
[92] *Ibid*, para. 73.

the national State of the detained person."[93] The Court did not deem it necessary to consider the additional argument of whether these rights have "today assumed the character of a human right."[94] The Court then elaborated on the reasons why the United States domestic rule of "procedural defaul" violated its international legal obligation to Germany to give full effect to Article 36 rights:

> The Court cannot accept the argument of the United States which proceeds, in part, on the assumption that paragraph 2 of Article 36 applies only to the rights of the sending State and not also to those of the detained individual. The Court has already determined that Article 36, paragraph 1, creates individual rights for the detained person in addition to the rights accorded the sending State, and that consequently the reference to "rights" in paragraph 2 must be read as applying not only to the rights of the sending State, but also to the rights of the detained individual [...].
>
> Turning now to the "procedural default" rule, the application of which in the present case Germany alleges violated Article 36, paragraph 2, the Court emphasizes that a distinction must be drawn between that rule as such and its specific application in the present case. In itself, the rule does not violate Article 36 of the Vienna Convention. The problem arises when the procedural default rule does not allow the detained individual to challenge a conviction and sentence by claiming, in reliance on Article 36, paragraph 1, of the Convention, that the competent national authorities failed to comply with their obligation to provide the requisite consular information "without delay", thus preventing the person from seeking and obtaining consular assistance from the sending State.
>
> In this case, Germany had the right at the request of the LaGrands "to arrange for [their] legal representation" and was eventually able to provide some assistance to that effect. By that time, however, because of the failure of the American authorities to comply with their obligation under Article 36, paragraph 1 (*b*), the procedural default rule prevented counsel for the LaGrands to effectively challenge their convictions and sentences other than on United States constitutional grounds. As a result, although United States courts could and did examine the professional competence of counsel assigned to the indigent LaGrands by reference to United States

[93] *Ibid*, para. 77.
[94] *Ibid*, para. 78.

> constitutional standards, the procedural default rule prevented them from attaching any legal significance to the fact, *inter alia,* that the violation of the rights set forth in Article 36, paragraph 1, prevented Germany, in a timely fashion, from retaining private counsel for them and otherwise assisting in their defence as provided for by the Convention. Under these circumstances, the procedural default rule had the effect of preventing "full effect [from being] given to the purposes for which the rights accorded under this article are intended", and thus violated paragraph 2 of Article 36.[95]

In his Declaration attached to the *Avena* judgment, Vice-President Ranjeva had this to say on the *LaGrand* case:

> [... L]ooking beyond the scope of diplomatic protection and the obligation to exhaust local remedies, the question to be determined is the significance of the interrelationship between the components of the consular protection system.
>
> The notion of interrelationship was used by the Court in 2001 to characterize the interdependence of the rights enumerated in Article 36, paragraph 1. The raison d'être or focus of that relationship is to seek to facilitate consular protection. However, the manner in which the various rights are defined consists in stating their content and how they are to be apportioned as between the sending State and the detainee; in other words, the 1963 Convention sought to identify the holders of the rights that it created, with individual rights being those belonging to the detained nationals. In these circumstances, the interrelationship contemplated by the 2001 Judgment concerns neither the nature nor the scope of the rights in question; it pertains to the effective implementation of the protection system. The effective exercise by a State of its right to provide for the protection of its nationals, who derive their rights from Article 36, paragraph 1 *(b),* is only possible if the detained national does not refuse such an initiative. The discretionary power of the sending State is thus confined to a right of initiative to activate the protection mechanism. And that right of initiative effectively arises "as soon as it is realized that the person is a foreign national, or once there are grounds lo think that the person is probably a foreign national" (Judgment, para. 88).[96]

---

[95] *Ibid,* paras. 89-91.
[96] Paras. 12 and 13 of the Declaration attached to the Judgment of March 31, 2004.

Different reactions have been registered as to the width of applicability of this judgment. It has been argued[97] that the declaration made by President Guillaume clarifies that the principles in the judgment apply to all nationalities. It has also been similarly argued[98] that the *LaGrand* case should apply equally to all member countries. In the *Avena* judgment,[99] the Court clarified the point beyond any shadow of doubt:

> To avoid any ambiguity, it should be made clear that, while what the Court has stated concerns the Mexican nationals whose cases have been brought before it by Mexico, the Court has been addressing the issues of principle raised in the course of the presence proceedings from the viewpoint of the general application of the Vienna Convention, and there can be no question of making an *a contrario* argument in respect of any of the Court's findings in the present Judgment. In other words, the fact that in this case the Court's ruling has concerned only Mexican nationals cannot be taken to imply that the conclusions reached by it in the present Judgment do not apply to other foreign nationals finding themselves in similar situations in the United States.[100]

The *LaGrand* case is also interesting for points of general international law: the prescription of claims[101] and the binding nature of provisional measures.[102]

[97] Macina, A. (2003): "The Future of Consular Relations in the United States" in *California Western International Law Journal*, Vol. 34, p. 130.
[98] Weinman, J.L. (2002): *op. cit.*, p. 867.
[99] Para. 151 of the Judgment.
[100] Para. 151 of the Judgment.
[101] See Mennecke, M., and Tams, C. (1999): "The Right to Consular Assistance under International Law: The *LaGrand Case* before the ICJ" in *Jahrbuch für Internationales Rechts*, Vol. 42, Germany, pp. 192-241.
[102] See Dupuy, P.-M. (2002): *Droit International Public*, France, pp. 569-570. He points out that in its 2001 decision, the ICJ cut short a doctrinal debate which had been going on practically speaking since the coming into effect of the Statute of its precursor, the PCIJ. The Court clearly declared that the provisional measures which it "orders" have a binding nature and not respecting them entails liability. This judgment, says Dupuy, is also important in order to signify to potential litigants that the ICJ is no less equipped than the International Tribunal on the Law of the Sea to deliver justice expediently in cases of urgency.

### 5.5.3.1 *Avena and Other Mexican Nationals* (Mexico v. United States of America), 2004

With the *LaGrand* case serving as a sort of cutwater, the *Avena Case* increased the "recognition of treaty obligations in [United States] domestic criminal cases." [103]

### 5.5.3.2 History of the Proceedings

Mexico alleged violations of Articles 5 and 36 VCCR by the United States in respect of 54 Mexican nationals sentenced to death in certain States of the United States. Mexico requested the Court that, pending final judgment in the case, the United States should take all measures necessary to ensure that no Mexican national be executed and that no execution dates be set for any Mexican national; that the United States report to the Court the actions it had taken in that respect; and that it ensure that no action be taken that might prejudice the rights of the United Mexican States or its nationals with respect to any decision the Court might render on the merits of the case.[104] The United States asked of the Court to reject the request since the it was "not a request seeking preservation of a right protected by the Vienna Convention" and that if accepted, it "would prejudice the sovereign right of the United States to operate its criminal justice system."

The Court was thus composed: (Provisional Measures Order) Guillaume, President; Shi, Vice-President; Judges: Oda, Ranjeva, Herczegh, Fleischhauer, Koroma, Vereshchetin, Higgins, Parra-Aranguren, Kooijmans, Rezek, Al-Khasawneh, Buergenthal, and Elaraby; (Judgment) Shi, President; Ranjeva, Vice-President; Judges: Guillaume, Koroma, Vereshchetin, Higgins, Parra-Aranguren, Kooijmans, Rezek, Al-Khasawneh, Buergenthal, Elaraby, Owada, Tomka; Sepúlveda (*ad hoc*).

### 5.5.3.3 Points of Law (Provisional Measures Order)

Unlike the provisional measures order in *LaGrand*, in which the Court used the phraseology "[t]he United States *should* take all measures at its disposal to ensure that Walter LaGrand [be] not executed pending the final decision in these proceedings... [emphasis added]," the *Avena* provisional measures

---

[103] Carter, L.E. (2003): "Compliance with ICJ Provisional Measures and the Meaning of Review and Reconsideration under the Vienna Convention on Consular Relations: *Avena and Other Mexican Nationals (Mex. v. U.S.)*" in *Michigan Journal of International Law*, Vol. 25, United States, p. 134.

[104] It is interesting to note that it would seem that Mexican officials routinely notify Americans they arrest that they may contact the American consulate. See Macina, A. (2003): "*Avena and Other Mexican Nationals*: The Litmus for *LaGrand* and the Future of Consular Rights in the United States" in *California Western International Law Journal*, Vol. 34, No. 1, United States, pp. 135-136.

order finds the Court using mandatory language: "[t]he United States *shall* take all measures necessary to ensure that [the Mexican nationals] are not executed pending final judgment in these proceedings [emphasis added]."

The shift is due to the *LaGrand* judgment which clarified the binding nature of provisional measures orders.[105]

As he had done in the *LaGrand Case*, Judge Oda appended a declaration:

> This case cannot be about domestic legal procedure in the United States because that lies within the sovereign discretion of that country. It does not concern a dispute over the interpretation or application of the Vienna Convention because the United States admits its violation. While there may be a question of the appropriate *remedy* for the violation, that is a matter of general international law, *not* of the interpretation or application of the Convention. What this case is about is abhorrence – by Mexico and others – of capital punishment.
>
> If the International Court of Justice interferes in a State's criminal law system (encompassing trial and appellate proceedings and clemency procedures), it fails to respect the sovereignty of the State and places itself on a par with the supreme court of the State. [...]

Raz seems to be addressing Judge Oda's declaration when he says that he considers "human rights to be rights which set limits to the sovereignty of States, in that their actual or anticipated violation is a (defeasible) reason for taking action against the violator in the international arena even when – in cases not involving violation of either human rights or the commission of other offences – the action would not be permissible, or normatively available on the grounds that it would infringe the sovereignty of the State."[106]

As the Court pointed out in the *LaGrand* case, these cases do "not concern the international legality *vel non* of the death penalty as such."[107] It may well be argued that the right to consular assistance exists independently of the degree of punishment meted out. Needless to say, the pathos is higher when

---

[105] Aceves, W.J. (2003): "The Vienna Convention on Consular Relations: Recent Developments" in *ACLU International Civil Liberties Report*, United States, p. 5.
[106] Raz, J. (2010): "Human Rights without Foundations" in *The Philosophy of International Law*, (Besson, S. & Tasioulas, J., eds.), United Kingdom, p. 328.
[107] Para. 20 of the Judgment.

the sanctity of human life is at stake, particularly because once it is carried out, an execution is irreversible. However, the right to consular notification is to be safeguarded also in countries which do not practise capital punishment.[108] And as the United States itself said in its brief to the Inter-American Court on Human Rights: "Consular notification is relevant in all cases and not just in those involving the death penalty."[109]

Hypothetical arguments as to the consequences, or lack of them, of non-notification are best avoided. To borrow one commentator's words, "[t]o say that the practical result would have been the same is to overlook the role of procedures in law."[110] As Quigley puts it, "A requirement is unrealistic if it would involve a court finding that a consul might have acted in a way that would have averted the conviction. [... However, s]o long as it appears that a consul might have participated had the obligation to inform been met, the presumption of unfairness stands. [...] Criminal trials can result in a variety of outcomes, not limited to simply acquittal or guilt on the charges filed. Charges can be reduced before or during trial, plea bargaining can be reached, and prosecutors can agree to recommend a particular sentence. One can never know how a consul might have taken action that could have affected these determinations."[111]

#### 5.5.3.4 Points of Law (Judgment)

The United Mexican States requested the Court to declare that the United States of America, in arresting, detaining, trying, convicting, and sentencing the 54 Mexican nationals on death row violated its international legal obligation to Mexico, in its own right and in the exercise of its right of consular protection of its nationals, as provided by Articles 5 and 36,

---

[108] The motivation ("abhorrence of capital punishment") as opposed to the intention of the applicant (to seek redress) ought not be judicially relevant. Even though, it has been argued (see Quigley, J. (2000): "Procedural Limitations on Capital Punishment: The Case of Foreign Nationals" in *ILSA Journal of International and Comparative Law*, Vol. 6, United States, p. 519) that the motivation of States (embracing abolitionist views) are deemed worthy of legal discussion and as a tenable premise to legal arguments.

[109] Inter-American Court of Human Rights: Advisory Opinion OC-16/99 of October 1, 1999 Requested by the United Mexican States, 'The Right To Information On Consular Assistance in the Framework of the Guarantees of the Due Process of Law', p. 17.

[110] Klabbers, J. (1998): "Executing Mr. Breard" in *Nordic Journal of International Law*, Vol. 67, the Netherlands, p. 362.

[111] Quigley, J. (2005): "Application of Consular Rights to Foreign Nationals: Standard for Reversal of a Criminal Conviction" in *ILSA Journal of International and Comparative Law*, Vol. 11, No. 2, United States, pp. 412-413.

respectively, of the VCCR; Mexico was therefore entitled to *restitutio in integrum*; the United States was under an international legal obligation not to apply the doctrine of procedural default, or any other doctrine of its municipal law, to preclude the exercise of the rights afforded by Article 36 of the VCCR; the United States was under an international legal obligation to carry out in conformity with the foregoing international legal obligations any future detention of or criminal proceedings against the 54 Mexican nationals on death row or any other Mexican national in its territory; the right to consular notification under the VCCR is a human right.

The Court made a linguistic clarification in the sense that it would be using the verb "to inform" when referring to an individual being made aware of his rights (under Article 36(1) VCCR) and the verb "to notify" when referring to the giving of notice to the consular post.

The Court interpreted the phrase "without delay" (with reference to the notice delivered to the detainee of his right to consular assistance) found in Article 36(1)(b) in terms of Article 31 and 32 of the Vienna Convention on the Law of Treaties given that it is not defined in the VCCR itself. Having found it impractical to resort to dictionaries to settle the matter, the Court looked elsewhere for an interpretation, namely at the VCCR itself. The Court argued that the consular function to assist nationals does not entail the Consul's acting as the legal representative of the national or more directly engaging in the criminal justice process. It followed, argued the Court, that, contrary to the interpretation suggested by Mexico, "without delay" does not mean "immediately upon arrest and before detention." This interpretation would seem to be corroborated by the *travaux préparatoires.* On the other hand, the Court argued that "there is nonetheless a duty upon the arresting authorities to give that information to an arrested person as soon as it is realized that the person is a foreign national, or once there are grounds to think that the person is probably a foreign national."[112]

The United States argued that the Court lacked jurisdiction to determine whether Article 36 rights are human rights. The Court, however, did not uphold this objection holding instead that it did have jurisdiction. But it then declared that "whether or not the Vienna Convention rights are human rights is not a matter that this Court need decide. The Court would, however, observe that neither the text nor the object and purpose of the Convention, nor any indication in the *travaux préparatoires*, support the conclusion that the right to consular notification is a human right".[113]

[112] Para. 88 of the Judgment

[113] Para. 124 of the Judgment.

Furthermore, the Court declared that it did not consider clemency procedures as being a sufficient means of review and reconsideration as envisaged in the *LaGrand* case.[114]

The Court found that the United States was in breach of its international obligations under Article 36(1)(a), (b), and (c) and (2) VCCR, but, contrary to Mexico's request for *restitutio in integrum* in the sense that the sentences be annulled, the Court ordered the United States to provide, by means of its own choosing, review and reconsideration of the convictions and sentences, so as to allow full weight to be given to the violation of the rights set forth in the VCCR.

It has been pointed out[115] that in this case, the Court referred to "other foreign nationals" rather than to nationals of other parties to the VCCR. This is markedly different from the *LaGrand* case in which the Court ordered remedies which concerned German nationals only. A possible interpretation of the Court's wording could be that Article 36 reflects customary international law.

Judge *ad hoc* Sepúlveda compared the *LaGrand* and *Avena* cases in his Separate Opinion:

> Had the Court followed its previous jurisprudence and applied it in the present case, it would have been acting in line with the *LaGrand* Judgment, where the Court rejected the argument made by the United States that "the right of a State to provide consular assistance to nationals detained in another country, and the right of a State to espouse the laws of its nationals through diplomatic protection, are legally different concepts" (*LaGrand, Judgment, I.C.J. Reports 2001,* p. 493, para. 76). The Court also rejected in *LaGrand* the contention of the United States that "rights of consular notification and access under the Vienna Convention are rights of States, and not of individuals, even though these rights may benefit individuals by permitting States to offer them consular assistance" *(ibid.).* One would have thought that these claims by the United States were put to rest, definitively and convincingly by the Court when it stated that:

[114] Para. 143 of the Judgment.
[115] Orakhelashvili, A. (2005): "Judicial Competence and Judicial Remedies in the Avena Case" in *Leiden Journal of International law*, Vol. 18, No. 1, the Netherlands, p. 47.

> the Court concludes that Article 36, paragraph 1, creates individual rights, which, by virtue of Article I of the Optional Protocol, may be invoked in this Court by the national State of the detained person. These rights were violated in the present case. (*LaGrand, Judgment, I.C.J. Reports 2001*, p. 494, para. 77.) [...]

[The *Avena* Judgment] departs substantially from the findings in the *LaGrand* Judgment in a number of other aspects, related to the circumstances in which local remedies must be exhausted, to application of the procedural default rule, and to the question of denial of justice. Some of the holdings are more modest than the ones that are to be found in the *LaGrand* Judgment. Some even contradict the rulings of *LaGrand*. The limited legal reach provided in the present Judgment may not sufficiently serve the purpose of establishing the grounds for reparations as a result of a wrongful act and the breach of an international obligation. The law of State responsibility may not find in [*Avena*] a source of further development.

Following the ICJ judgment, a Presidential memorandum was issued in the United States as a determination "that the United States will discharge its international obligations under the decisions of the International Court of Justice in ... [*Avena*] by having state courts give effect to the decision in accordance with general principles of comity in cases filed by the [...] Mexican nationals addressed in that decision."

In the *Request for Interpretation of the Judgment of 31 March 2004 in the Case Concerning* Avena and Other Mexican Nationals (Mexico *v.* United States of America) of 19 January 2009, the ICJ held that "the *Avena* judgment nowhere lays down or implies that the courts in the United States are required to give direct effect to [the obligation to provide review and reconsideration of the convictions and sentences of the Mexican nationals referred to therein]." That obligation "is indeed an obligation of result which clearly must be performed unconditionally; non-performance of it constitutes internationally wrongful conduct. However, the judgment leaves it to the United States to choose the means of implementation, not excluding the introduction within a reasonable time of appropriate legislation, if deemed necessary under domestic constitutional law. Nor moreover does the *Avena* judgment prevent direct enforceability of the obligation in question, if such an effect is permitted by domestic law."[116] However, the Court further

---

[116] Para. 44.

observed that "considerations of domestic law which have so far hindered the implementation of the obligation incumbent upon the United States, cannot relieve it of its obligation. A choice of means was allowed to the United States in the implementation of its obligation and, failing success within a reasonable period of time through the means chosen, it must rapidly turn to alternative and effective means of attaining that result."[117]

Optimistic opinions had been expressed about the outcome of the *Avena* affair, irrespective of the findings of the Court. The publicity given to the case, it was argued, would auspicate a renewed awareness of the obligation of all authorities detaining a foreigner to inform him of his right to consular protection, which emanates from his special juridical condition distinct from that of nationals of the arresting State. This would augur well as it is frequent for local authorities in many countries, though well-versed in their own municipal law, to ignore rights and obligations emanating from international law. The case would attract public attention and end up having beneficial effects for a better understanding of international law.[118]

[117] Para. 47.

[118] Vallarta Marrón, J.L. (2004): "*Obligación de informar a todo detenido extranjero de su derecho a la protección consular, según el derecho internacional*" in *Revista de la Facultad de Derecho*, Universidad Nacional Autónoma de Mexico, Vol. 54, Mexico, p. 312.

# *Chapter 6*

# NOTARIAL FUNCTIONS OF CONSULS

> *"If one were to offer men to choose out of all the customs in the world such as seemed to them best, they would examine the whole number, and end by preferring their own; so convinced are they that their own usages far surpass those of others."*
>
> Herodotus.

## 6.1 Introduction

These are Latin-type notarial functions, which are wider in scope than the functions of common-law notaries public.

If an event and a year were to be chosen to mark the divergence in the evolution of the two types of notaries, the Protestant reformation of Henry VIII and 1531 would probably fit the bill best. While the continental, Latin-type notariat proceeded from its medieval beginnings to the uniformity imposed by the Napoleonic codification, in common-law jurisdictions the notariat subdivided into two professions, the notary public (who notarizes) and the solicitor (who is a lawyer and draws up legal instruments).[1]

The International Union of Latin Notariats (UINL) defines Latin-type notaries as: "professional lawyers and public officials appointed by the State to confer authenticity on legal acts and contracts contained in documents drafted by them and to advise persons who call upon their services."[2]

The function of the United States[3] notary public is "to witness a signature to a document or administer an oath to a person signing a document in which the signing party swears to the accuracy and truthfulness of the signed document. The notarial jurat, entered on the document immediately after the signature, establishes the fact of signing or that an oath has been

---

[1] Morello, A. (1977): *L'Atto Notarile*, Italy, p. 118.

[2] http://www.uinl.net/notariado_mundo.asp?idioma=ing&submenu=NOTAIRE, last access on 31.7.2010.

[3] With the exception of Louisiana.

administered. Less frequently, the notarial jurat places the burden on the Notary to swear to the truth of the statements in the foregoing text."[4]

Understood in this sense, the rules of consular law regulating notarial functions of consuls presuppose the choice between two juridical systems: the juridical system of the sending State and the juridical system of the receiving State. Consular law sets to strike a balance between two opposing interests – the personal sovereignty of the sending State on its nationals abroad and the territorial sovereignty of the receiving State on foreigners residing on its territory. The application of the law of the sending State is limited by international law as well as by its compatibility with the rules of the juridical system of the receiving State. Each State regulates the competence and functions only of its own organs, and whereas it lays down the requisites for foreign public acts to be recognized and executed in its own juridical system, it cannot accord international efficacy to acts of its own organs. Consequently, the notarial capacity of consular (and diplomatic) agents has efficacy only insofar as the receiving State does not oppose it.[5]

## 6.2 Raison d'Être of the Consul's Notarial Functions

The consul's notarial functions respond to considerations of a practical nature and of international cooperation. Nationals of the sending State are not bound to ask for the intervention of local authorities for the execution of acts which are meant to produce effects within the sending State and would incur high costs if done according to procedures of the receiving State.[6] For the same reasons, even citizens of the receiving State may ask for the intervention of the consul of the sending State for the redaction of acts the juridical effects of which are to be enforced in the territory of the sending State. An illustration[7] of this latter case would be the case of a Frenchman living in France who wishes to donate an immovable situated in France to

---

[4] Sinnott, J.P. (2002 ed., 2001): *A Practical Guide to Document Authentication: Legalization of Notarized & Certified Documents 2002*, United States, p. ix.

[5] Article 5 (f) VCCR. There is an analogous provision in the European Convention on Consular Functions (Article 15) which lays down that such acts and contracts "shall have judicial effect in the receiving State only to the extent that there is nothing contrary thereto under the law of that State". Green, N. A. Maryan (1972): "European Convention on Consular Functions; a contribution by the Council of Europe to the development of international law" in *Revue belge de droit international, 8*, Belgium, pp.176-188, notes that nothing is said as to judicial effects in other Contracting States. The same comment may be passed on the VCCR article.

[6] In fact, acts received by the consul are enforceable in the sending State without the need for an exequatur.

[7] Revilland, M. (1980): "*Les attributions notariales et le règlement des successions par les consuls*" in *Annuaire de l'A.A.A.*, 1979-80, vol. 49-50, the Netherlands, p. 104.

one of his children residing in New York. The acceptance of the donation must be done in the authentic form (*forme authentique*). The simplest solution would be to make a power-of-attorney (*procuration*) for the child to accept the donation directly in the presence of the consul of France in New York. The *procuration* would abide by all the formalities required by French law. Having recourse to such a solution is particularly advisable given that the interested party lives in a common-law country where the notion of *acte authentique* is different from that of the Latin notariat.

### 6.3 Conventional Source of Notarial Functions

Notarial functions are not exercised by the consul if the consular convention operative between the sending State and the receiving State does not envisage them or if the law of the receiving State does not allow them.

In view of the possibility of the notarial functions of consuls being contrary to the laws of the receiving State, States insert a clause in their bilateral consular conventions to regulate the notarial functions of consuls. Such a clause could merely envisage the power of the consul to act in the capacity of notary. On the other hand, the consular convention may include a clause enumerating in detail the notarial functions of consuls.[8] Such clauses, whether of the one or the other type, are eminently practical in nature and concern both *inter vivos* and *mortis causa* acts.[9]

### 6.4 Nationality of the Contracting Parties

Notarial functions of consuls are only exercised at the request of the interested parties. The nationality of the parties to the act is a vital element to determine whether the consular (or diplomatic) agent may exercise notarial functions. The intervention of such agents, through the execution of a notarial act is generally limited to the nationals of the sending State, or at least to acts in which a person having that nationality is involved.

However, older conventions underline the nationality of the contracting parties and that the act should be of interest to nationals of the sending State more than to nationals of the receiving State. More recent conventions allow consuls to receive in the notarial form acts irrespective of the nationality of the parties provided that such acts deal with a *res* situated, or businesses to be conducted, on the territory of the sending State or that are meant to have

---

[8] This is French practice and the model followed by the European Convention on Consular Functions (Article 15).

[9] *Inter vivos* acts are, literally, acts "among the living" – e.g., sale, donation, loan. *Mortis causa* acts are, literally, acts "caused by death."

juridical effects on that territory (e.g., Convention between France and Tunisia, and Senegal and Italy).[10]

### 6.5 Exercise of Competence

The exercise of competence by extraterritorial authorities such as consulates depends on two principles. First, the authority must have received the power of intervention by the sending State, on the basis of the axiom that *auctor regit actum*. Furthermore, this competence must be recognized by the receiving State where the intervention has taken place, on the basis of *locus regit actum*. The law of the sending State and the treaties concluded between the sending State and the receiving State which determine this competence are to be interpreted restrictively. The same limitation on interpretation is to be applied to the law of the receiving State.

While notarial acts executed by consuls in accordance with the laws and regulations of the sending State may be valid in that State, they are not necessarily so in the receiving State.[11] The competence of the authority is to be distinguished from the effects of the act which said authority executes. That the consul is – under Public International Law – internationally competent to execute such acts does not imply that the effects of such acts must necessarily be recognized within the receiving State.

Such a dissociation of the foreign authority's competence from the recognition of its acts conforms with the *raison d'être* of the consular institution which, in these matters, exists mainly to satisfy the administrative needs of the sending State. For this reason, the consul may sometimes correctly advise the parties to have recourse to local rather than consular forms while stressing the point that the act's validity may nevertheless be questioned within the receiving State's internal structures. Even in such a case, the competence of the consul who gave such advice would not be questioned. This point is of particular importance when the act is to be utilized in the receiving State.

In the absence of consular conventions, before receiving notarial acts the consul is bound to verify whether the laws of the sending State oppose what he is about to do in the exercise of his notarial function. If there is such opposition, he must abstain from executing the act and the parties are to seek the intervention of appropriate local institutions.[12] It is uncontested that

---

[10] Revilland, M., *op. cit.*, p. 105.
[11] Gamboa, M.J. (1966): "Notarial Services of Consuls" in *Elements of Diplomatic and Consular Practice – A Glossary*, the Philippines, p. 309.
[12] Revilland, M., *op. cit.*, p. 106.

when exercising notarial functions, the consul has to abide by the laws of the sending State.

## 6.6 Consuls are not Notaries

In the exercise of notarial functions, consuls do not become notaries but carry out, as a State organ, notarial functions in the strict sense of the word.[13] The consul is thus not entitled to perform all the functions which the law permits the notary, but only those which fall within the ambit of his function. Hence, the consul can neither give legal advice to the contracting parties as a notary would,[14] nor perform notarial functions mentioned by laws other than the notarial statute of the sending State. For instance, a consul may not submit applications to courts even in those cases where a notary might, nor may he proceed to perform delegations made by judicial authorities. Similarly, notarial disciplinary sanctions are not applicable to consuls. Like notaries, consuls can be held responsible for errors committed in the exercise of their functions, but their responsibility is less than that of notaries because consuls are never equal to notaries.[15] In fact, consuls are never to be personally compensated for giving notarial services, any taxes or other dues are to be received by the State.

## 6.7 Unrecognized Regimes

Notarial acts done by consuls of unrecognized regimes raise two concomitant questions. First, whether such acts are valid. And secondly, whether acknowledging the validity of such acts implies recognition of the regime the consul represents. In numerous pre-World War II cases involving the United States and unrecognized regimes,[16] the United States recognized the *de facto* authorities of unrecognized regimes. However, in cases involving the then Soviet Republics of Latvia and Lithuania, the United States did not recognize notarial acts done by Soviet consuls, even though the reasoning in these decisions has been perceived as dubious because it seems to stem from a mixture of political considerations with administrative matters.[17] In fact, in

---

[13] Biscottini, G. (1969): *Manuale di Diritto Consolare*, Italy, pp. 164 *et seq.*

[14] A Latin-type notary usually advises the contracting parties as to the most efficacious and effective way to achieve their ends, while interpreting their volition and reducing it to writing. See Irti, N. (1997): *Studi sul Formalismo Negoziale*, Italy, pp. 199 *et seq.*

[15] Revillard, M., *op. cit.*, p. 108.

[16] Cited by El Ganzory, A.E. (1978): "Consular Relations and Unrecognised Regimes" in *Revue Egyptienne de Droit International*, Vol. 34, Egypt, ff. 43-46: Costa Rica (1917), Chile (1924), Panama (1931), Cuba (1933), Italy's occupation of Albania (1939).

[17] *Idem.*

the 1978 *Daniunas vs. Simutis* case, a distinction was made between notarial acts and political acts.[18]

## 6.8 Benefits for Sending State Nationals

The receipt of notarial acts by consuls facilitates commercial exchanges and saves time and money. When an act meant to produce its effects in the sending State is executed by a consul of that same State, supplementary translation and legalization expenses are avoided, because the act is considered as having been done in the sending State. Moreover, when such an act is executed by a consul of the sending State, there is the further advantage of achieving greater legal certainty as the consular authority will reproduce the notarial formalities imposed by the law of the sending State. Lastly, difficulties of interpretation are circumvented: the choice of the consular form indicates, in case of doubt, the intention of the parties to submit to the law of the State granting the consul his powers.

[18] McHugh, J.T., and Pacy, J.S. (2001): *Diplomats Without A Country, Baltic Diplomacy, International Law and the Cold War*, United States, p. 80.

*Chapter 7*

# THE CONSUL'S ROLE IN THE PROTECTION OF FOREIGN INTERESTS

*"The absent are always wrong."*
French Proverb

## 7.1 Introduction

The institution of the protecting power, i.e., a State (or an organization such as the International Committee of the Red Cross or the International Organisation for Migration[1]) (called the "protecting power") which protects the citizens and interests of another State (called the "commissioning power" or "protected power") in a third State (called the "local State"), is of particular relevance in time of war. Its possibilities for indirect communication between belligerents have been so extensively exploited as to constitute in effect an important modification of the traditional concept of severance of diplomatic relations between States at war.[2]

However, Berridge considers the older device of severing diplomatic relations while maintaining consular ones, thereby permitting the use of consular posts to conduct resident diplomacy, as being more advantageous:

> One advantage of using the older device of a consular post rather than the interests section sheltered by a protecting power is the avoidance of the general drawbacks of relying on a third party: indebtedness, possible misunderstandings, the necessity to share secrets, and so on. The unostentatious and outwardly mundane consular post is also unlikely to

[1] The International Organization for Migration (IOM) offers its services in the field of consular protection and assistance, acting as a *de facto* or independent consular post protecing migrants' rights in a given country. One such programme is being implemented in Kazakhstan, for instance. "This IOM role [is] particularly relevant in terms of stranded migrants or migrants in an irregular situation. In such circumstances, the IOM would perform quasi-consular services and act as a 'Consul-at-Large'." – Perruchoud, R. (2007): "Consular Protection and Assistance" in (2007) *International Migration Law*, Cholewinski, R., Perruchoud, R., and MacDonald, E. (eds.), the Netherlands, p. 84.

[2] Lowe, V. (1990): "Diplomatic Law: Protecting Powers" in *International and Comparative Law Quarterly*, vol. 39, United Kingdom, p. 471.

> carry overtones of political dealings between sending and receiving state. By contrast, interests sections are known to be more political – their denizens may have boasted too much about how little difference there is between them and the embassies they replaced. Consular posts may also be larger and more in multiples; spread around the country, they are better placed than the interests section to gather intelligence. Finally, with the general integration of the consular and diplomatic services in the course of the twentieth century, consular officers are now much more likely to have had previous diplomatic experience and thus to be able to cope with any diplomatic tasks thrust upon them. Consular representation may also be a convenient method of conducting limited relations with unrecognized states when these states were created out of provinces of larger ones in which external powers happened already to have consulates.[3]

Despite these advantages, the protection of the interests and nationals of third States still forms an integral part of consular practice. Historically speaking, down to the middle of the nineteenth century, the granting of protection to foreigners was considered as a personal prerogative of the (diplomatic or) consular officer.[4] This has, however, changed and the consul's role is not so much to make *ad hoc* decisions but to follow instructions given by the sending State. The authority to protect foreign nationals and interests emanates not from the consular officer himself but from the sending State.

Article 8 VCCR provides that upon appropriate notification to the receiving State a consular post of the sending State may, unless the receiving State objects, exercise consular functions in the receiving State on behalf of a third State. Article 27 (1) (b) and (c) VCCR provide that in the event of the severance of consular relations between two States, the sending State may entrust the custody of the consular premises together with the property contained therein and the consular archives, to a third State acceptable to the receiving State; the sending State may entrust the protection of its interests and those of its nationals to a third State acceptable to the receiving State. Article 27 (2) (b) VCCR provides that if the sending State has no diplomatic mission and no consular post in the receiving State, the provisions of sub-paragraphs (b) and (c) of paragraph 1 of the same Article apply. The VCCR has nothing more to say on this practice. Thus, in view of the VCCR Preamble which provides that "the rules of customary international law

---

[3] Berridge, G.R. (2002): *Diplomacy – Theory and Practice*, United Kingdom, p. 139.
[4] Franklin, W.M. (1947, reprinted 1969): *Protection of Foreign Interests*, United States, p. 119, and Chapter 1 generally.

continue to govern matters not expressly regulated by the provisions of the Convention," the practice is regulated by customary international law.

## 7.2 The Ten Requisites for Protection of Foreign Interests

Section 7.2 sets out to analyse the ten requisites of customary international law governing the practice of protecting foreign interests as enumerated by W.M. Franklin (1947) in his *Protection of Foreign Interests.*[5] It will also review two relevant instruments, namely the 1989 Agreement on Protection of British Interests in Iran between the United Kingdom and Sweden[6] and the 2001 Convention of GUUAM Member States on Rendering Mutual Assistance in Consular Matters[7] as practical applications of these norms. The main characteristics of the UK-Sweden Agreement (the complete text of which is found in Appendix 3) have been described as "novelty and importance" and "intended to be a model for future bilateral agreements."[8] The GUUAM Convention (the complete text of which is found in Appendix 4), signed between Azerbaijan, Georgia, Moldova, Uzbekistan, and Ukraine has been described as laying "a legal foundation for cooperation between the GUUAM states in protecting the rights and interests of citizens and organizations of Member States on the territories of third states."[9]

### 7.2.1 "The Temporary Absence of Diplomatic or Consular Representation by the Power Desiring Foreign Protection"[10]

This requisite presupposes that the absence of representation should be of a temporary nature, though not necessarily complete.

---

[5] Luke T. Lee (Lee, L.T. and Quigley, J. (2008): *Consular Law and Practice*, p. 55, fn 70, considers Franklin's work a "lucid treatment" of the subject.

[6] For reasons of security the representation of British interests in Tehran was assumed by Sweden from 1980 to 1988. The British embassy in Tehran reopened in 1988, but British diplomatic representation was withdrawn in 1989 when Iranian government officials issued death threats against Salman Rushdie, the (British) author of *The Satanic Verses*, a book deemed by some Muslims to be blasphemous. Sweden then resumed the representation of British interests in Iran. – Lowe, V., *op. cit.*, p. 471.

[7] Hereinafter referred to as GUUAM Convention.

[8] Lowe, V., *op. cit.*, p. 472.

[9] Press Release Number 7/2001 issued by the Embassy of Ukraine in the People's Republic of China, June 2001. The same Press Release quoted Presidents Aliyev of Azerbaijan, Shevardnadze of Georgia, Voronin of Moldova, Karimov of Uzbekistan, and Kuchma of Ukraine, who signed the GUUAM Convention, describing GUUAM as "unique in its nature as it binds together five states united by common interests, steady economic links, similar or even identical view on the modern world and global processes. These states acknowledge the importance of mutual support and coordination in efforts in the age of globalization."

[10] Franklin, W.M., *op. cit.*, p.116.

The absence of representation of the protected State does not cease with the temporary presence of a special envoy. On the contrary, the protection of the interests of one State by another State does not preclude direct negotiations between the protected State and the local State, despite hostilities or non-recognition. When war proper is being waged, talks of a politico-military nature between the warring parts may be carried out by the protecting State. However, often times, they are conducted by special emissaries, military commanders, or by diplomats in neutral capital cities, and the protecting States or the warring States themselves are not involved.[11]

The UK-Sweden Agreement opens with the parties "noting that diplomatic and consular relations between the United Kingdom and the Islamic Republic of Iran have been severed." The GUAAM Convention in Article 2 provides that the convention applies "in case any of the Parties should not have diplomatic representations or consular institutions" in third countries in the territory of which there would be citizens of the Parties.

### 7.2.2 "Except in Extreme Emergencies Protection is not Granted without an Official Request from the State whose Interests are to be Protected"[12]

The granting of protection without an official request by the State whose interests are to be protected but only on the request of a foreign national would be recognized by the government of the consular post only in cases of extreme emergency, when a moment of hesitation might seriously prejudice human life or property of high value. Thanks to modern developments in, and spreading of telecommunications, such emergencies have become increasingly rare and, whereas no government would deny *a priori* the right of its diplomatic or consular officials to extend protection in such circumstances, every government would tend to recommend a high degree of caution until an official request of protection was received from the State whose nationals were in danger.[13] On the other hand, the

[11] *Ibid.*, pp. 117-119.

[12] *Ibid.*, p. 119.

[13] Nava, S. (1956): *Corso di Diritto di legazione e consolare*, Italy, p. 139, argues that consular protection is a *raison d'État*, and the citizen has therefore no right to such protection and cannot sue his government for failure to protect. This opinion is shared by François, J.P.A. (1967): *Grondlijnen van het volkenrecht*, the Netherlands, p. 234. The Netherlands and Canada subscribe to this view. The United Kingdom, Hungary, and Brazil are but three countries which tend to view consular protection as a right of the national against the sending State. There are also cases involving dual nationality. In the 1979 Albino Cimini case, the Italian Government protected a (dual) national prompted by its sensitivity "to humanitarian reasons and to the sentimental motives of Cimini's parents (both of Italian nationality)," as quoted in the *Italian Yearbook of International Law* (1980-1), pp. 320-1. Developments in

government, rather than the individual official, may take the initiative and extend protection to foreign nationals who find themselves in precarious situations even before their government requests such protection. However, such cases are always fraught with the danger of political consequences: the State receiving unsolicited protection might construe such a move as an "infringement of its own sovereignty or as a patronizing assumption of its inability to protect its own nationals." Thus the need for an official request, through customary diplomatic channels from one foreign ministry to the other, from the State whose interests are to be protected, unless the situation is one of unexpected emergency in which it is reasonable to assume that the request from the foreign national represents the official volition of the foreign national's government.[14]

Article 1 (2) of the UK-Sweden Agreement applies this principle thus: "The commission as protecting power comprises administrative, humanitarian and consular matters. If the commission is to be extended to cover other matters, a separate agreement to that effect is required." In this particular case, this clause was added at the request of the protecting power, Sweden, as a result a domestic policy to conclude bilateral agreements with the countries whose interests it is protecting.[15] On the other hand, the Agreement contemplates, in Article 5 (1), the case in which the official makes a request: "The protecting power shall take good care of the property received. If an official sent out by the commissioning country has taken the property into his care, the responsibility for it shall rest with him. The representative of the protecting power shall assist him, if the official requests such assistance."

Article 2 of the GUUAM Convention provides that the parties thereto shall reciprocally assist each other upon "a reciprocal agreement for every separate case." Article 6 provides that "matters pertaining to the protection of the rights and interests of the Parties' citizens will be decided upon through diplomatic channels, with a reciprocal agreement for every separate case."

### 7.2.3 "The Government, not the Particular Officer, Assumes and Grants the Protection"[16]

As soon as a request for protection arrives at the diplomatic mission or consulate, it has to be immediately referred to the government of the sending State for approval. In cases of extreme emergency, protection may be proffered out of humanitarian considerations, but such action is always

---

Human Rights Law make these considerations which fall short of recognising a right, somewhat untenable. See Meron, Th. (2006): *The Humanization of International Law*, the Netherlands, for an in-depth study of these developments.

[14] Franklin, W.M., *op. cit.*, pp. 119-122.

[15] Lowe, V., *op. cit.*, p. 472.

[16] Franklin, W.M., *op. cit.*, p. 122.

dependent on the sending State's approval, since it is the government not the individual official who grants protection even if the official signs "in charge of" foreign interests. One upshot of this principle is that the transfer of the official does not interrupt the protective function. The same holds for change of the protecting State's mission. Another outcome is that the protecting State may impose any qualification it deems necessary.[17]

The UK-Sweden Agreement contemplates a qualification in Article 1 (3): "In dealing with protection matters, the protecting power may avoid taking action that could damage its position or good name in the receiving country, or in relation to any other country." Also, Article 4 (2) provides that "the protecting power is not under an obligation to accept care of the property of citizens of the commissioning power."

There are no similar provisions in the GUUAM Convention. The reason could be that the Convention is meant to serve as a legal framework, as is confirmed both by the Final Communiqué of the Yalta GUUAM Summit and by Article 9 of the Convention, which allows the integration of future protocols in the Convention aiming at amending or adding to the provisions of the Convention.

Protection being a favour granted by the protecting State to the protected State, the former may terminate it at its own discretion. However this rarely happens, and protection usually terminates with the approval or at the request of the protected State.[18]

Article 12 of the GUUAM Convention allows every Party to withdraw from the Convention by notifying in writing the depository through diplomatic channels of its decision to cease being a Party to the Convention. Article 9 of the UK-Sweden Agreement envisages recourse to arbitration (in the event that diplomatic means do not suffice) to settle "disputes arising in connection with the termination of the commission of the protecting power."

### 7.2.4 "The Consent of the Local Power is a Requirement"[19]

If there is strong objection to protection by the local State, the question must be abandoned forthwith, unless the protecting State aims to become for all ends and purposes "a party to unwarranted interposition or intervention." The consent of the local State, to borrow the words of United States Secretary of State William Jennings Bryan, "having been freely given, may as

[17] *Ibid.*, pp. 122-123.
[18] *Ibid.*, p. 124.
[19] *Idem.*

freely be withdrawn." The protected State may protest against such withdrawal, particularly during wartime.[20]

The necessity for the local State's consent is necessary both in wartime and in peacetime. The local State may refuse to give its consent to this delegated right of protection within its own territory.

The UK-Sweden Agreement mentions obtaining the receiving country's consent with regard to the employment of career officials sent out by the commissioning country (Article 2 (1) – "permission" sought), to the establishment of diplomatic courier and secure telegraphic communication between the commissioning country and its Interests Section at the protecting power (Article 2 (2) – "approval" sought), to direct communication between the commissioning country and the Swedish Embassy in Tehran (Article 3 – "consent" sought, in this case not only of the receiving country but also of the protecting power). Iran's consent to the arrangement between the United Kingdom and Sweden was taken for granted.[21]

Article 2 of the GUUAM Convention lays down that the consent of the receiving country is to be acquired before the Parties to the Convention mutually assist each other in that receiving country.

### 7.2.5 "A Resort to Foreign Protection does not necessarily imply Severance of Relations between the Protected Power and the Local State"[22]

The request for foreign protection may also be motivated by economic reasons or convenience, and does not necessarily imply the rupture of relations between the local State and the protected State. On certain occasions, the protection granted by one State to the nationals of another in a third one actually establishes as between the second and the third country, a temporary diplomatic or consular relation where none had existed before. Consuls of various nationalities have assumed responsibility for short periods of time for one of their colleagues' establishments in order that consular relations be maintained. Such relations would otherwise lapse after some time due to health problems, transport difficulties, delays in appointments, or economic reasons. In the protection of belligerent interests too, the practice aims not at the intensification of undesired reciprocal consequences of the rupture of direct relations between the warring States, but the attempt to counteract such consequences and better relations.[23]

---

[20] *Ibid.*, pp. 127-128.
[21] Lowe, V., *op. cit.*, p. 472.
[22] Franklin, W.M., *op. cit.*, p. 134.
[23] *Ibid.*, pp. 134-136.

The UK-Sweden Agreement explicitly states that it came into being because of the severance of relations between the United Kingdom and Iran. It would therefore be reasonable to conclude that in this case both Iran and the United Kingdom wanted to maintain a channel of communication through Sweden.

The GUUAM Convention is explicitly meant to provide a legal infrastructure for the Parties to the Convention mutually to assist each other in third countries where the protected Party (within the GUUAM framework) does not have diplomatic or consular representation.

### 7.2.5 "Officers in Charge of Foreign Interests do not become Officials of the Protected Power"[24]

The double role in which the consular official of the protecting State finds himself has engendered and perhaps could still engender ambiguity with regard to his position. However, given that consular officials are usually prohibited from accepting commissions from foreign governments without the prior approval of their own government (which is very rarely granted, if ever), it can be said that the officer in charge of foreign interests remains exclusively the official of his own government. He does not require another *exequatur* from the local government when he extends protection to foreign interests. He uses none of the insignia or any official symbol of the protected State, and he appends the qualification "in charge of -------- interests" to his signature on documents relating to the protected State. When acting in the capacity of the protecting power, the consul is an agent of the protected State. However, as decided in the 1931 arbitration on the "Chevron claims", the government of the protecting power "cannot be held responsible for the negligence of its consul in his capacity as *gérant* [manager] of the consulate of another Power."[25]

The UK-Sweden Agreement gives full application to this principle in Articles 2 and 3. Article 2 expressly permits the inclusion of "locally engaged personnel of the commissioning country" within the Interest Section for the United Kingdom at the Swedish Embassy in Tehran. Article 3 lays down that only "in appropriate cases direct communication may [...] be maintained between the commissioning power and the Swedish Embassy in Tehran," subject to the consent of the receiving power and on condition that the protecting power be "kept informed of the nature and extents of such contacts." It is abundantly clear that the officers of the protecting power are not meant to become officials of the protected power.

---

[24] *Ibid.*, p. 136.
[25] *Ibid.*, pp. 136-139.

The GUUAM Convention applies this principle indirectly in Articles 4 and 5 which establish financial procedures to regulate the potentially ambiguous relationship between the protecting and the protected power. It seems evident that Article 4 is based on the premise that the officers of the protecting power do not become officials of the protected power, for otherwise the necessity expressly to mention that the expenses are to be incurred by the protecting power would not logically arise. The same applies to Article 5 which lays down the procedure whereby the protected power reimburses the protecting power for expenses incurred. This is further confirmed by the otherwise tautological emphasis that consular charges to be levied by the protecting power should be equivalent to the consular tariffs of the protected power.

### 7.2.6 "Nationals of the Protected Power do not become Assimilated to Nationals of the Protecting Power"[26]

For a long time this principle was not accepted, the dominant theory being that the nationals of the protected power do become assimilated to the nationals of the protecting power. However, foreign protection became increasingly recognized as a "temporary delegation of the protective rights and duties of the power unable at the moment to exercise them through its own instrumentalities. [T]he protecting power cannot exercise any rights of protection not possessed by the protected power within the territory of the local state."[27] This seems to tally with the idea that the relationship between protecting and protected States is one of agency as reflected in the wording of Article 8 VCCR: "a consular post of the sending State may [...] exercise consular functions in the receiving State *on behalf of* a third State" (emphasis added). The collocation "on behalf of" would seem to denote a relationship of delegation or agency, not an assignment, of protective rights and duties.

The UK-Sweden Agreement is seemingly silent on this issue, probably because this principle is accepted by both parties. The GUUAM Convention seems to adhere to this principle, for it seems to lay the foundations for a vast communication network between nationals of GUUAM Member States and their respective governments through the "good offices" of the consular posts of other GUUAM Member States, without assimilating the nationals of one Member State with those of another.

[26] *Ibid.*, p. 139.
[27] *Ibid.*, pp. 142-143.

### 7.2.7 "The Presence of the Protecting Power does not alter the Responsibility of the Local States for Aliens within its Jurisdiction"[28]

The presence of a protecting power, in no way alters the primary responsibility of the local State to afford adequate protection to aliens admitted to its territory.[29]

The provisions of two international instruments being examined are irrelevant here, as this principle addresses the relationship between the protected power and the local State which is *res inter alios acta* in the context of the relationship between protecting and protected power.

### 7.2.8 "In Protecting Foreign Interests an Officer is not Expected to Engage in any Activities Contrary to the Interests of his Own Government"[30]

Not being an official of the protected State, the consul responsible for foreign interests is under no obligation to perform activities on behalf of the protected State which would be contrary to the interests of his own government. "This means no unneutral activities in protecting belligerent interests, no competitive activities in protecting non-belligerent interests, and no unessential activities on behalf of foreign interests in either peace or war."[31] The consul in charge of foreign interests is therefore expected to give his services in "current activities" of an essential nature and is not expected to undertake lengthy investigations or to compile periodic reports for the protected State.[32]

The UK-Sweden Agreement reflects this principle in Articles 1 (2) ("administrative, humanitarian and consular matters") and 1 (3) ("the protecting power may avoid taking action that could damage its position or good name in the receiving country"). The GUUAM Convention, being a convention on mutual assistance, seeks (in Articles 1, 2, and 3) almost to create a supranational network of consulates which goes beyond the mere protection of foreign interests. Thus the principle of not running counter to the interests of the protecting power is not only respected, but is taken one level higher, and the interests of the protected power are positively promoted as a priority equal to the interests of the protecting power.

---

[28] *Ibid.*, p. 143.
[29] *Ibid*, p. 145.
[30] *Ibid.*, p. 146.
[31] *Idem.*
[32] *Ibid.*, p. 148.

### 7.2.9 "Protection is Accorded to the Interests of a State, as Distinguished from a Government"[33]

This principle explains the absence of protection in the case of civil wars. It is also useful in the case of non-recognition of States (as opposed to the non-recognition of governments).[34] The distinction is not an abstract one, but firmly rooted in the conception of international relations as existing between national States and that the overarching humanitarian aim of the practice would be defeated if too much weight is given to short-term political situations.[35]

Needless to say, the two international instruments being analysed as case studies are irrelevant for this point.

## 7.3 Consular protection of European Union (EU) citizens in third countries

EU citizenship was created by the Maastricht Treaty (Treaty on European Union) of 1992. Following the Lisbon Treaty amending the Treaty on European Union and the Treaty Establishing the European Union of 2007,[36] it is currently regulated by Article 23 of the Treaty on the Functioning of the European Union which not only provides that citizens of Member States shall have EU citizenship (in addition to their national citizenship), but also enumerates some of the rights EU citizens are entitled to. Among these is the right to enjoy, in the territory of a third country in which the Member State of which they are nationals is not represented, the protection of the diplomatic and consular authorities of any Member State on the same conditions as the nationals of that State.[37]

The consent of the receiving State must always be sought before the sending EU State assumes the temporary protection of the interests of the national of the third EU State.[38] The wording of Article 8 VCCR – "appropriate notification" – is generic and gives no indication as to the form such

---

[33] *Idem.*

[34] *Ibid.*, p. 149.

[35] *Ibid.*, p. 153.

[36] "[...] the requirement for Member States' missions in third countries to assist each others' nationals on the same conditions as they would their own nationals already exists under the current Treaties, and this is not, therefore, a significant change." – House of Lords: European Union Committee 10th Report of Session (2007-2008): *The Treaty of Lisbon: an impact assessment*, Volume I, United Kingdom, p. 189.

[37] This right is taken up in the same terms in Article 46 of the EU Charter of Fundamental Rights.

[38] Verhoeven, J. (2001): *Droit de la Communauté européenne*, Belgium, p. 142-143.

notification should take. It could be assumed that a *note verbale*[39] by the EU Commissioner for Foreign Affairs or the EU Presidency would suffice.

The principle of the "sufficiently close link" allows the application of EU law to EU citizens who are on the territory of a third State.[40] The inverse reasoning could be invoked to allow the application of EU law to nationals of non-EU States who nonetheless have a sufficiently close link to the territory of the EU. This reasoning could lead to EU consular protection of persons who, though nationals of a third State, have a sufficiently close link to the territory of the EU and over whom a Member State exercises its sovereignty and jurisdiction.[41]

[39] Touzé, S. (2005): "*Le régime de la protection diplomatique et consulaire des citoyens de l'Union européenne*" in *Aktuelle juristische Praxis*, 14 (2005) 7, Switzerland, p. 848.
[40] See *Walgrave and Koch*, European Court of Justice, Case 36/74.
[41] Misson, P.L., Berthe E., Delree C, and Kaëns L. (2007): *La protection diplomatique et consulaire est-elle un droit fondamental?*, Belgium, http://ec.europa.eu/justice_home/news/consulting_public/consular_protection/contributions/contribution_mission_fr.pdf, pp. 4-5.

# *Chapter 8*

# THE HONORARY CONSUL

> *"The temper, qualities, and limitations of many a man can be divined on short acquaintance; those of a nation need a longer contact."* J.J. Jusserand, 1924.

### 8.1 The Institution of the Honorary Consul

Graham Greene's eponymous novel[1] portrays a fictional honorary consul who survives on selling, year in year out, his brand new Cadillac: his profit is equal to the import duty which in his capacity of honorary consul he is exempt from paying.[2] The 1916 *Practical Guide for Russian Consular Officers* used to warn that "Elective Consular Officers ought to bear in mind that their appointment is a high honour. It may be that their social and business standing will gain by such an appointment, but they should never exploit it for personal purposes [...]."[3]

The evil Greene portrayed and the Guide warned against, was probably the same to have inspired E.W.A. Tuson's words in *A Paper on Consular Law and Consular Duties*, when he spoke about honorary consuls:

> We may justly quote an old saying applied to this subject by the American writer Warden, in the following passage: "If he be obliged to seek support as a merchant or factor, his eye must be constantly directed to his private advantage, and in this position he insensibly adopts the doctrine of the trader: *Every man for himself, and God Almighty for us all!*"[4]

---

[1] Greene, G. (1973): *The Honorary Consul*, United Kingdom. A 1983 John Mackenzie British film with the same name but also released under the title *Beyond the Limit*, starring Richard Gere, Michael Caine, and Bob Hoskins, was based on the novel.

[2] For the veracity of this exemption, see section 8.3.5 below.

[3] Heyking, Baron A. (1916): *A Practical Guide for Russian Consular Officers and All Persons having Relations with Russia*, United Kingdom, p. 5.

[4] Tuson, E.W.A. (1857): *A Paper on Consular Law and Consular Duties* read on Saturday, February 14, 1857, before the Mercantile Law Commission at the rooms of

For these reasons, he argued that:

> [The Consul] ought to be a man unfettered by all commercial ties; such a one as is described by Mr. Macculloch in the following words: "To render the condition of the subjects of the country employing him within the limits of his consulship as comfortable, and their transactions as advantageous and secure as possible." This he cannot do if engaged in trade; for personal interest would cause him to endeavour that all this should be centred in himself.
>
> A good consul, therefore, should not be engaged in other pursuits.[5]

The League of Nations Committee of Experts had suggested the abolition of honorary consuls. Engelhardt would not even recognize their existence, saying that International Law recognizes the title of Consul only to *consules missi. Consules electi*, that is to say those consuls who are not subjects of the State appointing them, or who exercise commerce or trade, are given the title of commercial agents.[6] But authors such as Pérez Sarmiento, for instance, recognized the existence of non-career consuls, called *ad honorem* or *electi*, usually citizens of the country where they serve, who do not receive any remuneration and may be traders or industrialists and be engaged in any profession or calling, for whom the office is an honorific title.[7] Others justified their existence. Nava, for instance, says that unsalaried consuls are called "honorary consuls," because they are appointed *ad honorem* and are above salary-related considerations. The idea of being honorary, he points out, does not clash with the idea of being a representative. What counts is the title with which the given consul is introduced to the authorities, that is whether *missus* or *electus*.[8] There were favourable opinions, such as the one expressed by the 1916 *Practical Guide for Russian Consular Officers*: "in places where there is not sufficient reason for appointing State Consular Officers, and where there is occasion to assist [...] subjects and [...] Industrial and Trading interests, Elective Consular Officers are appointed."[9]

Communist countries, now surpassed by history, were adamantly against the practice of appointing and receiving honorary consuls.[10] Their reasoning, couched in Marxist terminology, was that the distinction between diplomats

the Law Amendment Society, London, and published by Longman & Co, United Kingdom, p. 5.

[5] *Ibid.*, p. 17.

[6] See Guesalaga, A. (1900): *Derecho Diplomático y Consular con los últimos casos de controversias entre los estados*, Argentina, p. 171.

[7] Pérez Sarmiento, J.M. (1915): *Manual Consular Colombiano*, Spain, p. 62.

[8] Nava, S. (1956): *Corso di Diritto di Legazione e Consolare*, Italy, p. 135.

[9] Heyking, Baron A., *op. cit.*, p. 5.

[10] Žourek, J. (1962): "*Le statut et les fonctions des consuls*" in *Recueil des Cours de l'Académie de Droit International, II*, p. 480.

and consuls has its roots in the feudal system: the diplomat represents the Prince, the consul represents the bourgeoisie. The modern successor of the Prince – the President, the Republican Government – is nowadays interested not only in high politics but also in commerce and economic affairs. The bourgeoisie, they argued, is no longer solely interested in economic affairs but it also wants to participate in politics, actively to boot. The conclusion, almost foregone: the two should be amalgamated.[11]

Article 68 VCCR allows each State the freedom to decide whether it will appoint or receive honorary consular officers. This freedom is to be understood in the context of Article 9 VCCR which enumerates the four classes of heads of consular posts, but also lays down (in paragraph 2) that this enumeration in no way restricts the right of any of the Contracting Parties to fix the designation of consular officers other than the heads of consular posts. The right of States to appoint non-nationals as (honorary) consuls is an exception to the principle enunciated in Article 22 VCCR, which lays down that consuls should have the nationality of the sending State. The appointment of a national of the receiving State as consul of the sending State is dependent on the consent of the former; the same holds for nationals of a third State residing in the receiving State.[12]

Although (or perhaps, because) some African States were also against the practice, during the Vienna Conference the delegate of the Congo made an important contribution in favour of the institution of honorary consular officers, arguing that newly-independent as well as small countries do not dispose of either financial means or of qualified staff to meet their obligations, a constatation which holds notably for their consulates.[13] This posed a veritable dilemma for newly-independent countries. As Lee points

---

[11] Nahlik, S. (1980): "*Tendance contemporaire à assimiler le statut juridique des consuls à celui des diplomates*" in *Annuaire de l'A.A.A.*, 1979/1980, vol. 49-50, the Netherlands, p. 69. As with many other issues tackled by communism, it is the present writer's view that the seventy-odd years of scientific socialism have demonstrated that the historical analysis was usually adroit, whereas the practical solutions supposedly stemming therefrom usually did not follow.

[12] Sinagra, A. (1995): "*Privilegi e Immunità dell'Agente Diplomatico o Consolare Cittadino dello Stato di Accreditamento*" in *Studi in Ricordo di Antonio Filippo Panzera Vol. II, Diritto Internazionale*, Italy, p. 883.

[13] Quoted by Yakemtchiuk, R. (1967): *Droit consulaire des États Africains*, Belgium, p. 79. The Congolese delegate's position echoed the argument proposed by Nava, S., *op. cit.*, p. 133, that the institution of honorary consuls appears to be dominated by financial concerns: it is offered to the sending State which is anxious to avoid providing for a consulate in which the career consul's work would not suffice to justify his salary.

out,[14] they were confronted with "either maintaining no consulates abroad, thus leaving their nationals unprotected, or relying upon the good offices and protection of foreign consuls, which, if done more than sparingly, would make a sham of independence." The Congolese delegate amplified[15] on this concern, saying that it was indispensable to set up an extended network of consulates covering all the regions having a sizable group of nationals of the sending State. In some cases, however, the interests to be protected do not justify the setting up of a full-scale consulate the maintenance of which is very expensive, apart from the consideration that if the consulates become numerous, they would impose too heavy a burden on the economy of some countries, particularly those that encounter economic difficulties or trouble in their balance of payments. For such countries, a network of consular posts run by honorary consuls represented a vital condition for economic development. Furthermore, embassies are usually found in the country's capital city and their area of action is too stretched to allow them to run business relations effectively.

The need for honorary consuls is also felt because the optimal performance of consular functions sometimes requires a profound and specific knowledge of the receiving State and its domestic set-up. This knowledge can obviously be possessed by a citizen or a permanent resident of the receiving State.[16]

As the Israeli representative pointed out during the Conference, the institution of honorary consuls was born of necessity, recognized by some States, rejected by others and tolerated by a few.

But it is here to stay.[17]

## 8.2 Functions of the Honorary Consul

"There are no honorary *consulates* – just honorary *consuls.*"[18] However, there are two categories of consuls[19] and two categories of consulates depending on the category of the head.[20]

---

[14] Lee, T.L. and Quigley, J. (2008): *Consular Law and Practice*, United Kingdom, p. 18.

[15] See Yakemtchiuk, R., *op. cit.*, p. 80.

[16] Sinagra, A. (1995), *Privilegi e Immunità dell'Agente Diplomatico e Consolare Cittadino dello Stato di Accreditamento*" in *Studi in Ricordo di Antonio Filippo Panzera, Vol. II, Diritto Internazionale*, Italy, p. 882.

[17] Bratt, M. (1980): "Status and functions of honorary consuls" in *Annuaire de l'A.A.A.*, 1979/1980, vol. 49-50, the Netherlands, p. 100, among others, including B. Sen and Luke T. Lee.

[18] Bratt, M., *op. cit.*, p. 96.

[19] As pointed out by Biscottini, G. (1969): *Manuale di Diritto Consolare*, Italy, p. 61.

[20] Nava, S., *op. cit.*, p. 135, states that consulates are of two categories, depending on the status of the head of consulate: the first category embraces those where career

It follows that generally speaking honorary consuls *can* perform all consular functions, but *may* perform only those delegated by the sending State. Some States, for instance, do not allow honorary consuls to carry out notarial functions (e.g., Latvia and Malta); others expect their honorary consuls to forge (all types of) relations ("*el fomento de relaciones entre ambos Estados*") between the two States (e.g., Costa Rica).[21]

## 8.3 Privileges and Immunities

During the Conference, doubts were raised by the Japanese delegation as to the wisdom of providing for the privileges and immunities of honorary consuls under Chapter III of the Convention, apart from those of career consuls. These doubts were assuaged and did not carry the day, because the separate enumeration of honorary consuls' privileges and immunities was motivated by the need to have the Convention acknowledge that the State practice of appointing honorary consuls is not universal.

Article 71 VCCR allows the receiving State to give "additional" privileges and immunities for consular officers who are citizens or permanent residents of the receiving State. But because of the fact that in most cases honorary consuls have the nationality of the receiving State and that the majority of States have the constitutional principle of equality for all their citizens, the VCCR itself limited the scope of privileges and immunities of honorary consuls only to those which are necessary for the conduct of their consular functions.[22] However, it has been argued that this provision in reality should be construed as to afford a wider interpretation, in the sense that honorary consuls are eligible to the application of all provisions of the Convention.[23] A rationale for such a position could stem from the consideration that honorary consuls are a necessity for poorer countries – as explained by the Congolese delegate at the Conference, quoted above – and the lack of equality in privileges and immunities would therefore put the poorer countries at a further disadvantage.

---

consuls are posted ("*consoli inviati apposta*"); the second, and lower, category is that of consulates where consuls chosen locally are posted ("*consoli scelti nel luogo dove [i consolati] sono istituiti*").

[21] Latvia's and Malta's positions given personally to the present writer by officials of the respective foreign ministries; for Costa Rica's position, see Mahlouf, A.M. (1990): *Derecho Diplomatico, Derecho Consular y Normativa Costaricense*, Costa Rica, p. 161.

[22] Czubinski, Z.A. (1980): "Consular Financial Privileges in the light of the 1963 Vienna Convention on Consular Relations" in *Annuaire de l'A.A.A.*, 1979/1980, vol. 49-50, the Netherlands, p. 166.

[23] Sinagra, A., *op. cit.*, p. 883.

### 8.3.1 Consular Premises

Consular posts headed by honorary consular officers are not accorded the privilege of inviolability. Indeed, the inviolability of a consular post headed by a honorary consular officer is limited to the receiving State's obligation to protect those premises, such obligation being neither special nor increased.[24]

### 8.3.2 Consular Archives

Stewart opines that:

> In its nature the exemption of the consular archives from the control of the local authorities is one which inheres in the consular office and is independent of the person of the consul. The immunity of is that of the government, not of the consular officer; and in consequence it may be waived only by the government. [...] As the right is one which may not be waived by the consul, it would seem that the government which has received him should never call upon him to give its officers access to any part of the consular records, addressing its request to the persons who have the right to grant such permission. Nor, of course, is such a request lightly to be made.[25]

There is therefore a net distinction between the archives and the premises. Article 33 VCCR lays down that consular archives shall be inviolable at all times irrespective of where they may be, and Article 61 extends this rule to consular posts headed by honorary consular officers on condition that the archives be kept separate from the materials, books or documents relating to the consul officer's profession or trade.

### 8.3.3 Personal Immunities of Honorary Consuls

It is almost universal State practice that the receiving State is to accord special protection to consular officers and treat them with due respect as befits their official position.[26] This obligation extends also to honorary consular officers[27] and forms part of customary international law. Its rationale is found in the notion that the consul is an official representing the

[24] Constantin, E. (1981): "Consular Relations" in *Max Planck Encyclopedia of Public International Law*, (ed. R. Bernhardt), Instalment 1, Vol. 9, the Netherlands, p. 38.
[25] Stewart, I. (1926): *Consular Privileges and Immunities*, United States, p. 21.
[26] Article 40 of the International Law Commission's Draft Articles.
[27] Article 61 of the International Law Commission's Draft Articles.

sending State and is charged with official functions on behalf of the same, in the receiving State.[28]

In the case of career consular officers, the receiving State is obliged to take appropriate steps to prevent any attack on their person, freedom or dignity, whereas in the case of honorary consuls the receiving State is under a duty to accord such protection as may be required by reason of their official position.[29] Personal inviolability is denied altogether to honorary consuls.

The VCCR provides that honorary consular officers shall be immune from jurisdiction in respect of their official acts.[30] It follows that in respect of all acts which are not done in the exercise of consular functions, the consul is amenable to local jurisdiction. This is even more so when the consul is engaged in a trade or profession, as is usually the case with an honorary consul.[31] However, immunity from jurisdiction as aforesaid applies only to honorary consular officers but not to consular employees or members of the honorary consul's family.[32]

The provisions of Article 41 (1) and (2) VCCR, which restrict the arrest or detention of consular officers, do not apply if the consular officer is honorary.[33] The same holds for restrictions with regard to giving of testimony in court: honorary consuls are not exempt,[34] except for matters concerned with the exercise of their functions.[35]

### 8.3.4 Freedom of Communication

The freedom of communication in respect of all official matters is enjoyed by both career and honorary consuls, in equal measure.[36] This includes not only the freedom to communicate with the sending State and diplomatic missions thereof, but also with nationals of the sending State, to whom the consular officer also has the right to access as per Article 36 (1) VCCR.

---

[28] Sen, B. (1988): *A Diplomat's Handbook of International Law and Practice*, the Netherlands, p. 289.
[29] Articles 40 and 64 VCCR.
[30] Article 43 (1) VCCR.
[31] Sen, B., *op. cit.*, p. 291.
[32] In fact, the final limb in Article 58 (3) VCCR is superfluous, as Article 43 VCCR applies only to honorary consular officers not to employees. – Sainio, T. (1979): "Immunity from Jurisdiction in Finland's Consular Treaties" in *Essays in Honour of Erik Castrén*, Finland, pp. 140-148.
[33] Article 58 VCCR.
[34] Sen, B., *op. cit.*, p. 296.
[35] Article 44 (3) VCCR.
[36] Sen, B., *op. cit.*, p. 299.

### 8.3.5 Fiscal Privileges

Posts headed by an honorary consular officer used for the offices of the consulate are exempt from national and local taxation only if the premises are owned or leased by the sending State.[37]

An honorary consular officer is exempt from all dues and taxes on the remuneration and emoluments which he may receive from the sending State in respect of the exercise of consular functions.[38] It follows that honorary consular officers do not enjoy a general tax exemption. Similarly, they are not exempt from customs duties and customs inspections of their personal luggage.[39] Customs privileges of honorary consuls are described in Article 62 VCCR: goods imported from the sending State for official use in a consular post are exempt from all customs duties, taxes and related charges with the exception of charges for storage, transport, and similar services. There is no thorough definition of articles which are for official use in a consular post, it only gives a list of certain articles which are in common use.[40] This exemption, however, is granted only subject to the condition that the goods are used exclusively for such purpose and remain the property of the government of the sending State. This exemption does not extend to the importation of motor cars, even for official use.[41]

### 8.3.6 Other Privileges and Immunities

Like career consuls, honorary consuls can exercise the right to display the national flag and the State coat-of-arms of the sending State and to fly the same flag on their means of transport if allowed by the consular treaty or the regulations of the receiving State. In the *Consular Premises (Austria)* case it was held that "it is necessary and customary to designate the office of a consul by means of a plate in order to facilitate the identification of the consulate by interested parties."[42]

Honorary consular officers, with the exception of those who carry on for personal profit any professional or commercial activity in the receiving State, are exempt from all obligations under the laws and regulations of the receiving State in regard to the registration of aliens and residence permits.[43] This, however, does not apply to members of their families.[44]

---

[37] Article 60 VCCR.
[38] Article 66 VCCR.
[39] Czubinski, Z.A., *op. cit.*, p. 166.
[40] *Ibid.*, p. 167.
[41] Sen, B., *op. cit.*, p. 302.
[42] *Ibid.*, pp. 303-304.
[43] Article 65 VCCR.
[44] Sen, B., *op. cit.*, p. 304.

Honorary consuls are not exempt from payment of contributions under the social security laws both for themselves and in regard to persons they employ.[45]

Honorary consular officers are exempt from all personal services and from all public services of any kind whatsoever and from military obligations such as those connected with requisitioning, military contributions and billeting.[46] Fire protection service and jury duty have also been mentioned as exemptions by authors. On the other hand, it has been opined that it is doubtful whether such exemptions ought to be granted when the honorary consul is engaged in trade or other occupation or profession because like all other persons residing in the receiving State, such honorary consul derives benefit from his private gainful activities conducted in that State.[47] Also, it is expected that honorary consuls should not use their official position in furtherance of their trade or any other gainful activity in which they may be engaged,[48] and avoiding such services may be construed as indirect furtherance of the gainful activity as no time is spent away from it. Yet, it would seem that such reasoning once again ignores the basic fact that consuls – be they career or honorary – represent the sending State and that not all sending States can afford a worldwide network of career consuls.[49] Thus, limiting the freedom of action of honorary consuls serves to diminish the effectiveness of the consular network of poorer or smaller countries. The delicate balance between the privileges and immunities of the consul who is a citizen or permanent resident of the receiving State and the attainment of the sending State's objectives should tend to tilt in favour of the latter. If the principle of equality of States is to be respected, the attainment of the sending State's objectives should be respected and facilitated by the receiving State.

---

[45] Article 48 (2) VCCR.
[46] Article 67 VCCR.
[47] Sen, B., *op. cit.*, p. 305.
[48] *Ibid.*, p. 309.
[49] Umpteenth example: Bettoni, G. (2003): "*Funzioni consolari e associazioni della categoria consolare onoraria*" in *Osservatorio diplomatico e consolare. Annuario diplomatico consolare UCOI*, Italy, p. 113: "*sono invero assai pochi gli Stati che possono intrattenere una rete di uffici consolari di prima categoria, non fosse che per manifeste esigenze finanziarie e ragioni attinenti alla disponibilità di risorse umane*" ["in reality only a few States can maintain a network of career consular posts, because of the evident financial commitment and due to the lack of availability of human resources" – translated by the present writer].

## 8.4 Associations of Honorary Consuls

It would seem that the experiment carried out in Italy in 1977, when the *UCOI* (*Unione dei Consoli Onorari in Italia* – Union of Honorary Consuls in Italy) was founded, prompted others to follow suit: Argentina, Belgium, Brazil, France, Germany, Hong Kong and Macao SAR China, Malta, San Marino, among others. In 1995, the *UCOI* spearheaded the *FUCHE* (*Fédération des Unions des Consuls Honoraires en Europe* – Federation of Honorary Consuls in Europe), which is made up of associations already formed in Europe.[50]

## 8.5 A Re-Evaluation of the Institution

The post-Berlin Wall world seems to resist less the institution of honorary consuls. The globalized world, with its mass migrations and its attempts at universalizing human rights, seems to be in need of vaster, stronger consular networks, with an increasing presence to help out nationals who are away from their homeland. This new world is however still riddled with poverty, and poor countries can only maintain worldwide consular networks if manned by honorary consuls. Even if poverty were ever to be eradicated, the international polity would still be made up of large, medium-sized, and small Nation States. The last two will never have enough human resources to man worldwide consular networks with career consuls. It follows that the institution of honorary consuls is not only useful but necessary. In the view of the present writer, it also follows that a re-evaluation of the institution is called for, leading to a radical review of the privileges and immunities accorded to such consuls.

---

[50] Fragola, M. (2004): *Nozioni di Diritto Diplomatico e Consolare – Tecnica Prassi Esperienza*, Italy, p. 144.

# *Conclusion*

The fact that this work has given so much space to consular assistance is not due to any implied priority being assigned to that particular consular function. On the contrary, it is the opinion of the present writer that all consular functions are of relatively equal importance. The national living in the receiving State who needs to use immovables situated in the sending State as collateral will view the notarial function of the consul as of supreme importance to him; similarly, the marriage-solemnizing function for the national who wishes to marry; similarly, consular assistance for the national who is detained in prison. To a certain extent, the consul's role is similar to that of the judge and the Latin-type notary. Whoever has recourse to the Law Courts – whether for a petty case relating to a mundane quarrel with a neighbour on a noisy air-conditioning unit or for a constitutional case concerning human rights – will deem his case more important than any other. The same applies to whoever needs the services of a Latin-type notary, whether he is bequeathing a baronial estate or the meagre savings of a pensioner. The generous amount of space which has been granted to consular assistance is justified by the far-reaching consequences of the decisions of the International Court of Justice.

The Vienna Convention on Consular Relations was, it almost goes without saying, the continuous backdrop to this work. It has been opined that "[t]he Vienna Convention on Consular Relations is no doubt one of the most outstanding codifications ever undertaken under the auspices of the United Nations. Considering the growing importance of consular relations in modern international society and the somewhat chaotic situation which had characterized the law before the conclusion of the Convention, the practical advantages of universally recognized legal rules in this field of international law are unquestionable and need no further justification."[1]

The Vienna Convention on Consular Relations together with the 1961 Vienna Convention on Diplomatic Relations can be regarded as one instance of the realization of the universalist ideal. However, as Koskenniemi points out, "universality still seems an essential part of progressive thought – but it also implies an imperial logic of identity: I will accept you, but only on the

[1] Kussbach, E. (1981): *Vienna Convention on Consular Relations (1963)* in *Max Planck Encylcopedia of Public International Law*, Instalment 1, vol. 9, (ed. R. Bernhardt), the Netherlands, p. 388.

condition that I may think of you as I think of myself."[2] To the mind of the present writer, this is the basic tenet underlying the psychology behind the Convention.

In contemporary times, it is noted that there is a tendency toward the independence of consular law, though maintaining a general dependence on public and private international law. However, it will be long before consular law's autonomy may be invoked.[3] In the eyes of the present writer, the relationship between consular law and public international law is very much akin to that between so-called "family law" and civil law.

Lastly, as Article 73 VCCR points out, "the apparent purpose of [the VCCR is] not to completely pre-empt the field of consular relations but to state the fundamental law on the subject."[4] In the final analysis, it points toward the ever-evolving role of the consul in international law and international relations, perceived as a necessary corollary of the co-existence of diverse human societies coping with various geophysical and geopolitical concerns and priorities.

---

[2] Koskenniemi, M. (2001): *The Gentle Civilizer of Nations – The Rise and Fall of International Law 1870-1960*, United Kingdom, p. 515.
[3] Ochaita, C.L. (1995): *Derecho Diplomatico y Consular*, Guatemala, p. 122.
[4] Kho, S. (1995): "Article 73 of the Vienna Convention on Consular Relations: the Relationship between the Vienna Consular Convention and Other International Agreements" in *Chinese Yearbook of International Law and Affairs*, vol. 13, Taiwan, pp. 235-276.

# *Appendix 1*

# WITHDRAWAL FROM THE OPTIONAL PROTOCOL

> *"Treaties at best are but complied with so long as interest requires their fulfilment. Consequently, they are virtually binding on the weaker party only; or, in plain truth, they are not binding at all."* Washington Irving, 1806.

## 1. Why do States obey or disobey international law?

> A government's determination to comply with (or to disregard) an international tribunal's decision may be informed by a variety of rational or irrational variables. While lawyers may often have an intuitive response to the question as to why a particular state 'obeyed' international law in a particular circumstance, legal method is poorly equipped for a systematic enquiry into this 'causal question'.[1]

On February 28, 2005, United States President George W. Bush issued a Memorandum for the Attorney General entitled "Compliance with the Decision of the International Court of Justice in *Avena*," stating:

> I have determined, pursuant to the authority vested in me as President by the Constitution and laws of the United States of America, that the United States will discharge its international obligations under the decision of the International Court of Justice in the Case Concerning Avena and Other Mexican Nationals (Mexico v. United States of America (Avena), 2004, I.C.J. 128 (Mar 31)), by having state courts give effect to the decision in accordance with

---

[1] Pulkowski, D. (2006): "Testing Compliance Theories: Towards United States Obedience of International Law in the *Avena Case*" in *Leiden Journal of International Law*, Vol. 19, No. 2, United Kingdom, p. 513.

general principles of comity in cases filed by the 51 Mexican nationals addressed in that decision.

## 2. The United States' Withdrawal from the Optional Protocol

Unlike the European Convention on Consular Functions, which provides for the duration and denunciation of the Convention and its Protocols,[2] the VCCR contains no such provision.

One week after the President's Memorandum to the Attorney General, the United States, through a letter dated March 7, 2005, signed by Secretary of State Condoleezza Rice, advised the Secretary-General of the United Nations that the United States were withdrawing from the Optional Protocol to the VCCR and that henceforth, the United States would no longer recognize the jurisdiction of the International Court of Justice reflected in that Protocol.

The questions raised by the United States' withdrawal need to be looked at from the law of treaties perspective. The United States withdrew from a *protocol*, a term which "usually denotes a treaty amending, or supplemental to, another treaty."[3]

The justification the Department of State gave for the withdrawal could be summed up as the need for protection "against future International Court of Justice judgments that might similarly interpret the consular convention or disrupt [the United States] domestic criminal system in ways [the United States] did not anticipate when [it] joined the convention."[4] The State Department thus briefed the Press on March 10, 2005:

> [No]body should conclude by our decision to withdraw from the Optional Protocol that we are any less committed to the international system or that we are in any way walking back from international commitments. On the contrary, we remain a party to the Vienna Convention, we remain committed to fulfilling its provisions and we stand by it. [...]
>
> When we signed up to the Optional Protocol, it [was] not anticipated that the [...] Optional Protocol would be used to review cases of domestic criminal law. [...] The way [the

---

[2] Article 55. See also Articles 6 and 7 of the Protocol.

[3] McNair, A. (1961): *Law of Treaties*, United Kingdom, p. 23.

[4] *Washington Post*, March 10, 2005.

> Optional Protocol] is being interpreted go[es] against the ideas – the original ideas – that we signed up for. [...]
>
> This is a really unexpected and unwelcome precedent where people who don't like decisions of our state courts can use an international court as a court of appeal. And that doesn't make any sense at all. [...]
>
> We have a system of justice that works [...] and provides people with due process and review of their case. And it's not appropriate that there be some international court that comes in and can reverse decisions of our national courts. [...]
>
> We're also saying that in the future we're going to find other ways to resolve disputes that come under the Vienna Convention other than submitting them to the ICJ. [...W]e're still committed to the Vienna Convention [and...] to upholding its principles and fulfilling our obligations under that convention.[5]

It is significant that the original position of the United States at the Conference leading to the Convention had been not the inclusion of an Optional Protocol but of a dispute settlement clause within the Convention itself, as Article 72. Had that been accepted, all disputes relating to the Convention would have fallen under the ICJ's compulsory jurisdiction.

The compulsory nature of the United States position on dispute resolution would seem to suggest that the United States was contemplating the impossibility to withdraw when it chose to become a party to the VCCR.

### 3. A Subjective United States Perspective

Other parties to the VCCR have not echoed the United States position on whether Article 36 VCCR provides for an individual right and whether a consular access violation calls for a judicial remedy; they have actually strongly condemned it for those positions. Foreign governments filed *amicus curiae* briefs in United States state and federal courts – this is not usually done and denotes criticism of the receiving State.[6] Such briefs were filed in

---

[5] www.usinfo.state.gov.

[6] Shabtai Rosenne's observation in *The Perplexities of Modern International Law* (2004, The Netherlands, p. 72) sheds more light: "only four cases introduced by unilateral application have not led to a serious deterioration in the relations between

cases involving own nationals, as well as in support of nationals of other States. Foreign States even filed as groups of Sates. In one United States Supreme Court case, a group of thirteen Latin American States filed a brief seeking judicial remedy for a consular access violation. In the same case, the European Union filed such a brief which was backed not only by its then twenty-five Member States, but also by an additional twenty-one other European States. The juridical system of these States does not contemplate capital punishment, and they were concerned that their nationals could be executed in the United States.[7]

Yet, the United States withdrawal could be viewed as a coherent continuation of a particular United States tradition. Luke T. Lee[8] hails the United States accession to the Optional Protocol as a departure from its traditional notion of sovereign equality which barred compulsory submission to a higher or impartial tribunal when no express agreements existed. Under both Permanent Court of International Justice and International Court of Justice regimes, States could accept an "Optional Clause" whereby they would accept the Court's compulsory jurisdiction, subject to such conditions as reciprocity and time limit as the States themselves set. In addition to these conditions, the United States excluded also "disputes with regard to matters which are essentially within the domestic jurisdiction of the United States of America as determined by the United States," referred to as the Connally Amendment.[9]

For Lee, the Optional Protocol was a sort of second-best alternative the United States Delegation at the Vienna Conference had: "the United States gave its vote to the Optional Protocol in the belief that the Protocol, even though 'Optional', would still be preferable to no dispute settlement provision at all. Thus ended a little-known episode in which the United States, widely associated in the public mind as the jealous guardian of its

the two States concerned: the *Passage through the Great Belt*; the *Delimitation in the Jan Mayen Area*, the *La Grand* and the *Avena and other Mexican nationals* cases. It appears that in the last twenty years the unilateral institution of proceedings is an unfriendly act."

7 Quigley, J. (2009): "The United States' Withdrawal from International Court of Justice Jurisdiction in consular cases" in *Duke Journal of Comparative and International Law*, United States, Vol. 19, No. 2, pp. 275, 279, 285, 296. See also Lou Ann Bohn (2003): "Understanding the Imposition of Capital Punishment on Foreign Nationals in the United States as a Human Rights Violation" in *Wisconsin International Law Journal*, Vol. 21 No. 4, United States, pp. 435 *et seq.*.

8 Lee, L.T. & Quigley, J (2008): *Consular Law and Consular Practice*, United Kingdom, pp. 574-579.

9 *Ibid.*, p. 574.

juridical sovereignty on account of its Connally Amendment, appears as the champion of the Court's compulsory jurisdiction."[10]

The United States' withdrawal might thus be construed as the reaction of either an outward-looking United States deeming its departure from its traditional stance abused of, or an inward-looking United States deeming its traditional stance vindicated. In both cases, from its own subjective point of view, there is reason enough to justify the withdrawal. However, it is accepted that domestic complications should not be invoked to justify failures to perform obligations or as grounds for exemption.

The Connally Amendment domestic jurisdiction perspective is implied in the following argument:

> The United States had indicated (and the evidence seems to substantiate the good faith of its effort) that it would henceforth try to ensure that the rights available to foreign nationals under Article 36 of the VCCR would be made as operational as the federal government of the United States was capable of making them. This satisfied the obligation under the Convention.
> {...}
> The essential objective of VCCR Article 36 was fulfilled; exercises of jurisdiction could not likely achieve much more and, if initiated, would probably be covert efforts at securing abolition of the death penalty. It appears likely that the United States felt that states and, increasingly, non-governmental organizations committed to abolitionism, would be able to continue to bring cases allegedly arising under Article 36 of the VCCR to an international tribunal that could well prove to be increasingly abolitionist in its orientation. Given the federal structure of the American system, the proliferation of these cases could have presented serious, if not insoluble domestic legal and political problems for any United States government. Hence the decision to pre-empt the problem by denouncing the Optional Protocol.[11]

---

[10] *Ibid.*, p. 579.

[11] Reisman, W.M., and Arsanjani, M.H. (2006): "No Exit? A Preliminary Examination of the Legal Consequences of United States' Notification of Withdrawal from the Optional Protocol to the Vienna Convention on Consular Relations" in *Promoting Justice, Human Rights and Conflict Resolution Through International*

However, to borrow Shabtai Rosenne's words, "it is axiomatic that a treaty, made between States, is binding upon each State as a whole, upon each of its organs."[12]

## 4. *Rebus sic stantibus*

Since Article 56 of the Vienna Convention on the Law of Treaties expresses the grounds for justifying withdrawal "as an exception, the onus of establishing that the exception applies lies on the party wishing to withdraw."[13]

The United States withdrawal was based on the *rebus sic stantibus* doctrine, which is an exception to the "*loi des lois*"[14] of international law, namely *pacta sunt servanda* ("agreements are binding and are to be implemented in good faith"[15]). According to the *rebus sic stantibus* doctrine, a party may withdraw from an agreement if circumstances independent of its conduct fail to remain as they were at the moment of signing up to the agreement. The origins of the doctrine lie in Medieval Canon Law.[16] Kelsen denied its existence, whereas Brierly warned that "if [such a doctrine] is to be accepted into the law, [it] clearly needs careful definition. Otherwise it is capable of being used, and it often has been used, merely to excuse the breach of a treaty obligation that a state finds it inconvenient to fulfil."[17]

The essentials of this doctrine are encapsulated in Article 62 of the Vienna Convention on the Law of Treaties:[18]

---

*Law - Liber Amicorum Lucius Caflisch* (M. G. Kohen (ed.)), The Netherlands, pp. 897, 925.

[12] Rosenne, Sh. (1989): *Developments in the law of treaties, 1946-1986*, United States, p. 39.

[13] Aust, A. (2000): *Modern Treaty Law and Practice*, United Kingdom, p. 290.

[14] "Law of laws" – Dupuy, P.-M. (2002): *Droit international public*, France, p. 284.

[15] Brownlie, I. (1998): *Principles of Public International Law*, United Kingdom, p. xlviii.

[16] See Lesaffer, R. (2000): "Medieval Canon Law of Contract and Early Modern Treaty Law" in *Journal of the History of International Law*, Vol. 2, Issue 2, Germany, pp. 178-198.

[17] Brierly, J.L. (1963): *The Law of Nations*, United Kingdom, p. 335.

[18] The Vienna Convention on the Law of Treaties has not been ratified by the United States. Nevertheless, the United States considers many provisions of this Convention to represent international customary law. In the *Fisheries Jurisdiction* case (Federal Republic of Germany *v.* Iceland), 1973, the ICJ held that Article 62 constituted a codification of existing customary law.

> 1. A fundamental change of circumstances which has occurred with regard to those existing at the time of the conclusion of a treaty, and which was not foreseen by the parties, may not be invoked as a ground for terminating or withdrawing from the treaty unless:
>
> a. the existence of those circumstances constituted an essential basis of the consent of the parties to be bound by the treaty; and
>
> b. the effect of the change is radically to transform the extent of obligations still to be performed under the treaty.
>
> 2. A fundamental change of circumstances may not be invoked as a ground for terminating or withdrawing from a treaty:
>
> a. if the treaty establishes a boundary; or
>
> b. if the fundamental change is the result of a breach by the party invoking it either of an obligation under the treaty or of any other international obligation owed to any other party to the treaty.

## 5. Validity of the Withdrawal

There is no denunciation clause in either VCCR or its Optional Protocol.

Since denunciation clauses are well-known to drafters of treaties, the omission of such a clause would imply that denunciation is prohibited.[19] There is a counterargument: the omission of a denunciation clause may be due to the negligence or inexperience of a treaty's drafter.[20] State practice would seem to allow withdrawal only in certain cases. Article 56 (2) of the Vienna Convention on the Law of Treaties allows withdrawal when the right is implied by the nature of the treaty.

In the *Fisheries Jurisdiction* case (Federal Republic of Germany *v.* Iceland), 1973, the Court noted the "views expressed by certain authorities to the effect that treaties of judicial settlement or declarations of acceptance of the

[19] Aust, A., *op. cit.*, p. 290.
[20] Haraszti, G. (1973): *Some Fundamental Problems of the Law of Treaties*, Hungary, p. 269.

compulsory jurisdiction of the Court are among those treaty provisions which, by their very nature, may be subject to unilateral denunciation in the absence of express provisions regarding their duration or termination."[21] The Court did not explicate the principle underlying these views, considering it "sufficient to remark that such views have reference only to instruments in which the parties had assumed a general obligation to submit to judicial settlement all or certain categories of disputes which might arise between them in the unpredictable future."[22]

It has been argued that the withdrawal from a general treaty for the settlement of disputes between the parties even when it has no withdrawal provision is usually a possibility. The rationale behind such a position seems to stem from the fact that such a withdrawal would be consistent with the consensual nature of international jurisdiction. State practice shows that "States have withdrawn from such optional dispute settlement protocols to several UN treaties without (at least legal) objection even when they contain no provision for this."[23]

**6. Was there (i) a fundamental change of those circumstances which constituted an essential basis of the consent of the parties to be bound by the treaty? and (ii) a radical transformation of the extent of obligations still to be performed under the treaty by the US?**

In the *Case Concerning The Gabcíkovo-Nagymaros Project* (Hungary *v.* Slovakia), 1997, the ICJ expressed itself thus:

> A fundamental change of circumstances must have been unforeseen; the existence of the circumstances at the time of the treaty's conclusion must have constituted an essential basis of the consent of the parties to be bound by the treaty. The negative and conditional wording of Article 62 of the Vienna Convention on the Law of Treaties is a clear indication moreover that the stability of treaty relations requires that a plea of fundamental change of circumstances be applied only in exceptional cases.[24]

Lee reports this: "The United States delegation to the Vienna Convention did not view these compromissory clauses [which call for the submission of disputes to the ICJ, without any self-judging domestic-jurisdiction

---

[21] I.C.J. Reports, 1973, p. 15.
[22] *Idem.*
[23] Aust, A., *op. cit.*, p. 235.
[24] Judgment at 8, para. 1.6.

reservation] as incompatible with the Connally Amendment, in light of ICJ Statute Art. 36(3)"[25]

It would therefore seem that there was no fundamental change in circumstances or a radical transformation of the obligations originally undertaken.

**7. Was there a fundamental change as a result of a breach by the party invoking an obligation under the treaty?**

"It seems that the only viable description of a breach of a treaty is one that can be deduced not from the law of the treaty-instrument but from the law of the treaty-obligation, the law of State responsibility. On that basis it can be described as conduct consisting of an action or omission attributable to a State or to an international organization under international law, that State or organization being a party to a treaty in force and the conduct being incompatible with an obligation grounded in that treaty."[26] An anonymous Memorandum (later established to have been penned by Lauterpacht) submitted to the nascent International Law Commission *Survey of International Law in Relation to the Work and Codification of the International Law Commission* read thus: "Persuasive reasons may be adduced in support of the view that it is desirable to include the entire subject of treaties within the orbit of codification [...] if the principle of fidelity in treaties is to be maintained and strengthened."[27] "That is the philosophical, political and psychological context within which the Commission treated the problem of breach of treaty (as an instrument) and certain related issues, which may include difficulties imposed by the State's internal law in the way of the application of the treaty (something which may lead to a breach of the treaty), or the concept (politically indistinguishable on many occasions) of *rebus sic stantibus.*"[28]

It would seem the United States was not entitled to withdraw, as it was the party in breach of a treaty obligation and it invoked the doctrine.

**8. Was the withdrawal procedure followed by the United States correct?**

In the *Fisheries Jurisdiction* case, the ICJ addressed the question of the relationship between Article 62 and Articles 65 and 66 of the Vienna Convention on the Law of Treaties, and the procedure set forth in those two provisions. The Court termed this relationship the "procedural complement

---

[25] *Op. cit.*, p. 576.
[26] Rosenne, Sh. (1984): *Breach of Treaty*, United Kingdom, p. 123.
[27] *Ibid.*, p. 11.
[28] *Ibid.*, p. 12.

to the doctrine of changed circumstances," that is to say "the requirement that a State invoking a fundamental change of circumstances should be prepared to allow a third party to determine whether the conditions for the operation of the doctrine are present."[29] Whereas some authors hold that the Court enjoys "seeming approval,"[30] others argue that as a matter of positive international law there seems to be no inherent link "in the sense that the invocation of the rule must follow the prescribed procedure or an equivalent."[31]

Rosenne invariably criticizes the ICJ's pronouncement in the *Military and Paramilitary Activities in and Against Nicaragua* case (The Republic of Nicaragua *v.* United States of America), 1986, which refers to the "law of treaties" and its requirement of "a reasonable time for withdrawal from or termination of treaties that contain no provision regarding the duration of their validity."[32]

There would seem to have been no violation of any rule in this respect.

### 9. Effects of the Withdrawal

There has been, and will be, no effect on cases already filed. The withdrawal did not preclude Mexico from seeking an interpretation on the *Avena* judgment. In fact, the ICJ affirmed that "the withdrawal of the United States from the Optional Protocol to the Vienna Convention on Consular Relations Concerning Settlement of Disputes since the rendering of the *Avena* judgment had no bearing on the Court's jurisdiction [...]."[33]

It cannot be excluded that a State party to the VCCR might file an action against the United States for a violation of a VCCR obligation, having as a preliminary plea the invalidity of the withdrawal and a request for the withdrawal to be impugned. Such an action would obligate the ICJ to analyse the *rebus sic stantibus* doctrine invoked by the United States, in all its ramifications, including procedural aspects.

---

[29] Sinclair, I. (1984): *The Vienna Convention on the Law of Treaties*, United Kingdom, p. 195.

[30] Sinclair, *loc. cit.* Brownlie (*op. cit.*) too accepts the ruling of the Court without expressing any reservation thereto.

[31] Rosenne, Sh. (1989): *Developments in the law of treaties 1946-1986*, pp. 350-351.

[32] *Loc. cit.*, pp. 27, 101, 121, 170, 195, 231, 235, 241, 251, with reference to para. 63 of the judgment.

[33] *Request for Interpretation of the Judgment of 31 March 2004 in the Case Concerning* Avena and Other Mexican Nationals (Mexico *v.* United States of America), 19 January 2009, para. 15.

From a purely internal point of view, the good faith of the United States in implementing its obligations under Article 36 VCCR has been recognized by the ICJ in *Avena*. However, from a "psychological" point of view, the withdrawal might have confirmed the impression that Article 36 VCCR is just a "toothless, clawless lion."[34]

**10. Can the United States accede to the Protocol again?**

Not only it can, be it would seem advisable for the United States to do so, particularly with a view to the protection of its nationals abroad.[35]

It has been argued that a State may withdraw and then immediately accede in order to make a reservation.[36] It is doubtful whether this is now possible in this case.

Nevertheless, the United States did not exclude finding "ways to resolve disputes that come under the Vienna Convention other than submitting them to the ICJ."[37]

---

[34] *Lombera-Camorlinga*, 206 F. 3d at 888 (Browning, J., dissenting).
[35] Quigley, J., *op. cit.*, p. 305.
[36] Aust, A., *op. cit.*, p. 240.
[37] See Press Briefing *supra*.

# *Appendix 2*

## VIENNA CONVENTION ON CONSULAR RELATIONS, 1963

Done at Vienna on 24 April 1963. Entered into force on 19 March 1967.

*The States Parties to the present Convention,*
*Recalling* that consular relations have been established between peoples since ancient times,

*Having in mind* the Purposes and Principles of the Charter of the United Nations concerning the sovereign equality of States, the maintenance of international peace and security, and the promotion of friendly relations among nations,

*Considering* that the United Nations Conference on Diplomatic Intercourse and Immunities adopted the Vienna Convention on Diplomatic Relations which was opened for signature on 18 April 1961,

*Believing* that an international convention on consular relations, privileges and immunities would also contribute to the development of friendly relations among nations, irrespective of their differing constitutional and social systems,

*Realizing* that the purpose of such privileges and immunities is not to benefit individuals but to ensure the efficient performance of functions by consular posts on behalf of their respective States,

*Affirming* that the rules of customary international law continue to govern matters not expressly regulated by the provisions of the present Convention,

*Have agreed* as follows:

*Article 1*

*Definitions*
1. For the purposes of the present Convention, the following expressions shall have the meanings hereunder assigned to them:

(*a*) "consular post" means any consulate-general, consulate, vice-consulate or consular agency;

(*b*) "consular district" means the area assigned to a consular post for the exercise of consular functions;

(*c*) "head of consular post" means the person charged with the duty of acting in that capacity;

(*d*) "consular officer" means any person, including the head of a consular post, entrusted in that capacity with the exercise of consular functions;

(*e*) "consular employee" means any person employed in the administrative or technical service of a consular post;

(*f*) "member of the service staff" means any person employed in the domestic service of a consular post;

(*g*) "members of the consular post" means consular officers, consular employees and members of the service staff;

(*h*) "members of the consular staff" means consular officers, other than the head of a consular post, consular employees and members of the service staff;

(*i*) "member of the private staff" means a person who is employed exclusively in the private service of a member of the consular post;

(*j*) "consular premises" means the buildings or parts of buildings and the land ancillary thereto, irrespective of ownership, used exclusively for the purposes of the consular post;

(*k*) "consular archives" includes all the papers, documents, correspondence, books, films, tapes and registers of the consular post, together with the ciphers and codes, the card-indexes and any article of furniture intended for their protection or safe keeping.

2. Consular officers are of two categories, namely career consular officers and honorary consular officers. The provisions of Chapter II of the present Convention apply to consular posts headed by career consular officers, the provisions of Chapter III govern consular posts headed by honorary consular officers.

3. The particular status of members of the consular posts who are nationals or permanent residents of the receiving State is governed by article 71 of the present Convention.

## CHAPTER I. CONSULAR RELATIONS IN GENERAL

### SECTION I. ESTABLISHMENT AND CONDUCT OF CONSULAR RELATIONS

*Article 2*

*Establishment of consular relations*
1. The establishment of consular relations between States takes place by mutual consent.

2. The consent given to the establishment of diplomatic relations between two States implies, unless otherwise stated, consent to the establishment of consular relations.

3. The severance of diplomatic relations shall not ipso facto involve the severance of consular relations.

*Article 3*

*Exercise of consular functions*
Consular functions are exercised by consular posts. They are also exercised by diplomatic missions in accordance with the provisions of the present Convention.

*Article 4*

*Establishment of a consular post*
1. A consular post may be established in the territory of the receiving State only with that State's consent.

2. The seat of the consular post, its classification and the consular district shall be established by the sending State and shall be subject to the approval of the receiving State.

3. Subsequent changes in the seat of the consular post, its classification or the consular district may be made by the sending State only with the consent of the receiving State.

4. The consent of the receiving State shall also be required if a consulate-general or a consulate desires to open a vice-consulate or a consular agency in a locality other than that in which it is itself established.

5. The prior express consent of the receiving State shall also be required for the opening of an office forming part of an existing consular post elsewhere than at the seat thereof.

*Article 5*

*Consular functions*
Consular functions consist in:
(*a*) protecting in the receiving State the interests of the sending State and of its nationals, both individuals and bodies corporate, within the limits permitted by international law;

(*b*) furthering the development of commercial, economic, cultural and scientific relations between the sending State and the receiving State and otherwise promoting friendly relations between them in accordance with the provisions of the present Convention;

(*c*) ascertaining by all lawful means conditions and developments in the commercial, economic, cultural and scientific life of the receiving State, reporting thereon to the Government of the sending State and giving information to persons interested;

(*d*) issuing passports and travel documents to nationals of the sending State, and visas or appropriate documents to persons wishing to travel to the sending State;

(*e*) helping and assisting nationals, both individuals and bodies corporate, of the sending State;

(*f*) acting as notary and civil registrar and in capacities of a similar kind, and performing certain functions of an administrative nature, provided that there is nothing contrary thereto in the laws and regulations of the receiving State;

(*g*) safeguarding the interests of nationals, both individuals and bodies corporate, of the sending States in cases of succession *mortis causa* in the territory of the receiving State, in accordance with the laws and regulations of the receiving State;

(*h*) safeguarding, within the limits imposed by the laws and regulations of the receiving State, the interests of minors and other persons lacking full capacity who are nationals of the sending State, particularly where any guardianship or trusteeship is required with respect to such persons;

(*i*) subject to the practices and procedures obtaining in the receiving State, representing or arranging appropriate representation for nationals of the sending State before the tribunals and other authorities of the receiving State, for the purpose of obtaining, in accordance with the laws and regulations of the receiving State, provisional measures for the preservation of the rights and interests of these nationals, where, because of absence or any other reason, such nationals are unable at the proper time to assume the defence of their rights and interests;

(*j*) transmitting judicial and extrajudicial documents or executing letters rogatory or commissions to take evidence for the courts of the sending State in accordance with international agreements in force or, in the absence of such international agreements, in any other manner compatible with the laws and regulations of the receiving State;

(*k*) exercising rights of supervision and inspection provided for in the laws and regulations of the sending State in respect of vessels having the nationality of the sending State, and of aircraft registered in that State, and in respect of their crews;

(*l*) extending assistance to vessels and aircraft mentioned in subparagraph (*k*) of this article, and to their crews, taking statements regarding the voyage of a vessel, examining and stamping the ship's papers, and, without prejudice to the powers of the authorities of the receiving State, conducting investigations into any incidents which occurred during the voyage, and settling disputes of any kind between the master, the officers and the seamen insofar as this may be authorized by the laws and regulations of the sending State;

(*m*) performing any other functions entrusted to a consular post by the sending State which are not prohibited by the laws and regulations of the receiving State or to which no objection is taken by the receiving State or which are referred to in the international agreements in force between the sending State and the receiving State.

*Article 6*

*Exercise of consular functions outside the consular district*

A consular officer may, in special circumstances, with the consent of the receiving State, exercise his functions outside his consular district.

*Article 7*

*Exercise of consular functions in a third State*
The sending State may, after notifying the States concerned, entrust a consular post established in a particular State with the exercise of consular functions in another State, unless there is express objection by one of the States concerned.

*Article 8*

*Exercise of consular functions on behalf of a third State*
Upon appropriate notification to the receiving State, a consular post of the sending State may, unless the receiving State objects, exercise consular functions in the receiving State on behalf of a third State.

*Article 9*

*Classes of heads of consular posts*
1. Heads of consular posts are divided into four classes, namely (*a*) consuls-general; (*b*) consuls; (*c*) vice-consuls; (*d*) consular agents.

2. Paragraph 1 of this article in no way restricts the right of any of the Contracting Parties to fix the designation of consular officers other than the heads of consular posts.

*Article 10*

*Appointment and admission of heads of consular posts*
1. Heads of consular posts are appointed by the sending State and are admitted to the exercise of their functions by the receiving State.

2. Subject to the provisions of the present Convention, the formalities for the appointment and for the admission of the head of a consular post are determined by the laws, regulations and usages of the sending State and of the receiving State respectively.

*Article 11*

*The consular commission or notification of appointment*
1. The head of a consular post shall be provided by the sending State with a document, in the form of a commission or similar instrument, made out for each appointment, certifying his capacity and showing, as a general rule, his full name, his category and class, the consular district and the seat of the consular post.

2. The sending State shall transmit the commission or similar instrument through the diplomatic or other appropriate channel to the Government of the State in whose territory the head of a consular post is to exercise his functions.

3. If the receiving State agrees, the sending State may, instead of a commission or similar instrument, send to the receiving State a notification containing the particulars required by paragraph 1 of this article.

*Article 12*

*The exequatur*
1. The head of a consular post is admitted to the exercise of his functions by an authorization from the receiving State termed an *exequatur*, whatever the form of this authorization.

2. A State which refused to grant an *exequatur* is not obliged to give to the sending State reasons for such refusal.

3. Subject to the provisions of articles 13 and 15, the head of a consular post shall not enter upon his duties until he has received an *exequatur*.

*Article 13*

*Provisional admission of heads of consular posts*
Pending delivery of the *exequatur*, the head of a consular post may be admitted on a provisional basis to the exercise of his functions. In that case, the provisions of the present Convention shall apply.

*Article 14*

*Notification to the authorities of the consular district*
As soon as the head of a consular post is admitted even provisionally to the exercise of his functions, the receiving State shall immediately notify the competent authorities of the consular district. It shall also ensure that the necessary measures are taken to enable the head of a consular post to carry out the duties of his office and to have the benefit of the provisions of the present Convention.

*Article 15*

*Temporary exercise of the functions of the head of a consular post*
1. If the head of a consular post is unable to carry out his functions or the position of head of consular post is vacant, an acting head of post may act provisionally as head of the consular post.

2. The full name of the acting head of post shall be notified either by the diplomatic mission of the sending State or, if that State has no such mission in the receiving State, by the head of the consular post, or, if he is unable to do so, by any competent authority of the sending State, to the Ministry for Foreign Affairs of the receiving State or to the authority designated by that Ministry. As a general rule, this notification shall be given in advance. The receiving State may make the admission as acting head of post of a person who is neither a diplomatic agent nor a consular officer of the sending State in the receiving State conditional on its consent.

3. The competent authorities of the receiving State shall afford assistance and protection to the acting head of post. While he is in charge of the post, the provisions of the present Convention shall apply to him on the same basis as to the head of the consular post concerned. The receiving State shall not, however, be obliged to grant to an acting head of post any facility, privilege or immunity which the head of the consular post enjoys only subject to conditions not fulfilled by the acting head of post.

4. When, in the circumstances referred to in paragraph 1 of this article, a member of the diplomatic staff of the diplomatic mission of the sending State in the receiving State is designated by the sending State as an acting head of post, he shall, if the receiving State does not object thereto, continue to enjoy diplomatic privileges and immunities.

*Article 16*

*Precedence as between heads of consular posts*
1. Heads of consular posts shall rank in each class according to the date of the grant of the *exequatur.*

2. If, however, the head of a consular post before obtaining the *exequatur* is admitted to the exercise of his functions provisionally, his precedence shall be determined according to the date of the provisional admission; this precedence shall be maintained after the granting of the *exequatur.*

3. The order of precedence as between two or more heads of consular posts who obtained the *exequatur* or provisional admission on the same date shall

be determined according to the dates on which their commissions or similar instruments or the notifications referred to in paragraph 3 of article 11 were presented to the receiving State.

4. Acting heads of posts shall rank after all heads of consular posts and, as between themselves, they shall rank according to the dates on which they assumed their functions as acting heads of posts as indicated in the notifications given under paragraph 2 of article 15.

5. Honorary consular officers who are heads of consular posts shall rank in each class after career heads of consular posts, in the order and according to the rules laid down in the foregoing paragraphs.

6. Heads of consular posts shall have precedence over consular officers not having that status.

*Article 17*

*Performance of diplomatic acts by consular officers*
1. In a State where the sending State has no diplomatic mission and is not represented by a diplomatic mission of a third State, a consular officer may, with the consent of the receiving State, and without affecting his consular status, be authorized to perform diplomatic acts. The performance of such acts by a consular officer shall not confer upon him any right to claim diplomatic privileges and immunities.

2. A consular officer may, after notification addressed to the receiving State, act as representative of the sending State to any intergovernmental organization. When so acting, he shall be entitled to enjoy any privileges and immunities accorded to such a representative by customary international law or by international agreements; however, in respect of the performance by him of any consular function, he shall not be entitled to any greater immunity from jurisdiction than that to which a consular officer is entitled under the present Convention.

*Article 18*

*Appointment of the same person by two or more States as a consular officer*
Two or more States may, with the consent of the receiving State, appoint the same person as a consular officer in that State.

*Article 19*

*Appointment of members of consular staff*
1. Subject to the provisions of articles 20, 22 and 23, the sending State may freely appoint the members of the consular staff.

2. The full name, category and class of all consular officers, other than the head of a consular post, shall be notified by the sending State to the receiving State in sufficient time for the receiving State, if it so wishes, to exercise its rights under paragraph 3 of article 23.

3. The sending State may, if required by its laws and regulations, request the receiving State to grant an *exequatur* to a consular officer other than the head of a consular post.

4. The receiving State may, if required by its laws and regulations, grant an *exequatur* to a consular officer other than the head of a consular post.

*Article 20*

*Size of the consular staff*
In the absence of an express agreement as to the size of the consular staff, the receiving State may require that the size of the staff be kept within limits considered by it to be reasonable and normal, having regard to circumstances and conditions in the consular district and to the needs of the particular consular post.

*Article 21*

*Precedence as between consular officers of a consular post*
The order of precedence as between the consular officers of a consular post and any change thereof shall be notified by the diplomatic mission of the sending State or, if that State has no such mission in the receiving State, by the head of the consular post, to the Ministry for Foreign Affairs of the receiving State or to the authority designated by that Ministry.

*Article 22*

*Nationality of consular officers*
1. Consular officers should, in principle, have the nationality of the sending State.

2. Consular officers may not be appointed from among persons having the nationality of the receiving State except with the express consent of that State which may be withdrawn at any time.

3. The receiving State may reserve the same right with regard to nationals of a third State who are not also nationals of the sending State.

*Article 23*

*Persons declared* "non grata"
1. The receiving State may at any time notify the sending State that a consular officer is persona non grata or that any other member of the consular staff is not acceptable. In that event, the sending State shall, as the case may be, either recall the person concerned or terminate his functions with the consular post.

2. If the sending State refuses or fails within a reasonable time to carry out its obligations under paragraph 1 of this article, the receiving State may, as the case may be, either withdraw the *exequatur* from the person concerned or cease to consider him as a member of the consular staff.

3. A person appointed as a member of a consular post may be declared unacceptable before arriving in the territory of the receiving State or, if already in the receiving State, before entering on his duties with the consular post. In any such case, the sending State shall withdraw his appointment.

4. In the cases mentioned in paragraphs 1 and 3 of this article, the receiving State is not obliged to give to the sending State reasons for its decision.

*Article 24*

*Notification to the receiving State of appointments, arrivals and departures*
1. The Ministry for Foreign Affairs of the receiving State or the authority designated by that Ministry shall be notified of:

(*a*) the appointment of members of a consular post, their arrival after appointment to the consular post, their final departure or the termination of their functions and any other changes affecting their status that may occur in the course of their service with the consular post;

(*b*) the arrival and final departure of a person belonging to the family of a member of a consular post forming part of his household and, where appropriate, the fact that a person becomes or ceases to be such a member of the family;

(*c*) the arrival and final departure of members of the private staff and, where appropriate, the termination of their service as such;

(*d*) the engagement and discharge of persons resident in the receiving State as members of a consular post or as members of the private staff entitled to privileges and immunities.

2. When possible, prior notification of arrival and final departure shall also be given.

## SECTION II.
## END OF CONSULAR FUNCTIONS

*Article 25*

*Termination of the functions of a member of a consular post*
The functions of a member of a consular post shall come to an end, inter alia:
(*a*) on notification by the sending State to the receiving State that his functions have come to an end;

(*b*) on withdrawal of the *exequatur*;

(*c*) on notification by the receiving State to the sending State that the receiving State has ceased to consider him as a member of the consular staff.

*Article 26*

*Departure from the territory of the receiving State*
The receiving State shall, even in case of armed conflict, grant to members of the consular post and members of the private staff, other than nationals of the receiving State, and to members of their families forming part of their households irrespective of nationality, the necessary time and facilities to enable them to prepare their departure and to leave at the earliest possible moment after the termination of the functions of the members concerned. In particular, it shall, in case of need, place at their disposal the necessary means of transport for themselves and their property other than property acquired in the receiving State the export of which is prohibited at the time of departure.

*Article 27*

*Protection of consular premises and archives and of the interests of the sending State in exceptional circumstances*
1. In the event of the severance of consular relations between two States:

(*a*) the receiving State shall, even in case of armed conflict, respect and protect the consular premises, together with the property of the consular post and the consular archives;

(*b*) the sending State may entrust the custody of the consular premises, together with the property contained therein and the consular archives, to a third State acceptable to the receiving State;

(*c*) the sending State may entrust the protection of its interests and those of its nationals to a third State acceptable to the receiving State.

2. In the event of the temporary or permanent closure of a consular post, the provisions of subparagraph (*a*) of paragraph 1 of this article shall apply. In addition,

(*a*) if the sending State, although not represented in the receiving State by a diplomatic mission, has another consular post in the territory of that State, that consular post may be entrusted with the custody of the premises of the consular post which has been closed, together with the property contained therein and the consular archives, and, with the consent of the receiving State, with the exercise of consular functions in the district of that consular post; or

(*b*) if the sending State has no diplomatic mission and no other consular post in the receiving State, the provisions of subparagraphs (*b*) and (*c*) of paragraph 1 of this article shall apply.

## CHAPTER II.
## FACILITIES, PRIVILEGES AND IMMUNITIES RELATING TO CONSULAR POSTS, CAREER CONSULAR OFFICERS AND OTHER MEMBERS OF A CONSULAR POST

### SECTION I.
### FACILITIES, PRIVILEGES AND IMMUNITIES RELATING TO A CONSULAR POST

*Article 28*

*Facilities for the work of the consular post*
The receiving State shall accord full facilities for the performance of the functions of the consular post.

*Article 29*

*Use of national flag and coat-of-arms*
1. The sending State shall have the right to the use of its national flag and coat-of-arms in the receiving State in accordance with the provisions of this article.

2. The national flag of the sending State may be flown and its coat-of-arms displayed on the building occupied by the consular post and at the entrance door thereof, on the residence of the head of the consular post and on his means of transport when used on official business.

3. In the exercise of the right accorded by this article regard shall be had to the laws, regulations and usages of the receiving State.

*Article 30*

*Accommodation*
1. The receiving State shall either facilitate the acquisition on its territory, in accordance with its laws and regulations, by the sending State of premises necessary for its consular post or assist the latter in obtaining accommodation in some other way.

2. It shall also, where necessary, assist the consular post in obtaining suitable accommodation for its members.

*Article 31*

*Inviolability of the consular premises*
1. Consular premises shall be inviolable to the extent provided in this article.
2. The authorities of the receiving State shall not enter that part of the consular premises which is used exclusively for the purpose of the work of the consular post except with the consent of the head of the consular post or of his designee or of the head of the diplomatic mission of the sending State. The consent of the head of the consular post may, however, be assumed in case of fire or other disaster requiring prompt protective action.

3. Subject to the provisions of paragraph 2 of this article, the receiving State is under a special duty to take all appropriate steps to protect the consular premises against any intrusion or damage and to prevent any disturbance of the peace of the consular post or impairment of its dignity.

4. The consular premises, their furnishings, the property of the consular post and its means of transport shall be immune from any form of requisition for purposes of national defence or public utility. If expropriation is necessary for such purposes, all possible steps shall be taken to avoid impeding the performance of consular functions, and prompt, adequate and effective compensation shall be paid to the sending State.

*Article 32*

*Exemption from taxation of consular premises*
1. Consular premises and the residence of the career head of consular post of which the sending State or any person acting on its behalf is the owner or lessee shall be exempt from all national, regional or municipal dues and taxes whatsoever, other than such as represent payment for specific services rendered.

2. The exemption from taxation referred to paragraph 1 of this article shall not apply to such dues and taxes if, under the law of the receiving State, they are payable by the person who contracted with the sending State or with the person acting on its behalf.

*Article 33*

*Inviolability of the consular archives and documents*
The consular archives and documents shall be inviolable at all times and wherever they may be.

*Article 34*

*Freedom of movement*
Subject to its laws and regulations concerning zones entry into which is prohibited or regulated for reasons of national security, the receiving State shall ensure freedom of movement and travel in its territory to all members of the consular post.

*Article 35*

*Freedom of communication*
1. The receiving State shall permit and protect freedom of communication on the part of the consular post for all official purposes. In communicating with the Government, the diplomatic missions and other consular posts, wherever situated, of the sending State, the consular post may employ all appropriate means, including diplomatic or consular couriers, diplomatic or consular bags and messages in code or cipher. However, the consular post may install and use a wireless transmitter only with the consent of the receiving State.

2. The official correspondence of the consular post shall be inviolable. Official correspondence means all correspondence relating to the consular post and its functions.

3. The consular bag shall be neither opened nor detained. Nevertheless, if the competent authorities of the receiving State have serious reason to believe that the bag contains something other than the correspondence, documents or articles referred to in paragraph 4 of this article, they may request that the bag be opened in their presence by an authorized representative of the sending State. If this request is refused by the authorities of the sending State, the bag shall be returned to its place of origin.

4. The packages constituting the consular bag shall bear visible external marks of their character and may contain only official correspondence and documents or articles intended exclusively for official use.

5. The consular courier shall be provided with an official document indicating his status and the number of packages constituting the consular bag. Except with the consent of the receiving State he shall be neither a national of the receiving State, nor, unless he is a national of the sending State, a permanent resident of the receiving State. In the performance of his functions he shall be protected by the receiving State. He shall enjoy personal inviolability and shall not be liable to any form of arrest or detention.

6. The sending State, its diplomatic missions and its consular posts may designate consular couriers ad hoc. In such cases the provisions of paragraph 5 of this article shall also apply except that the immunities therein mentioned shall cease to apply when such a courier has delivered to the consignee the consular bag in his charge.
7. A consular bag may be entrusted to the captain of a ship or of a commercial aircraft scheduled to land at an authorized port of entry. He shall be provided with an official document indicating the number of packages constituting the bag, but he shall not be considered to be a consular courier. By arrangement with the appropriate local authorities, the consular post may send one of its members to take possession of the bag directly and freely from the captain of the ship or of the aircraft.

*Article 36*

*Communication and contact with nationals of the sending State*
1. With a view to facilitating the exercise of consular functions relating to nationals of the sending State:

*(a)* consular officers shall be free to communicate with nationals of the sending State and to have access to them. Nationals of the sending State shall have the same freedom with respect to communication with and access to consular officers of the sending State;

(*b*) if he so requests, the competent authorities of the receiving State shall, without delay, inform the consular post of the sending State if, within its consular district, a national of that State is arrested or committed to prison or to custody pending trial or is detained in any other manner. Any communication addressed to the consular post by the person arrested, in prison, custody or detention shall be forwarded by the said authorities without delay. The said authorities shall inform the person concerned without delay of his rights under this subparagraph;

(*c*) consular officers shall have the right to visit a national of the sending State who is in prison, custody or detention, to converse and correspond with him and to arrange for his legal representation. They shall also have the right to visit any national of the sending State who is in prison, custody or detention in their district in pursuance of a judgement. Nevertheless, consular officers shall refrain from taking action on behalf of a national who is in prison, custody or detention if he expressly opposes such action.

2. The rights referred to in paragraph 1 of this article shall be exercised in conformity with the laws and regulations of the receiving State, subject to the proviso, however, that the said laws and regulations must enable full effect

to be given to the purposes for which the rights accorded under this article are intended.

*Article 37*

*Information in cases of deaths, guardianship or trusteeship, wrecks and air accidents*
If the relevant information is available to the competent authorities of the receiving State, such authorities shall have the duty:

(*a*) in the case of the death of a national of the sending State, to inform without delay the consular post in whose district the death occurred;

(*b*) to inform the competent consular post without delay of any case where the appointment of a guardian or trustee appears to be in the interests of a minor or other person lacking full capacity who is a national of the sending State. The giving of this information shall, however, be without prejudice to the operation of the laws and regulations of the receiving State concerning such appointments;

(*c*) if a vessel, having the nationality of the sending State, is wrecked or runs aground in the territorial sea or internal waters of the receiving State, or if an aircraft registered in the sending State suffers an accident on the territory of the receiving State, to inform without delay the consular post nearest to the scene of the occurrence.

*Article 38*

*Communication with the authorities of the receiving State*
In the exercise of their functions, consular officers may address:

(*a*) the competent local authorities of their consular district;

(*b*) the competent central authorities of the receiving State if and to the extent that this is allowed by the laws, regulations and usages of the receiving State or by the relevant international agreements.

*Article 39*

*Consular fees and charges*
1. The consular post may levy in the territory of the receiving State the fees and charges provided by the laws and regulations of the sending State for consular acts.

2. The sums collected in the form of the fees and charges referred to in paragraph 1 of this article, and the receipts for such fees and charges, shall be exempt from all dues and taxes in the receiving State.

## SECTION II.
## FACILITIES, PRIVILEGES AND IMMUNITIES RELATING TO CAREER CONSULAR OFFICERS AND OTHER MEMBERS OF A CONSULAR POST

*Article 40*

*Protection of consular officers*
The receiving State shall treat consular officers with due respect and shall take all appropriate steps to prevent any attack on their person, freedom or dignity.

*Article 41*

*Personal inviolability of consular officers*
1. Consular officers shall not be liable to arrest or detention pending trial, except in the case of a grave crime and pursuant to a decision by the competent judicial authority.

2. Except in the case specified in paragraph 1 of this article, consular officers shall not be committed to prison or be liable to any other form of restriction on their personal freedom save in execution of a judicial decision of final effect.

3. If criminal proceedings are instituted against a consular officer, he must appear before the competent authorities. Nevertheless, the proceedings shall be conducted with the respect due to him by reason of his official position and, except in the case specified in paragraph 1 of this article, in a manner which will hamper the exercise of consular functions as little as possible. When, in the circumstances mentioned in paragraph 1 of this article, it has become necessary to detain a consular officer, the proceedings against him shall be instituted with the minimum of delay.

*Article 42*

*Notification of arrest, detention or prosecution*
In the event of the arrest or detention, pending trial, of a member of the consular staff, or of criminal proceedings being instituted against him, the receiving State shall promptly notify the head of the consular post. Should

the latter be himself the object of any such measure, the receiving State shall notify the sending State through the diplomatic channel.

*Article 43*

*Immunity from jurisdiction*
1. Consular officers and consular employees shall not be amenable to the jurisdiction of the judicial or administrative authorities of the receiving State in respect of acts performed in the exercise of consular functions.

2. The provisions of paragraph 1 of this article shall not, however, apply in respect of a civil action either:

(*a*) arising out of a contract concluded by a consular officer or a consular employee in which he did not contract expressly or impliedly as an agent of the sending State; or

(*b*) by a third party for damage arising from an accident in the receiving State caused by a vehicle, vessel or aircraft.

*Article 44*

*Liability to give evidence*
1. Members of a consular post may be called upon to attend as witnesses in the course of judicial or administrative proceedings. A consular employee or a member of the service staff shall not, except in the cases mentioned in paragraph 3 of this article, decline to give evidence. If a consular officer should decline to do so, no coercive measure or penalty may be applied to him.

2. The authority requiring the evidence of a consular officer shall avoid interference with the performance of his functions. It may, when possible, take such evidence at his residence or at the consular post or accept a statement from him in writing.

3. Members of a consular post are under no obligation to give evidence concerning matters connected with the exercise of their functions or to produce official correspondence and documents relating thereto. They are also entitled to decline to give evidence as expert witnesses with regard to the law of the sending State.

*Article 45*

*Waiver of privileges and immunities*
1. The sending State may waive, with regard to a member of the consular post, any of the privileges and immunities provided for in articles 41, 43 and 44.
2. The waiver shall in all cases be express, except as provided in paragraph 3 of this article, and shall be communicated to the receiving State in writing.

3. The initiation of proceedings by a consular officer or a consular employee in a matter where he might enjoy immunity from jurisdiction under article 43 shall preclude him from invoking immunity from jurisdiction in respect of any counterclaim directly connected with the principal claim.

4. The waiver of immunity from jurisdiction for the purposes of civil or administrative proceedings shall not be deemed to imply the waiver of immunity from the measures of execution resulting from the judicial decision; in respect of such measures, a separate waiver shall be necessary.

*Article 46*

*Exemption from registration of aliens and residence permits*
1. Consular officers and consular employees and members of their families forming part of their households shall be exempt from all obligations under the laws and regulations of the receiving State in regard to the registration of aliens and residence permits.

2. The provisions of paragraph 1 of this article shall not, however, apply to any consular employee who is not a permanent employee of the sending State or who carries on any private gainful occupation in the receiving State or to any member of the family of any such employee.

*Article 47*

*Exemption from work permits*
1. Members of the consular post shall, with respect to services rendered for the sending State, be exempt from any obligations in regard to work permits imposed by the laws and regulations of the receiving State concerning the employment of foreign labour.

2. Members of the private staff of consular officers and of consular employees shall, if they do not carry on any other gainful occupation in the receiving State, be exempt from the obligations referred to in paragraph 1 of this article.

*Article 48*

*Social security exemption*
1. Subject to the provisions of paragraph 3 of this article, members of the consular post with respect to services rendered by them for the sending State, and members of their families forming part of their households, shall be exempt from social security provisions which may be in force in the receiving State.

2. The exemption provided for in paragraph 1 of this article shall apply also to members of the private staff who are in the sole employ of members of the consular post, on condition:

(*a*) that they are not nationals of or permanently resident in the receiving State; and

(*b*) that they are covered by the social security provisions which are in force in the sending State or a third State.

3. Members of the consular post who employ persons to whom the exemption provided for in paragraph 2 of this article does not apply shall observe the obligations which the social security provisions of the receiving State impose upon employers.

4. The exemption provided for in paragraphs 1 and 2 of this article shall not preclude voluntary participation in the social security system of the receiving State, provided that such participation is permitted by that State.

*Article 49*

*Exemption from taxation*
1. Consular officers and consular employees and members of their families forming part of their households shall be exempt from all dues and taxes, personal or real, national, regional or municipal, except:

(*a*) indirect taxes of a kind which are normally incorporated in the price of goods or services;

(*b*) dues or taxes on private immovable property situated in the territory of the receiving State, subject to the provisions of article 32;

(*c*) estate, succession or inheritance duties, and duties on transfers, levied by the receiving State, subject to the provisions of paragraph (*b*) of article 51;

(*d*) dues and taxes on private income, including capital gains, having its source in the receiving State and capital taxes relating to investments made in commercial or financial undertakings in the receiving State;

(*e*) charges levied for specific services rendered;
(*f*) registration, court or record fees, mortgage dues and stamp duties, subject to the provisions of article 32.

2. Members of the service staff shall be exempt from dues and taxes on the wages which they receive for their services.

3. Members of the consular post who employ persons whose wages or salaries are not exempt from income tax in the receiving State shall observe the obligations which the laws and regulations of that State impose upon employers concerning the levying of income tax.

*Article 50*

*Exemption from customs duties and inspection*
1. The receiving State shall, in accordance with such laws and regulations as it may adopt, permit entry of and grant exemption from all customs duties, taxes, and related charges other than charges for storage, cartage and similar services, on:

(*a*) articles for the official use of the consular post;

(*b*) articles for the personal use of a consular officer or members of his family forming part of his household, including articles intended for his establishment. The articles intended for consumption shall not exceed the quantities necessary for direct utilization by the persons concerned.

2. Consular employees shall enjoy the privileges and exemptions specified in paragraph 1 of this article in respect of articles imported at the time of first installation.

3. Personal baggage accompanying consular officers and members of their families forming part of their households shall be exempt from inspection. It may be inspected only if there is serious reason to believe that it contains articles other than those referred to in subparagraph (*b*) of paragraph 1 of this article, or articles the import or export of which is prohibited by the laws and regulations of the receiving State or which are subject to its quarantine laws and regulations. Such inspection shall be carried out in the presence of the consular officer or member of his family concerned.

*Article 51*

*Estate of a member of the consular post or of a member of his family*
In the event of the death of a member of the consular post or of a member of his family forming part of his household, the receiving State:
(*a*) shall permit the export of the movable property of the deceased, with the exception of any such property acquired in the receiving State the export of which was prohibited at the time of his death;

(*b*) shall not levy national, regional or municipal estate, succession or inheritance duties, and duties on transfers, on movable property the presence of which in the receiving State was due solely to the presence in that State of the deceased as a member of the consular post or as a member of the family of a member of the consular post.

*Article 52*

*Exemption from personal services and contributions*
The receiving State shall exempt members of the consular post and members of their families forming part of their households from all personal services, from all public service of any kind whatsoever, and from military obligations such as those connected with requisitioning, military contributions and billeting.

*Article 53*

*Beginning and end of consular privileges and immunities*
1. Every member of the consular post shall enjoy the privileges and immunities provided in the present Convention from the moment he enters the territory of the receiving State on proceeding to take up his post or, if already in its territory, from the moment when he enters on his duties with the consular post.

2. Members of the family of a member of the consular post forming part of his household and members of his private staff shall receive the privileges and immunities provided in the present Convention from the date from which he enjoys privileges and immunities in accordance with paragraph 1 of this article or from the date of their entry into the territory of the receiving State or from the date of their becoming a member of such family or private staff, whichever is the latest.

3. When the functions of a member of the consular post have come to an end, his privileges and immunities and those of a member of his family forming part of his household or a member of his private staff shall normally

cease at the moment when the person concerned leaves the receiving State or on the expiry of a reasonable period in which to do so, whichever is the sooner, but shall subsist until that time, even in case of armed conflict. In the case of the persons referred to in paragraph 2 of this article, their privileges and immunities shall come to an end when they cease to belong to the household or to be in the service of a member of the consular post provided, however, that if such persons intend leaving the receiving State within a reasonable period thereafter, their privileges and immunities shall subsist until the time of their departure.

4. However, with respect to acts performed by a consular officer or a consular employee in the exercise of his functions, immunity from jurisdiction shall continue to subsist without limitation of time.

5. In the event of the death of a member of the consular post, the members of his family forming part of his household shall continue to enjoy the privileges and immunities accorded to them until they leave the receiving State or until the expiry of a reasonable period enabling them to do so, whichever is the sooner.

*Article 54*

*Obligations of third States*

1. If a consular officer passes through or is in the territory of a third State, which has granted him a visa if a visa was necessary, while proceeding to take up or return to his post or when returning to the sending State, the third State shall accord to him all immunities provided for by the other articles of the present Convention as may be required to ensure his transit or return. The same shall apply in the case of any member of his family forming part of his household enjoying such privileges and immunities who are accompanying the consular officer or travelling separately to join him or to return to the sending State.

2. In circumstances similar to those specified in paragraph 1 of this article, third States shall not hinder the transit through their territory of other members of the consular post or of members of their families forming part of their households.

3. Third States shall accord to official correspondence and to other official communications in transit, including messages in code or cipher, the same freedom and protection as the receiving State is bound to accord under the present Convention. They shall accord to consular couriers who have been granted a visa, if a visa was necessary, and to consular bags in transit, the

same inviolability and protection as the receiving State is bound to accord under the present Convention.

4. The obligations of third States under paragraphs 1, 2 and 3 of this article shall also apply to the persons mentioned respectively in those paragraphs, and to official communications and to consular bags, whose presence in the territory of the third State is due to force majeure.

*Article 55*

*Respect for the laws and regulations of the receiving State*
1. Without prejudice to their privileges and immunities, it is the duty of all persons enjoying such privileges and immunities to respect the laws and regulations of the receiving State. They also have a duty not to interfere in the internal affairs of the State.

2. The consular premises shall not be used in any manner incompatible with the exercise of consular functions.

3. The provisions of paragraph 2 of this article shall not exclude the possibility of offices of other institutions or agencies being installed in part of the building in which the consular premises are situated, provided that the premises assigned to them are separate from those used by the consular post. In that event, the said offices shall not, for the purposes of the present Convention, be considered to form part of the consular premises.

*Article 56*

*Insurance against third party risks*
Members of the consular post shall comply with any requirements imposed by the laws and regulations of the receiving State, in respect of insurance against third party risks arising from the use of any vehicle, vessel or aircraft.

*Article 57*

*Special provisions concerning private gainful occupation*
1. Career consular officers shall not carry on for personal profit any professional or commercial activity in the receiving State.

2. Privileges and immunities provided in this chapter shall not be accorded:

(*a*) to consular employees or to members of the service staff who carry on any private gainful occupation in the receiving State;

(*b*) to members of the family of a person referred to in subparagraph (*a*) of this paragraph or to members of his private staff;

(c) to members of the family of a member of a consular post who themselves carry on any private gainful occupation in the receiving State.

## CHAPTER III.
## REGIME RELATING TO HONORARY CONSULAR OFFICERS AND CONSULAR POSTS HEADED BY SUCH OFFICERS

*Article 58*

*General provisions relating to facilities, privileges and immunities*
1. Articles 28, 29, 30, 34, 35, 36, 37, 38 and 39, paragraph 3 of article 54 and paragraphs 2 and 3 of article 55 shall apply to consular posts headed by an honorary consular officer. In addition, the facilities, privileges and immunities of such consular posts shall be governed by articles 59, 60, 61 and 62.

2. Articles 42 and 43, paragraph 3 of article 44, articles 45 and 53 and paragraph 1 of article 55 shall apply to honorary consular officers. In addition, the facilities, privileges and immunities of such consular officers shall be governed by articles 63, 64, 65, 66 and 67.

3. Privileges and immunities provided in the present Convention shall not be accorded to members of the family of an honorary consular officer or of a consular employee employed at a consular post headed by an honorary consular officer.

4. The exchange of consular bags between two consular posts headed by honorary consular officers in different States shall not be allowed without the consent of the two receiving States concerned.

*Article 59*

*Protection of the consular premises*
The receiving State shall take such steps as may be necessary to protect the consular premises of a consular post headed by an honorary consular officer against any intrusion or damage and to prevent any disturbance of the peace of the consular post or impairment of its dignity.

*Article 60*

*Exemption from taxation of consular premises*
1. Consular premises of a consular post headed by an honorary consular officer of which the sending State is the owner or lessee shall be exempt from all national, regional or municipal dues and taxes whatsoever, other than such as represent payment for specific services rendered.

2. The exemption from taxation referred to in paragraph l of this article shall not apply to such dues and taxes if, under the laws and regulations of the receiving State, they are payable by the person who contracted with the sending State.

*Article 61*

*Inviolability of consular archives and documents*
The consular archives and documents of a consular post headed by an honorary consular officer shall be inviolable at all times and wherever they may be, provided that they are kept separate from other papers and documents and, in particular, from the private correspondence of the head of a consular post and of any person working with him, and from the materials, books or documents relating to their profession or trade.

*Article 62*

*Exemption from customs duties*
The receiving State shall, in accordance with such laws and regulations as it may adopt, permit entry of, and grant exemption from all customs duties, taxes, and related charges other than charges for storage, cartage and similar services on the following articles, provided that they are for the official use of a consular post headed by an honorary consular officer: coats-of-arms, flags, signboards, seals and stamps, books, official printed matter, office furniture, office equipment and similar articles supplied by or at the instance of the sending State to the consular post.

*Article 63*

*Criminal proceedings*
If criminal proceedings are instituted against an honorary consular officer, he must appear before the competent authorities. Nevertheless, the proceedings shall be conducted with the respect due to him by reason of his official position and, except when he is under arrest or detention, in a manner which will hamper the exercise of consular functions as little as possible. When it

has become necessary to detain an honorary consular officer, the proceedings against him shall be instituted with the minimum of delay.

*Article 64*

*Protection of honorary consular officers*
The receiving State is under a duty to accord to an honorary consular officer such protection as may be required by reason of his official position.

*Article 65*

*Exemption from registration of aliens and residence permits*
Honorary consular officers, with the exception of those who carry on for personal profit any professional or commercial activity in the receiving State, shall be exempt from all obligations under the laws and regulations of the receiving State in regard to the registration of aliens and residence permits.

*Article 66*

*Exemption from taxation*
An honorary consular officer shall be exempt from all dues and taxes on the remuneration and emoluments which he receives from the sending State in respect of the exercise of consular functions.

*Article 67*

*Exemption from personal services and contributions*
The receiving State shall exempt honorary consular officers from all personal services and from all public services of any kind whatsoever and from military obligations such as those connected with requisitioning, military contributions and billeting.

*Article 68*

*Optional character of the institution of honorary consular officers*
Each State is free to decide whether it will appoint or receive honorary consular officers.

## CHAPTER IV. GENERAL PROVISIONS

*Article 69*

*Consular agents who are not heads of consular posts*

1. Each State is free to decide whether it will establish or admit consular agencies conducted by consular agents not designated as heads of consular post by the sending State.

2. The conditions under which the consular agencies referred to in paragraph 1 of this article may carry on their activities and the privileges and immunities which may be enjoyed by the consular agents in charge of them shall be determined by agreement between the sending State and the receiving State.

*Article 70*

*Exercise of consular functions by diplomatic missions*

1. The provisions of the present Convention apply also, so far as the context permits, to the exercise of consular functions by a diplomatic mission.

2. The names of members of a diplomatic mission assigned to the consular section or otherwise charged with the exercise of the consular functions of the mission shall be notified to the Ministry for Foreign Affairs of the receiving State or to the authority designated by that Ministry.

3. In the exercise of consular functions a diplomatic mission may address:

(*a*) the local authorities of the consular district;

(*b*) the central authorities of the receiving State if this is allowed by the laws, regulations and usages of the receiving State or by relevant international agreements.

4. The privileges and immunities of the members of a diplomatic mission referred to in paragraph 2 of this article shall continue to be governed by the rules of international law concerning diplomatic relations.

*Article 71*

*Nationals or permanent residents of the receiving State*

1. Except insofar as additional facilities, privileges and immunities may be granted by the receiving State, consular officers who are nationals of or permanently resident in the receiving State shall enjoy only immunity from jurisdiction and personal inviolability in respect of official acts performed in the exercise of their functions, and the privileges provided in paragraph 3 of article 44. So far as these consular officers are concerned, the receiving State shall likewise be bound by the obligation laid down in article 42. If criminal proceedings are instituted against such a consular officer, the proceedings

shall, except when he is under arrest or detention, be conducted in a manner which will hamper the exercise of consular functions as little as possible.

2. Other members of the consular post who are nationals of or permanently resident in the receiving State and members of their families, as well as members of the families of consular officers referred to in paragraph 1 of this article, shall enjoy facilities, privileges and immunities only insofar as these are granted to them by the receiving State. Those members of the families of members of the consular post and those members of the private staff who are themselves nationals of or permanently resident in the receiving State shall likewise enjoy facilities, privileges and immunities only insofar as these are granted to them by the receiving State. The receiving State shall, however, exercise its jurisdiction over those persons in such a way as not to hinder unduly the performance of the functions of the consular post.

*Article 72*

*Non-discrimination*

1. In the application of the provisions of the present Convention the receiving State shall not discriminate as between States.

2. However, discrimination shall not be regarded as taking place:

(*a*) where the receiving State applies any of the provisions of the present Convention restrictively because of a restrictive application of that provision to its consular posts in the sending State;

(*b*) where by custom or agreement States extend to each other more favourable treatment than is required by the provisions of the present Convention.

*Article 73*

*Relationship between the present Convention and other international agreements*

1. The provisions of the present Convention shall not affect other international agreements in force as between States Parties to them.

2. Nothing in the present Convention shall preclude States from concluding international agreements confirming or supplementing or extending or amplifying the provisions thereof.

## CHAPTER V.
## FINAL PROVISIONS

*Article 74*

*Signature*
The present Convention shall be open for signature by all States Members of the United Nations or of any of the specialized agencies or Parties to the Statute of the International Court of Justice, and by any other State invited by the General Assembly of the United Nations to become a Party to the Convention, as follows: until 31 October 1963 at the Federal Ministry for Foreign Affairs of the Republic of Austria and subsequently, until 31 March 1964, at the United Nations Headquarters in New York.

*Article 75*

*Ratification*
The present Convention is subject to ratification. The instruments of ratification shall be deposited with the Secretary-General of the United Nations.

*Article 76*

*Accession*
The present Convention shall remain open for accession by any State belonging to any of the four categories mentioned in article 74. The instruments of accession shall be deposited with the Secretary-General of the United Nations.

*Article 77*

*Entry into force*
1. The present Convention shall enter into force on the thirtieth day following the date of deposit of the twenty-second instrument of ratification or accession with the Secretary-General of the United Nations.

2. For each State ratifying or acceding to the Convention after the deposit of the twenty-second instrument of ratification or accession, the Convention shall enter into force on the thirtieth day after deposit by such State of its instrument of ratification or accession.

*Article 78*

*Notifications by the Secretary-General*
The Secretary-General of the United Nations shall inform all States belonging to any of the four categories mentioned in article 74:

(*a*) of signatures to the present Convention and of the deposit of instruments of ratification or accession, in accordance with articles 74, 75 and 76;

(*b*) of the date on which the present Convention will enter into force, in accordance with article 77.

*Article 79*

*Authentic texts*
The original of the present Convention, of which the Chinese, English, French, Russian and Spanish texts are equally authentic, shall be deposited with the Secretary-General of the United Nations, who shall send certified copies thereof to all States belonging to any of the four categories mentioned in article 74.

IN WITNESS WHEREOF the undersigned Plenipotentiaries, being duly authorized thereto by their respective Governments, have signed the present Convention.

DONE at Vienna this twenty-fourth day of April, one thousand nine hundred and sixty-three.

# *Appendix 3*

## UNITED KINGDOM OF GREAT BRITAIN AND NORTHERN IRELAND and SWEDEN

**Agreement concerning the assumption of responsibility for the protection of the diplomatic and consular interests of the United Kingdom Government in the Islamic Republic of Iran by the Government of the Kingdom of Sweden. Signed at London on 27 July 1989**

*Authentic text: English.*
*Registered by the United Kingdom of Great Britain and Northern Ireland on 23 November 1990.*

AGREEMENT BETWEEN THE GOVERNMENT OF THE UNITED KINGDOM OF GREAT BRITAIN AND NORTHERN IRELAND AND THE GOVERNMENT OF THE KINGDOM OF SWEDEN CONCERNING THE ASSUMPTION OF RESPONSIBILITY FOR THE PROTECTION OF THE DIPLOMATIC AND CONSULAR INTERESTS OF THE UNITED KINGDOM GOVERNMENT IN THE ISLAMIC REPUBLIC OF IRAN BY THE GOVERNMENT OF THE KINGDOM OF SWEDEN

The Government of the United Kingdom of Great Britain and Northern Ireland and the Government of the Kingdom of Sweden;

Noting that diplomatic and consular relations between the United Kingdom and the Islamic Republic of Iran have been severed;

Have agreed as follows:

**Article 1**
(1) Sweden undertakes to represent the United Kingdom as protecting power in the Islamic Republic of Iran.

(2) The commission as protecting power comprises administrative, humanitarian and consular matters. If the commission is to be extended to cover other matters, a separate agreement to that effect is required.

(3) In dealing with protection matters, the protecting power may avoid taking action that could damage its position or good name in the receiving country, or in relation to any other country. In case of doubt in dealing with a matter, the Ministry for Foreign Affairs in Stockholm shall take the decision. This always applies to letters and other messages from the commissioning country to the receiving country.

**Article 2**

(1) An Interests Section for the commissioning country under the Swedish Ambassador shall be set up at the Swedish Embassy in Tehran. Staff employed at the Interests Section may on the one hand be Swedish officials, on the other locally engaged personnel of the commissioning country. The protecting power undertakes, where necessary, to obtain permission from the receiving country with regard to the employment of career officials sent out by the commissioning country.

(2) The Parties agree that diplomatic courier and secure telegraphic communications may not be established between the commissioning country and its Interests Section at the protecting power without the approval of the receiving country.

**Article 3**

The Department for the commission as protecting power at the Ministry for Foreign Affairs (B Department) shall maintain contact with the commissioning country's representatives in Sweden in all matters relating to the commission. In appropriate cases direct communication may, with the consent of the protecting power, be maintained between the commissioning country and the Swedish Embassy in Tehran. However, the protecting power shall be kept informed of the nature and extent of such contacts.

**Article 4**

(1) The premises taken into custody by the protecting power are listed in the annex to this Agreement. The Parties shall exchange information about the contents of the premises taken into custody.

(2) The protecting power is not under an obligation to accept care of the property of citizens of the commissioning power.

**Article 5**

( 1 ) The protecting power shall take good care of the property received. If an official sent out by the commissioning country has taken the property into his care, the responsibility for it rests with him. The representatives of the protecting power shall assist him, if the official requests such assistance.

(2) If property belonging to the commissioning country is used by agreement between the Parties as a residence or office for a member of the staff connected with the mission of protection, no rent shall be charged, but the protecting power shall be responsible for the maintenance of the property. Other properties may be leased by the protecting power on terms to be agreed.

(3) Sale of property belonging to the commissioning country through the agency of the protecting power may not take place without the permission of the commissioning country.

**Article 6**
The commissioning country undertakes to reimburse the protecting power for all expenses incurred in the protection of its interests. B Department shall inform the commissioning country's Embassy in Stockholm of the amount.

**Article 7**
The bank deposits of the commissioning country in the name of the British Interests Section Tehran shall be transferred to special accounts in the Swedish Embassy's name.

**Article 8**
Disputes arising between the Parties to this Agreement relating to the commission as protecting power shall be settled by diplomatic means. If a settlement cannot be reached in that way, the dispute shall be submitted to arbitration according to a procedure agreed between the Parties.

**Article 9**
This Agreement shall enter into force on the date of signature and shall remain valid until the commissioning country, having re-established relations with the receiving country, notifies the protecting power of the assumption of normal diplomatic and consular functions. The provisions of Article 8 of this Agreement shall also apply to disputes arising in connection with the termination of the commission as protecting power.

In witness whereof, the undersigned, duly authorized thereto by their respective Governments, have signed this Agreement.

Done in duplicate in the English language at London this 27th day of July 1989.

*Appendix 4*

# CONVENTION OF GUUAM MEMBER STATES ON MUTUAL RENDERING OF ASSISTANCE IN CONSULAR MATTERS

**(entry into force 9 December 2002)**

The States Parties to the present Convention, hereinafter referred to as "the Parties", with the purposes of further development of the cooperation in consular field, striving in the interests of its citizens to improve the system of protection of their legitimate rights and interests within the territories of third countries, striving to develop the provisions of Vienna Convention on Consular Relations dated 24 April 1963, as well as of relevant bilateral conventions, reaffirming that the norms of international law, multilateral and bilateral international treaties shall be applied relating to the issues that are not stipulated for by this Convention, have decided to conclude the present Convention and have agreed as follows:

**Article 1**
The Parties shall promote comprehensive cooperation of consular services in various spheres of consular activities and shall exchange the experience of their work through consultations, organization of seminars, exchange of trainees and establishment of various types of connections between themselves.

**Article 2**
The Parties by mutual consent in each specific case shall render each other mutual assistance in third states by approbation of the latter in cases when there are no diplomatic and consular missions of one of the Parties, regarding protection of rights and interests of the citizens of the Parties.
This assistance shall be rendered within the framework of competence of diplomatic or consular mission and shall concern:

- informing through diplomatic channels about accidents or deaths of citizens of the Parties;

- rendering of assistance, when possible, to the persons who have suffered from accidents or emergencies, and informing of consular service of relevant Party;

- assistance to the search of missing persons with subsequent transmission of obtained information to consular service of the state of their citizenship;

- obtaining information about the citizens of the Parties who have been detained or arrested within the state of residence, and informing of consular service of the state of their citizenship;

- informing about the issues of medical and legal assistance within the state of residence through providing data about relevant specialists;

- requesting and transmission of documents necessary for protection of legitimate interests of citizens regarding social, legal, hereditary, property and other matters;

- study of consular-related matters of activity of the state of residence and mutual informing about them.

**Article 3**
The Parties shall inform each other about attempts of use of forged passports and visas and falsification of other documents by the citizens of the Parties.

**Article 4**
Financial assistance, repatriation costs and other possible expenditures caused by rendering assistance in accordance with Article 2 of this Convention, shall be covered at the expense of the country of citizenship of the victim.

**Article 5**
Consular fees for the actions of a Party conducted to protect the rights and interests of legal entities and individuals of other Parties shall be collected at the rate of consular fees of the first Party to compensate its expenditures for the mentioned actions.

**Article 6**
The issues of protection of rights and interests of the citizens of the Parties shall be settled through diplomatic channels by mutual consent in each specific case, proceeding from possibilities and competence of diplomatic and consular missions of the Parties.

**Article 7**
The Parties shall exchange through diplomatic channels the lists of their diplomatic and consular missions in third countries and shall subsequently inform each other about their opening and closing.

**Article 8**
The present Convention is without prejudice to the obligations of the Parties under other international treaties to which they are parties.

**Article 9**
The present Convention may be amended and supplemented by mutual consent. Amendments and supplements shall be made in the form of separate protocols, which shall constitute integral part of the present Convention and shall enter into force in accordance with Article 10 of the present Convention.

**Article 10**
The present Convention shall enter into force-on the date of deposit of the third notification about fulfillment by the states parties to the present Convention of internal procedures necessary for the present Convention to enter into force. In respect of the Parties that deposit their notifications after such date, the Convention shall enter into force on the date of receipt by the depositary of such notification.

**Article 11**
The present Convention shall be open for accession by other states that acquired membership in the GUUAM and share the objectives and principles of the Convention.

The accession to the present Convention shall be effected by the deposit of the instrument of accession with the depositary. For acceding Party the Convention shall enter into force on the date of receipt by the depositary of the instrument of accession.

**Article 12**
Each Party may denounce the present Convention by written notification addressed to the depositary and sent through diplomatic channels. For such Party denunciation shall take effect three months after the date of receipt of the notification by the depositary.

Done at the city of Yalta on the 7th of June 2001 in a single true copy in the Azerbaijani, English, Georgian, Moldovian, Russian, Uzbek and Ukrainian languages, each of them being authentic.

The true copy shall be deposited in the Cabinet of Ministers of Ukraine, which shall be depositary of the present Convention, and which shall send its certified copy to the each member state of the present Convention.

# *Bibliography*


Aceves, W.J.: "International Decisions" in *The American Journal of International Law*, Vol. 92, No. 3, United States, 1998

---------. "The Vienna Convention on Consular Relations: Recent Development" in *ACLU International Civil Liberties Report*, United States, 2003

Addo, M.K.: "Interim Measures of Protection for Rights under the Vienna Convention on Consular Relations" in *European Journal of International Law*, Vol. 10, No. 4, Italy, 1998

Aeschleman, N.L.: "The Vienna Convention on Consular Relations: Quo Vadis America?" in *Santa Clara Law Review*, Vol. 45, No. 4, United States, 2005

Agüeras, J.M.P.: *La Adopción Consular*, Spain, 1990

Ahmad, M.A.: "*L'institution consulaire et le droit international*" in *Études de la Convention du 24 avril 1963 sur les Relations Consulaires et la pratique des États dans ce domaine*, France, 1973

Allary-Valentin, J.: "*Consuls et Navigation Maritime*" in *Annuaire de l'A.A.A.*, Vol. 49-50, the Netherlands, 1980

Amerasinghe, C.F.: *Diplomatic Protection*, United Kingdom, 2008

Antokoletz, D.: *Manual Diplomático y Consular*, Argentina, 1928

---------. *Tratado Teorico y Practico de Derecho Diplomatico y Consular*, Argentina, 1948

*Annuaire de la Commission du Droit International*, 1957, Vol. II

*Annuaire de la Commission du Droit International*, 1960, Vol. II

*Annuaire de la Commission du Droit International*, 1961, Vol. II

*Annuaire de la Commission du Droit International*, 1966, Vol. II

*Annuaire de l'Institut de Droit International*, 1889-1892

*Annuaire de l'Institut de Droit International*, Vol. XVII, 1892-1894

*Annuaire de l'Institut de Droit International*, 1896

Arangio-Ruiz, V., Guarino, A., and Pugliese, G.: *Il Diritto Romano*, Italy, 1980

Aust, A.: *Modern Treaty Law and Practice*, United Kingdom, 2000

Barduzzi, C.E.: *La Giurisdizione Consolare nelle terre islamiche, nell'Estremo Oriente, negli Stati Vassalli, nei Protettorati, con un'appendice sugli ordinamenti giudiziari coloniali*, Italy, 1909

Beckett, W.E.: "Consular Immunities" in *British Yearbook of International Law*, Vol. XXI, United Kingdom, 1944

Berridge, G.R., *et al.*: *Diplomatic Theory from Machiavelli to Kissinger*, United Kingdom, 2001
Berridge, G.R.: *Diplomacy – Theory and Practice*, United Kingdom, 2002
Biscottini, G.: *Manuale di Diritto Consolare*, Italy, 1969
Bishop, A. N.: "The enforceable rights to consular notification and access in the United States: What's changed since in the *LaGrand case*?" in *Houston Journal of International Law*, Vol. 25. No. 1, 2002
Bleimaier, J.K.: "Recognition to be accorded the Quasi-Judicial acts of foreign consul" in *Annuaire de l'A.A.A.*, vol. 49-50, the Netherlands, 1980
Bohn, L.A.: "Understanding the Imposition of Capital Punishment on Foreign Nationals in the United States as a Human Rights Violation" in *Wisconsin International Law Journal*, Vol. 21 No. 4, United States, 2003
Bonfils, H.: *Droit International Publique*, France, 1914
Borchard, E.M.: *The Diplomatic Protection of Citizens Abroad or the Law of International Claims*, United States, 1915
Bourgnon, E.: *Consulats et consuls*, Switzerland, 1968
Bradley, C.A.: "*Sanchez-Llamas v. Oregon*" in *The American Journal of International Law*, United States, 2006
Bratt, M. : "Status and functions of honorary consuls" in *Annuaire de l'A.A.A.*, Vol. 49-50, the Netherlands, 1980
Brierly, J.L.: *The Law of Nations*, United Kingdom, 1963
Brownlie, I.: *Principles of Public International Law*, United Kingdom, 1998

Cançado Trindade, A.A.: "The Humanization of Consular Law: The Impact of Advisory Opinion No. 16 (1999) of the Inter-American Court of Human Rights on International Case-law and Practice" in *Chinese Journal of International Law*, Vol. 6, No. 1, China, 2007
Candela, M.: "Judicial Notification: A Simple Solution to Ensure Compliance with the Vienna Convention on Consular Relations" in *Pace International Review*, Vol. 18, No. 1, 2006
Candioti, A.M.: *Historia de la Institución Consular en la Antigüedad y en la Edad Media*, Argentina, 1925
Calvo, C.: *Le Droit International, Théorique et Pratique*, France, 1870
Carter, L.E.: "Lessons from *Avena*: The Inadequacy of Clemency and Judicial Proceedings for Violations of the Vienna Convention on Consular Relations" in *Duke Journal of International and Comparative Law*, Vol. 15, United States, 2005
Cerna, C.M.: "The right to consular notification as a human right" in *Suffolk Transnational Law Review*, Vol. 31, No. 2, United States, 2008
Chin, D.C.: "The Cultural Defense: Beyond Exclusion, Assimilation, and Guilty Liberalism" in *California Law Review*, Vol. 82, United States, 1994

Choi, W.M.: "Diplomatic and Consular Law in the Internet Age" in *Singapore Yearbook of International Law*, Vol. 10, Singapore, 2006

Constantin, E.: "Consular Relations" in *Encyclopedia of Public International Law* (R. Bernhardt, ed.), the Netherlands, 1981

Cussy, de, F.: *Dictionnaire ou Manuel-Lexique du Diplomate et du Consul*, Leipzig, 1846

---------. *Réglements Consulaires des Principaux États Maritimes de l'Europe et de l'Amerique*, Leipzig, 1851

Czubinski, Z.A.: "Consular Financial Privileges in the light of the 1963 Vienna Convention on Consular Relations" in *Annuaire de l'A.A.A.*, Vol. 49-50, the Netherlands, 1980

Deck Harrill, E.: "Exorcising the Ghost: Finding a Right and a Remedy in Article 36 of the Vienna Convention on Consular Relations" in *South Carolina Law Review*, Vol. 55, United States, 2004

Deek, J.A.: "A New Miranda" in *Vanderbilt Journal of Transnational Law*, Vol. 31, United States, 1998

Denza, E.: *Diplomatic Law, a Commentary on the Vienna Convention on Diplomatic Relations*, United Kingdom, 1998

Dervishi, P.: "No remedies for violations of the foreign national's right to consular notification" in *Florida Journal of International Law*, Vol. 15, No. 4, United States, 2003

Diamond, J.: *Guns, Germs, and Steel – The Fates of Human Societies*, United States, 1997

Dinstein, Y.: *Consular Immunity from Judicial Process*, Israel, 1966

Doumbe-Bille, S., and Gherari, H. , eds.: *La Protection Consulaire*, France, 2006

Dugard, J.R.: *First Report on Diplomatic Protection*, International Law Commission, 52nd session, A/C.N.4/506, 2000

Dupuy, P.-M.: *Droit international public*, France, 2002

El Ganzory, A.E.: "Consular Relations and Unrecognized Regimes" in *Revue Egyptienne de Droit International*, Vol. 34, Egypt, 1978

Elkind, J.B.: *Interim Protection: A Functional Approach*, the Netherlands, 1981

Esperson: *Diritto Diplomatico e Giuridizione Internazionale Marittima*, Italy, 1874

Faucille, P.: *Traité de Droit International Publique*, France, 1921-26

Faust, J.P.: "*Breard* and Treaty-Based Rights Under the Consular Convention" in *The American Journal of International Law*, Vol. 92, United States, 1998

Ferris, K.E.: "Violation of Vienna Convention on Consular Relations does not warrant suppression of evidence" in *Suffolk Transnational Law Review*, Vol. XXIX, No. 1, United States, 2005

Fragola, M.: *Nozioni di Diritto Diplomatico e Consolare – Tecnica Prassi Esperienza*, Italy, 2004

Franklin, W.M.: *Protection of Foreign Interests: A Study in Diplomatic and Consular Practice*, United States, 1946

Freeman, C.W., Jr.: *The Diplomat's Handbook*, United States, 1997

Gamboa, M.J.: "Notarial Services of Consuls" in *Elements of Diplomatic and Consular Practice – A Glossary*, the Philippines, 1966

Garbesi, G.C.: *Consular Authority over Seamen from the United States Point of View*, the Netherlands, 1968

Garnett, R.: "The precarious position of embassy and consular employees in the United Kingdom" in *The International and Comparative Law Quarterly*, Vol. 54, No. 3, United Kingdom, 2005

Giuliano, M., Scovazzi, T., and Treves, T.: *Diritto Internazionale – II, Gli Aspetti Giuridici della Coesitenza degli Stati*, Italy, 1983

Gray, C.: "The Choice between Restitution and Compensation" in *European Journal of International Law*, 10, Italy, 1999

Greene, G.: *The Honorary Consul*, United Kingdom, 1973

Greffenius, R.: "Selling *Medellín*: The Entourage of Litigation Surrounding the Vienna Convention on Consular Relations and the Weight of ICJ Opinions in the Domestic Sphere" in *American University International Law*, Vol. 23, No. 5, United States, 2008

Gross, L.: *Selected Essays on International Law and Organization*, United States, 1993

Guesalaga, A.: *Derecho Diplomático y Consular con los últimos casos de controversias entre los estados*, Argentina, 1900

Guggenheim, P.: *Traité de Droit International Publique*, Switzerland, 1953

Haraszti, G.: *Some Fundamental Problems of the Law of Treaties*, Hungary, 1973

Heyking, A.: *A Practical Guide for Russian Consular Officers and All Persons having Relations with Russia*, United Kingdom, 1916

---------. "*La théorie et la pratique des services consulaires*" in *Receuil des Cours, The Hague Academy of International Law*, Vol. 34, 1930-IV, 1930

Herrada, Z.R.M.: "*El Surgimiento de un Nuevo Derecho Consular Internacional (Política Exterior, Migraciones, Derechos Humanos y Relaciones Consulares en el Contexto de la Globalización)*" in *Revista de la Sociedad Peruana de Derecho Internacional*, No. 132, Peru, 2006

Herz, M., ed.: *The Consular Dimension of Diplomacy*, United States, 1983

Holladay Latané, J.: *A History of American Foreign Policy*, United States, 1934

House of Lords: European Union Committee 10th Report of Session: *The Treaty of Lisbon: an impact assessment*, Volume I, United Kingdom, 2007-2008

Iovane, M.: *La riparazione nella teoria e nella prassi dell'illecito internazionale*, Italy, 1990

Irti, N.: *Studi sul Formalismo Negoziale*, Italy, 1997

Irrizarry, Y.: *Traité sur les Functions Internationales des Consuls*, France, 1937

James, A., and Warren, M.: *Equal Protection: Consular Assistance and Criminal Justice Procedures in the USA, An Introductory Guide for Consulates*, United States, 2002

Jennings, R., and Watts, A.: *Oppenheim's International Law*, United Kingdom, 1992

Kemp Parker, P.: "When a Foreign Child Comes Into Care: Has the Consul Been Notified?" in *Child Law Practice*, Vol. 19, United States, 2001

Kadish, M.J.: "Article 36 of the Vienna Convention on Consular Relations: A Search for the Right to Consul" in *Michigan Journal of International Law*, Vol. 18, issue 4, United States, 1997

Kadish, M.J. and Olson, C.C.: "*Sanchez-Llamas v. Oregon* and Article 36 of the Vienna Convention on Consular Relations: The Supreme Court, the Right to Consul and Remediation" in *Michigan Journal of International Law,* Vol. 27, No. 4, United States, 2006

Kelsen, H.: *Principles of International Law*, United States, 1952

Kessler, J.B.: "Perspective: The Lawyer's Intercultural Communication Problems with Clients of Diverse Cultures" in *North Western Journal of International Law and Business*, Vol. 9, United States, 1988

Kho, S.: "Article 73 of the Vienna Convention on Consular Relations: the Relationship between the Vienna Consular Convention and Other International Consular Agreements" in *Chinese Yearbook of International Law and Affairs*, Vol. 13, Taiwan, 1995

Klabbers, J.: "Executing Mr. Breard" in *Nordic Journal of International Law*, Vol. 67, Denmark, 1998

Kontou, N.: *The Termination and Revision of Treaties in the Light of New Customary International Law*, United Kingdom, 1994

Koskenniemi, M.: *The Gentle Civilizer of Nations – The Rise and Fall of International Law 1870-1960*, United Kingdom, 2001

Kundera, M.: *Testaments Betrayed*, United Kingdom, 1993

Künzli, A.: "Case Concerning Mexican Nationals" in *Leiden Journal of International Law*, Vol. 18, No. 1, United Kingdom, 2005

---------. "Exercising Diplomatic Protection: The Fine Line Between Litigation, Demarches and Consular Assistance" in *Heildelberg Journal of International Law*, Vol. 66, No. 2, Germany, 2006

Kussbach, E.: "Vienna Convention on Consular Relations (1963)" in *Encylcopedia of Public International Law* (R. Bernhardt, ed.), the Netherlands, 1981

Lauterpacht, E.: *International Law Reports*, United Kingdom, 2001

Lauterpacht, H.: Lauterpacht's Revision of Oppenheim in *International Protection of Human Rights* (L.B. Sohn and T. Buergenthal, eds.), United States, 1973

---------. *International Law: The Law of Peace*, United Kingdom, 1978

Lee, L.T.: *Consular Law and Practice*, United Kingdom, 1961

---------. *Vienna Convention on Consular Relations*, the Netherlands, 1966

---------. *Consular Law and Consular Practice*, United Kingdom, 1991

Lee, L.T., and Quigley, J.: *Consular Law and Consular Practice*, United Kingdom, 2008

Lehr, E.: "*De quelques modifications à apporter à l'organisation du corps consulaire et de la création d'agents commerciaux*" in *Revue de Droit International et de Législation Comparée*, Tome XXII, Belgium, 1890

Lesaffer, R.: "Medieval Canon Law of Contract and Early Modern Treaty Law" in *Journal of the History of International Law*, Vol. 2, Issue 2, Germany, 2000

Libera, K.: *Principles of International Consular Law*, Poland, 1960

Lillich, R.B.: *The Human Rights of Aliens in Contemporary International Law*, United States, 1984

Lowe, V.: "Diplomatic Law: Protecting Powers" in *International and Comparative Law Quarterly*, Vol. 39, United Kingdom, 1990

Macina, A.: "*Avena and Other Mexican Nationals*: The Litmus for *LaGrand* and the Future of Consular Rights in the United States" in *California Western International Law Journal*, Vol. 34, No. 1, United States, 2003

Mahlouf, A.M.: *Derecho Diplomático, Derecho Consular y Normativa Costaricense*, Costa Rica, 1990

Mahmoud Mostafa, M.: "Crisis in diplomatic relations case concerning United States diplomatic and consular staff in Tehran" in *Egyptian Review of International Law*, No. 4, Egypt, 1981

Mani, V.S.: "The Right to Consular Assistance as a Basic Human Right of Aliens: A Review of the ICJ Order dated 3 March 1999" in *The Indian Journal of International Law*, Vol. 39, India, 1999

Marcantonatos, L.G.: *Les Relations Consulaires aux termes de la Convention de Vienne du 24 avril 1963*, Greece, 1974

Maresca, A.: *Convenzione di Vienna sulle relazioni consolari*, Italy, 1984

McNair, A.: *Law of Treaties*, United Kingdom, 1961

McHugh, J.T, and Pacy, J.S.: *Diplomats Without a Country - Baltic Diplomacy, International Law, and the Cold War*, United States, 2001

Mendenhall, M.: "A Case for Consular Notification: Treaty Obligation as a Matter of Life and Death" in *Southwestern University Journal of Law and Trade in the Americas*, Vol. 8, United States, 2002

Mennecke, M.: "Towards the Humanization of the Vienna Convention on Consular Relations – The *LaGrand* case before the ICJ" in *The German Yearbook of International Law*, No. 44, Germany, 2001

Misson, P.L., Berthe E., Delree C, and Kaëns L.: *La protection diplomatique et consulaire est-elle un droit fondamental?*, Belgium, 2007

Montero, R.A.: *El Matrimonio Consular*, Spain, 1991

Morello, A.: *L'Atto Notarile*, Italy, 1977

Moroeiul, M.: *Manuel des Agents Consulaires Française et Étrangers*, France, 1850

Murphy, S.D.: "Implementation of ICJ's LaGrand Decision" in *The American Journal of International Law*, Vol. 97, United States, 2003

Nafziger, J.A.R.: "Review of Visa Denials by Consular Officers" in *Washington Law Review*, Vol. 66, No.1, United States, 1991

Nahlik, S.: "*Tendance contemporaine à assimiler le statut juridique des consuls à celui des diplomates*" in *Annuaire de l'A.A.A.*, Vol. 49-50, the Netherlands, 1980

(do) Nascimento e Silva, G.E.: *Dictionary in International Law*, the Netherlands, 1972

Nava, S.: *Corso di Diritto di legazione e consolare*, Italy, 1956

Nicolson, H.: *The Congress of Vienna*, United Kingdom, 1946

Ninagawa, A.: "*L'histoire ancienne du Japon et le droit international*" in *Revue Générale de Droit International Public, Deuxième Série, Tome I*, France, 1918

Obregón, L.: "The Forgotten 19th Century: A New History of a 'Latin American' International Law" in *The Hague Yearbook of International Law*, the Netherlands, 2000

Ochaita, Carlos Laios: *Derecho Diplomático y Consular*, Guatemala, 1995

Orakhelashvili, A.: "Judicial Competence and Judicial Remedies in the *Avena* case" in *Leiden Journal of International Law*, United Kingdom, 2005

Ostrovsky, A.A. and REavis, B.E.: "*Rebus Sic Stantibus*: Notification of Consular Rights after *Medellín*" in *Michigan Journal of International Law*, Vol. 27, United States, 2006

Oxman, B.H.: "Jurisdiction and the Power to Indicate Interim Measures" in *The International Court of Justice at a Crossroads* (L.F. Domrosch, ed.), 1987

Pérez Sarmiento, J.M.: *Manual Consular Colombiano*, Colombia, 1915

Pergantis, V.: "Towards a 'Humanization' of Diplomatic Protection?" in 66 *Zeitschrift für Ausländisches Offentliches Recht und Völkerrecht*, Germany, 2006

Perruchoud, R.: "Consular Protection and Assistance" in *International Migration Law* (Cholewinski, R., Perruchoud, R., and MacDonald, E., eds.) , the Netherlands, 2007

Piotrowicz, R.: "The Australian-Hungarian Consular Treaty of 1988 and the Regulation of Dual Nationality" in *Sydney Law Review*, Vol. 12, Australia, 1990

Politi, M.: *Funzioni Consolari e Rapporti tra Ordinamenti*, Italy, 1978

Pradier-Fodéré, P.: *Traité de Droit International Publique, Tome IV*, France, 1888

Przetacznik, F.: "The Protection of Individual Persons in Traditional International Law (Diplomatic and Consular Protection)" in *Österreichische Zeitschrift für öffentliches Recht*, Vol. 21, Austria, 1971

Pulkowski, D.: "Testing Compliance Theories: Towards United States Obedience of International Law in the *Avena Case*" in *Leiden Journal of International Law*, Vol. 19, No. 2, United Kingdom, 2006

Quercia, P., ed.: *Fare Italia nel Mondo: le sfide post-globali delle nuove relazioni internazionali*, Italy, 2009

Quigley, J.: "Procedural Limitations on Capital Punishment: The Case of Foreign Nationals" in *ILSA Journal of International and Comparative Law*, Vol. 6, United States, 2000

---------. "Application of Consular Rights to Foreign Nationals: Standard for Reversal of a Criminal Conviction" in *ILSA Journal of International and Comparative Law*, Vol. 11, No. 2, United States, 2005

---------. "The United States' Withdrawal from International Court of Justice Jurisdiction in consular cases" in *Duke Journal of Comparative and International Law*, United States, Vol. 19, No. 2, 2009

Raz, J. : "Human Rights Without Foundations" in *The Philosophy of International Law* (Besson, S. and Tasioulas, J., eds.), United Kingdom, 2010

Reisman, W.M., and Arsanjani, M.H.: "No Exit? A Preliminary Examination of the Legal Consequences of United States' Notification of Withdrawal from the Optional Protocol to the Vienna Convention on Consular Relations" in *Promoting Justice, Human Rights and Conflict Resolution Through International Law - Liber Amicorum Lucius Caflisch* (M. G. Kohen, ed.), The Netherlands, 2006

Reuter, P.: *Introduction to Law of Treaties*, Switzerland, 1995

Revillard, M.: "*Les attributions notariales et le règlement des successions par les consuls*" in *Annuaire de l'A.A.A.*, Vol. 49-50, the Netherlands, 1980

Rigaux, F., and Fallon, M.: *Droit international privé, Tome II*, Belgium, 1993

Röling, B.V.A.: "Aspects of the case concerning United States diplomatic and consular staff in Tehran" in *Netherlands Yearbook of International Law*, Vol. XI, the Netherlands, 1980

Rosenne, Sh.: *The Law of Treaties, Guide to Legislative History of Vienna Convention*, the Netherlands, 1970

---------. *Breach of Treaty*, United Kingdom, 1984

---------. *Developments in the law of treaties, 1946-1986*, United States, 1989

---------. *The Perplexities of Modern International Law*, The Netherlands, 2004

Root, E.: "The Basis of Protection of Citizens Residing Abroad" in *The American Journal of International Law*, Vol. 4, United States, 1910

Sainio, T.: "Immunity from Jurisdiction in Finland's Consular Treaties" in *Essays in Honour of Erik Castrén*, Finland, 1979

Salles, G.: *L'Institution des Consulats*, France, 1898

Samson, E.: "Revisiting *Miranda* After *Avena*: The Implications of *Mexico v. United States of America* for the Implementation of the Vienna Convention on Consular Relations in the United States" in *Fordham International Law Journal*, Vol. 29, United States, 2006

Schiffman, H. S.: "The Evolving Legal Landscape of the Vienna Convention on Consular Relations in US Death Penalty Cases" in *Santa Clara Law Review*, Vol. 42, No. 4, United States, 2002

Sen, B.: *A Diplomat's Handbook of International Law and Practice*, the Netherlands, 1988

Shank, S.A., and Quigley, J.: "Foreigners on Texas' Death Row and the Right to Access to a Consul" in *St. Mary's Law Journal*, Vol. 26, no. 3, United States, 1995

Sinagra, A.: "*Privilegi e Immunità dell'Agente Diplomatico e Consolare Cittadino dello Stato di Accreditamento*" in *Studi in Ricordo di Antonio Filippo Panzera, Vol. II, Diritto Internazionale*, Italy, 2000

Sinclair, I.: *The Vienna Convention on the Law of Treaties*, United Kingdom, 1984

Sinnott, J.P.: *A Practical Guide to Document Authentication: Legalization of Notarised & Certified Documents 2002*, United States, 2001

Slaughter, A.M.: "Court to Court" in *The American Journal of International Law*, Vol. 92, United States, 1998

Springrose, L.J.: "Strangers in a Strange Land: the Rights of Non-Citizens under article 36 of the Vienna Convention on Consular Relations" in *Georgetown Immigration Law Review*, Vol. 14, No. 1, United States, 1999

Sridhar, A.: "Creating juridical remedies for violations of the Vienna Convention on Consular Relations: A Proposed Resolution to *Medellín v. Dretke*" in *Stanford Journal of Civil Rights and Civil Liberties*, Vol. 2, United States, 2006

Starke, J.G.: *Introduction to International Law*, United Kingdom, 1989

Stewart, I.: *Consular Privileges and Immunities*, United States, 1926

Stirling-Zanda, S.: "Obtaining judicial enforcement of individual conventional rights: The Consular Convention at the ICJ and at the Inter-American Court" in *Archiv des Völkerrechts*, Vol. 42, No. 2, Germany, 2004

Svarlien, O.: *An Introduction to the Law of Nations*, United States, 1955

Thomas, C.: "Neo-Victorianism and the Ideology of Globalization" in *The Hague Yearbook of International Law*, the Netherlands, 2000

Thirlway, H.: *International Customary Law and Codification – An Examination of the Continuing Role of Custom in the Present Period of Codification of International Law*, United Kingdom, 1972

*Time Magazine*, No. 4, January 26 1980

---------. No. 4, January 26, 1981

Tinta, M.F.: "Due process and the Right to Life in the Context of the Vienna Convention on Consular Relations: Arguing the *LaGrand case*" in *European Journal of International Law*, Vol. 12, no. 2, Italy, 2001

Torroba Sacristan, J.: *Derecho Consular*, Spain, 1993

Trainer, K.: "The Vienna Convention on Consular Relations in the United States Courts" in *The Transnational Lawyer*, Vol. 13, No. 1, United States, 2000

Trajano Mera, J.: *Cónsules y Consulados*, Argentina, 1910

Tranel, A. M.: "The ruling of the ICJ in *Avena And Other Mexican Nationals*: Enforcing the Right to Consular Assistance in US Jurisprudence" in *American University International Law Review*, Vol. 20, No. 2, United States, 2004

Uribe, V.M.: "Consuls at Work: Universal Instruments o Human Rights and Consular Protection in the Context of Consular Justice" in *Houston Journal of International Law*, Vol. 19, United States, 1997

Vadnais, M.: "A Diplomatic Morass: An Argument Against Judicial Involvement in Article 36 of the Vienna Convention on Consular Relations" in *UCLA Law Review*, Vol. 47, No. 1, United States, 1999

Vallarta Marión, J.L.: "*Obligación de informar a todo detenido extranjero de su derecho a la protección consular, según el derecho internacional*" in *Revista de la Facultad de Derecho de México, Universidad Autónoma de México*, Vol. 54, No. 243, Mexico, 2004

Viault, B.S.: *Modern European History*, United States, 1990

Vignali, H.A.: *Lecciónes de Derecho Diplomático y Consular, Tomo I*, Uruguay, 1992

Villiger, M.E.: *Customary International Law and Treaties*, the Netherlands, 1985

Von Asbeck, F.M.: "*Le régime des étrangers dans les colonies*" in *Recueil des cours III Tome 61 de la Collection*, The Hague Academy of International Law, the Netherlands, 1937

Weiland, S. J.: "The Vienna Convention on Consular Relations: persuasive force or binding law?" in *The Denver Journal of International Law and Policy*, Vol. 33, No. 4, United States, 2005

Weinman, J.L.: "The Clash between U.S. Criminal Procedure and the Vienna Convention on Consular Relations: An Analysis of the International Court of Justice Decision in the *LaGrand Case*" in *American University International Law Review*, 17 (2002) 4, United States, 2002

Westlake, J.: *Chapter on the Principle of International Law*, United Kingdom, 1894

Williams, D.W.: "Consular Access to Detained Persons" in *International and Comparative Law Quarterly*, Vol. 29, United Kingdom, 1980

Willemarck, L.: "*La competence des agents diplomatiques et consulaires en matière notariale. Théorie et analyse de la pratique*" in *Revue du notariat belge*, Belgium, 2002

Whitesell, B.P.: "Mining Article 36(1)(b) of the Vienna Convention on Consular Relations for an individual right to due process" in *Duke Law Journal*, Vol. 54, No. 2, United States, 2004

Yakemtchiuk, R.: *Droit consulaire des États Africains*, Belgium, 1967

Zaccaria, G.: *L'arte dell'interpretazione*, Italy, 1990

Zas, M.: "Consular Absolutism: The Need for Judicial Review in the Adjudication of Immigrants Visas for Permanent Residence" in *The John Marshall Law Review*, Vol. 37, No. 2., United States, 2004

Zlotnik, H.: *International Migration Trends Since 1980*, Population Division Department of Economic and Social Affairs, United Nations Organization, 2002

Žourek, J.: "*Le statut et les fonctions des consuls*" in *Recueil des Cours Tome 106*, The Hague Academy of International Law, the Netherlands, 1962

---------. "*Quelques problèmes théoriques du droit consulaires*" in *Journal du Droit International*, No. 1., France, 1963

# Index

www.ingramcontent.com/pod-product-compliance
Ingram Content Group UK Ltd.
Pitfield, Milton Keynes, MK11 3LW, UK
UKHW020142290926
15471UKWH00004B/643